VAGABOND PRINCESS

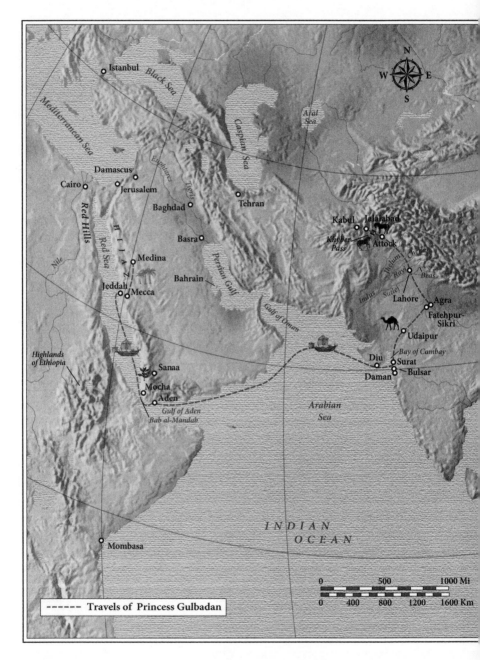

The travels of Princess Gulbadan

VAGABOND PRINCESS

The Great Adventures of Gulbadan

Ruby Lal

~

Yale
UNIVERSITY PRESS
NEW HAVEN & LONDON

Published with assistance from the Mary Cady Tew Memorial Fund.

Yale University Press books may be purchased in quantity for
educational, business, or promotional use. For information, please e-mail
sales.press@yale.edu (U.S. office) or sales@yaleup.co.uk (U.K. office).

Set in Spectral type by Newgen North America, Inc.
Printed in the United States of America.

Library of Congress Control Number: 2023941958
ISBN 978-0-300-25127-2 (hardcover : alk. paper)

A catalogue record for this book is available from the British Library.

This paper meets the requirements of
ANSI/NISO Z39.48-1992 (Permanence of Paper).

10 9 8 7 6 5 4 3 2 1

Also by Ruby Lal

Empress: The Astonishing Reign of Nur Jahan

Coming of Age in Nineteenth-Century India:
The Girl-Child and the Art of Playfulness

Domesticity and Power in the Early Mughal World

For Homa Bazyar—exile-adventurer, linguist par excellence, friend, and teacher—in fond memory of lavish late-afternoon readings of Princess Gulbadan's memoir

Contents

Plates follow page 122

Dramatis Personae

~

The following list is arranged alphabetically by first name.
I provide birth and death dates where known.

ʿABD AL-QADIR BADAUNI (1540–1605)

A courtier in Akbar's court and a committed Sunni Muslim, he disapproved of the emperor's eclectic policies and politics. A prolific translator of many Sanskrit and Persian works, he wrote his history, the *Muntakhab-ut-Tawarikh,* secretly. The work contains unusual information not found in other court documents about the times of Emperor Akbar and is a valuable counter to the panegyric *Akbarnama* of Abul Fazl.

ABUL BAQA

Amir Abul Baqa, well versed in Unani medicine, was also a close confidant of Emperor Babur. He advised both Babur and Humayun during important political and personal moments in their lives as kings.

ABUL FAZL (1551–1602)

Abul Fazl was the son of Shaikh Mubarak, a man with humble beginnings who later became renowned for his expertise in philosophy and the Islamic sciences. After his early learning with his father, Abul Fazl joined Akbar's court in 1574 and became known for his forceful debates with the jurists in the Ibadat Khana, or the house of worship that Akbar built in 1575. Here, Akbar held discussions with thinkers and leaders of many schools of thought and on varied spiritual themes. Emperor Akbar selected him to write the first official history of the Mughal court, the three-volume *Akbarnama,* including the imperial gazetteer, the *Aʾin-i Akbari.* At the instigation of Prince Salim, Bir Singh Bundela, later the king of Orchha, murdered Abul Fazl in 1602.

AKBAR (1542–1605)

Born in October 1542 in Amarkot (now in Sindh province, Pakistan), Akbar was one of the greatest emperors of India. The son of Hamida Banu Begum and the second Mughal king, Humayun, Akbar succeeded to the throne at the age of thirteen. A contemporary of Elizabeth I, he reigned for four decades, extending Mughal power over the greater part of India and securing the northwest frontier by recapturing Kabul and Kandahar. A humanist, he remained dedicated to Islam and took an active interest in other religions and denominations. His court drew world attention and attracted a wave of aristocrats and creative people from Persia, Afghanistan, and Central Asia. At the heart of Akbar's success was his pluralistic outlook.

'ASAS

Khwaja Muhammad 'Ali 'Asas, a devoted ally of Emperor Babur, supported the emperor in many critical times and was the first to follow him when he renounced wine. He appears at various entertainments in Babur's and Gulbadan's accounts. His last known public role was as caretaker of Babur's tomb.

'ASKARI (1516–57)

'Askari was the son of Babur and Gulrukh Begum and blood brother of Prince Kamran. After he participated in early Mughal conquests of India, Babur appointed him governor of Sambhal. He died in 1557 while he was on a hajj.

ATUN MAMA

She was an intimate assistant of Babur's mother. In 1501, when Babur lost the city of Samarkand, Atun was left behind because there was no horse for her to ride. She walked for days in the snow to be reunited with the Mughals. She was a legendary figure; Gulbadan mentions her many times and includes her in the list of women who attended her brother Hindal's wedding feast.

BABUR (1483–1556)

The first Mughal king, Babur, a poet, a wanderer, and the author of the *Baburnama*, descended from Central Asian heroes: Chingiz Khan (1167–1227) on his mother's side and Timur (1336–1405) on his father's. Babur's paternal grandfather parceled out his empire to his sons. For much of Babur's life he fought for these provinces, controlled by uncles or cousins of varying degrees. During a protracted struggle for the coveted city Samarkand, Timur's capital, Babur lost the territory his father had bequeathed to him. By about 1504, he was driven to Kabul. Eventually, in 1526, he defeated Ibrahim Lodi of Delhi and inaugurated Mughal rule.

BAIRAM KHAN (1501–61)

Of Persian origin, Bairam Khan was a skilled military commander and a powerful statesman who served during the reigns of Humayun and Akbar. He is remembered for his role as the regent of Akbar during his boyhood years as well as his chief mentor, adviser, and most trusted ally. As Akbar began to robustly take charge of the affairs of his empire, he dismissed Bairam in 1560. Bairam was murdered en route to Mecca.

BAYAZID BAYAT

Bayazid Bayat first emerged on the pages of Mughal history when he accompanied Bairam Khan to Kabul in late 1545. From aboard his ship, Bayazid sent a letter to Gulbadan when she was stranded in Aden. He was among the officers Emperor Akbar asked to record their memories for the *Akbarnama*, which led to Bayazid's *Tazkireh-i Humayun va Akbar*, a history of the reigns of Humayun and Akbar from 1542 to 1591.

BEGA BEGUM (1511–81)

Bega was the senior wife of the second Mughal king, Humayun, and mother of Al-Aman, their first child, who died in Badakhshan soon after his birth. Bega was captured in 1539 by Sher Shah in the battle of Chausa—where she also lost her daughter 'Aqiqa—but she later returned to the Mughals. Famous in history as Hajji Begum, she was honored in the aftermath of the pilgrimage she undertook to western Arabia in 1564–65, a decade before Gulbadan led the royal women's group there.

BIBI FATIMA (B. 1490S)

A wet nurse of Humayun, she played significant roles, including as the *Ordu-begi,* an armed woman/warrior of Humayun's harem and as envoy in an important political marriage of the emperor. Some sources indicate that in the early part of Akbar's reign she may have served as the *sadr-i anas,* the superintendent of the harem. Gulbadan mentions her repeatedly, and so does Bayazid Bayat.

BIBI MUBARIKA

Bibi Mubarika Yusufzai was the daughter of Malik Shah Mansur, the chief of the Yusufzai tribe of the Pashtuns. She was the fifth wife of Babur, the first Mughal emperor. Their marriage took place in 1519 and established friendly relations between the Mughals and the Yusufzais. Along with her co-wife Maham Begum and stepdaughter Gulbadan, Mubarika was among the first women from the Kabul household to travel to Hindustan in 1529 after Babur's victory over Delhi and Agra. She is frequently mentioned by Gulbadan; the two had a playful relationship and the princess fondly called her *Afghani Aghacha,* or the Afghan Lady.

BUWA BEGUM (D. 1528)

Mother of Sultan Ibrahim Lodi of Delhi, whom Babur defeated in the battle of Panipat. She was responsible for poisoning Babur. On her enforced journey to Kabul, she drowned herself in the river Indus.

DILDAR BEGUM

Dildar Begum's ancestry is not discussed in the contemporary records. Her marriage to Babur took place between 1508 and 1519 (these years of the *Baburnama* are missing from the manuscripts), and she came to the Kabul household as his second wife. She gave birth to Gulrang, Gulchihra, Hindal, Gulbadan, and Alwar (the last of the five children died in childhood). She shared Hindal and Gulbadan with her senior co-wife Maham Begum. Gulbadan discusses several episodes of Dildar's fine intervention and firm speech and calls her mother Acam in Turkish.

GULBADAN BEGUM (1523–1603)

Gulbadan Begum, the daughter of Dildar and Babur, traveled to Agra from Afghanistan at the age of six and a half after her father had made substantial conquests in that region. An unusual witness to the emerging Mughal monarchy, from its inception in the early conquests of Babur to its majesty in the reign of Akbar, she recorded what she had seen in her memoir, the *Ahval-i Humayun Badshah* (literally, Conditions in the Age of Humayun Badshah). The *Ahval,* a unique piece of writing and the only example of prose by a Mughal woman, is the best source describing Mughal domestic life and the character of the empire as it was taking shape. From Fatehpur-Sikri, she led the *haraman,* the women of the harem, on an unprecedented group pilgrimage to Mecca, braving the hazards of treacherous seas and unknown territories—including a year at Aden in the Red Sea after their ship was wrecked. This book centers on her life and adventures, and the scandals caused by her presence and actions in the Ottoman territories.

GULRUKH BEGUM

Gulrukh's family background is not mentioned in the contemporary records, and nor is the date of her marriage to Babur, which likely took place some-time between 1508 and 1519 (these years of the *Baburnama* are missing from the manuscripts). She bore Shahrukh, Ahmad, Gul'izar (all three died young), Kamran, and 'Askari.

HAMIDA BANU BEGUM (1527–1604)

It is difficult to chart Hamida Banu's family tree precisely, but sources suggest she was a descendant of a renowned saint. Revered as the mother of Emperor Akbar, Hamida fits well the trajectory of Mughal women who animated the royal circles with their presence, support, and wisdom. She married Humayun, the second Mughal king, at Paat in the summer of 1541, and gave birth to Akbar in 1542 while the royals were in exile. Hamida surfaces frequently in the Mughal sources, especially in the *Akbarnama.* She sought forgiveness on behalf of Prince Salim, future Jahangir. She did not join the party of senior women pilgrims that her close ally Gulbadan Begum led, likely staying back to support Akbar.

HARKHA BAI (1542–1623)

Daughter of Raja Bharmal, the Kachhwaha ruler of Amer, she was the first Rajput Hindu woman to marry Emperor Akbar. She gave birth to Prince Salim. Ennobled later in Akbari histories as Maryam-uz-Zamani, she lived into her son's reign.

HINDAL (1519–51)

Son of Babur and Dildar Begum, 'Abdul Nasir was born in Kabul as his father was on his way to conquer the regions across the river Hind. Taking his birth as a good omen, Babur called him Hindal—of Hind—and commemorated the birth of his son in his memoir. He was placed in the care of Babur's senior wife, Maham Begum, as was his younger sister Gulbadan. By age nineteen, he had emerged as a strong contender for the newly emerging Mughal throne in India. Eventually he pledged allegiance to Humayun and remained faithful to him until 1551, when he died fighting for the Mughals in a battle against Kamran's forces.

HUMAYUN (1508–56)

Humayun was born in March 1508 in Kabul, the son and successor of Babur, the founder of Mughal rule in northern Hindustan. Humayun inherited in 1530 an empire that was still in the making: the Afghans and the Rajputs were only restrained but not subdued by Mughal power after his father's victories of Panipat (1526), Khanua (1527), and the Ghaghara (1529). His biggest challenge came from the Afghan Sher Shah Suri, who had consolidated his power in Bihar and Bengal. He defeated Humayun in Chausa in 1539 and at Kannauj in 1540, expelling him from northern India. After years of exile, during which time he married his beloved Hamida Banu and she gave birth to Akbar, Humayun regained Kabul and eventually returned to Hindustan. He ruled again from 1555 to 1556.

ISAN DAULAT KHANUM

Babur's maternal grandmother, she married Yunas Khan Chagatai, the Great Khan of the Mughals, around 1456. She gave birth to three daughters. Isan Daulat shared bravely the vicissitudes of her husband's career and was four times taken captive by her enemies. Sagacious and far-sighted, she was revered for her good judgment. Toward the end of her life, she lived in a garden house in Andijan.

JAWHAR AFTABCHI

Jawhar is known for his valiant act of saving Emperor Humayun from drowning during the battle of Chausa. He accompanied the exiled Humayun to Sind and Persia, and then to Hindustan. He wrote the *Tazkirat-ul-Vaqi'at,* a candid account of Humayun's reign, in response to Akbar's 1587 order.

KAMRAN (1512–57)

Son of Babur and Gulrukh Begum, he had a fraught relationship with Humayun, his half brother. After Humayun returned from the battle of Chausa,

Kamran refused to place his troops under Humayun's command. Kamran forcibly took Gulbadan during the Mughal clan's coerced relocation to Kabul, when Humayun left for Sind and eventually Persia. By 1545 Humayun took over Kabul. Although Humayun resisted pressure to put his rebellious brother to death, he was persuaded that something needed to be done, and so he had him blinded. Humayun banished him to Mecca, where he later died. Two of his daughters accompanied Gulbadan on the pilgrimage to Mecca.

KHANZADA BEGUM (B. 1478)
Khanzada Begum was the formidable sister of Babur. Accounts of her life emerge in her brother's and niece Gulbadan's histories. She is lauded in the chronicles for the "sacrifice" she made by marrying Shaibani Khan Uzbek in order to establish peace between the Mughals and the Uzbeks. She came back to her family ten years later and acquired immense respect, discussed and underlined by Gulbadan, whose rendering of Khanzada's special status as *aka janam*, "my dearest *aka*," marked her privileged status, enhanced age, and the deference due her. Her nephews, sons of Babur, regularly sought her out as an elder. Khanzada's guidance to the fighting sons of Babur in the matter of reading their name in the Friday sermons, called the *khutba*, is memorable, and a striking statement of how senior women collaborated in the process of the promotion of kings.

KHWAJA KALAN
Among Babur's prominent men, he served in the right wing of the armed forces that fought against Ibrahim Lodi and played an important role in the takeover of Agra. After the victories, he was assigned the task of taking bounties of Hind for the royal household. Kalan served for a few years in Hindustan and then returned to Kabul. Babur, fond of and reliant on him, was loath to see him leave. The emperor sent him poems that he wrote in Agra.

MAHAM BEGUM
She was the influential senior wife of Babur and mother of the second Mughal king Humayun, but her ancestry is unknown. Babur met her in 1506 in Herat and they were married soon afterward. After Humayun, she had four other children, all of whom died. She took over Hindal and Gulbadan

from her co-wife Dildar. Gulbadan is the best chronicler of her guardian mother's life events.

MAHDI KHWAJA

The second husband of Khanzada Begum, the powerful sister of Babur, Muhammad Mahdi Khwaja served in the emperor's armed forces, against Ibrahim Lodi. It is unclear when he and Khanzada married or what the nature of their relationship was. At the instigation of Babur's senior courtier Nizam al-Din Barlas, he attempted to win the Mughal courtiers to secure nomination to the Mughal throne. But the entire saga ended terribly.

MURAD III, OTTOMAN SULTAN OF TURKEY (1546–95)

From 1574 until his death in 1595, Murad III ruled the Ottoman Empire, which included, among other places in Arabia, the Holy Cities Mecca and Medina, and Egypt to the north. He ordered the eviction of the Mughal royal ladies who had gone on a pilgrimage under the leadership of Princess Gulbadan, charging that the royal visitors as well as the caravans of Hind had overcrowded the Holy Cities. But the story was more complicated, as this book shows.

NIZAM AL-DIN BARLAS (KHALIFA)

Along with his wife, he received the six-year-old Gulbadan in Aligarh in 1529, when she arrived there from Kabul. His brother was married to Babur's half sister, and he and the emperor were friends of long standing. Initially he was opposed to Humayun's accession to the throne, but eventually he endorsed his rule.

RUQAYYA BEGUM (D. 1626)

One of the longest-living matriarchs of the Mughal Empire, she was the first wife of Emperor Akbar. She was also the emperor's first cousin, a Mughal princess by birth. She had no children of her own and raised Akbar's grandson Khurram. As a senior Mughal woman, she was instrumental in forging peace between Akbar and her stepson Jahangir, paving the way for his accession to the throne. Jahangir wrote fondly of Ruqayya in his memoirs and recorded her death. Her burial place is in the Garden of Babur (Bagh-e Babur) in Kabul.

SALIMA SULTAN BEGUM (D. 1613)

Salima was the granddaughter of Babur. In 1557 she accompanied Gulbadan and Hamida Banu to Agra. Shortly after that she was married to Akbar's regent Bairam Khan. After Bairam's death 1561, Salima married her first cousin Akbar. A senior wife, she was central in pleading for forgiveness on behalf of Prince Salim and wielded much influence in his eventual succession to the throne. She was one of the senior women who accompanied Gulbadan on the hajj. Along with Ruqayya, she guided Mihr-un-nisa—future Mughal co-sovereign Nur Jahan—upon her arrival in the harem. There is some uncertainty about the date of her death, but Jahangir records it as 1613 in Agra. Mentioning her repeatedly as a cultured and wise woman, Jahangir notes particulars of her birth and descent, her marriages, and her death.

SHER SHAH (D. 1545)

Founder of the Suri dynasty in Bihar, he was born Farid Khan. A brilliant strategist and a gifted administrator, he defeated the second Mughal king Humayun in the 1540s, which led to the migration of the Mughal clan to Kabul and Sind. His monetary, fiscal, and administrative reforms were the bedrock for Mughal rule in Hindustan.

VAGABOND PRINCESS

Introduction

Complex Messages

⁓

I WAITED WITH NERVOUS ANTICIPATION AS I SKIMMED through the card catalogue in the tall wooden cabinets behind the service desk of the Asian and African Studies reading room. A majestic, high-ceilinged rectangular room, it had several long tables, each of which could comfortably seat up to four readers on each side. Lamps with light-blue shades stood in contrast to the yellow tables. Large portraits of Indian rajas and other aristocrats from the former British colonies dominated one side of the high walls. Rows of bookshelves holding printed guides and other catalogues drew patrons' attention. Every now and then, the library staff looked toward the area where readers pored over the special collections.

Earlier in the day, I had asked to see the sixteenth-century princess Gulbadan Begum's book, classified as Or. 166 in the British Library. Gulbadan, literally "Rosebody," was the beloved daughter of Babur, the patriarch of the magnificent Mughals of India, and the first and only woman historian of the Mughal Empire. Writing as events unfolded, she captured the gritty and fabulous daily lives of ambitious men, subversive women, brilliant eunuchs, devoted nurses, gentle and perceptive guards, and captive women and children who died in war zones. Yet Gulbadan's stellar book was relegated to the margins of history—to mere footnotes in volumes on Mughal politics, war, economy, and agrarian histories, all written by men.

Before I left India for Oxford, I had seen a 1902 English translation of Gulbadan's work by Annette Beveridge, a British colonial-era scholar. It was obvious that Gulbadan was a woman of many quests and journeys. Yet her work had been sidelined by modern historians, who shared Beveridge's publisher's belief, articulated in a letter accepting the translation for publication, that it was "of unique interest. . . . A little history . . . it is but a little thing."[1]

The "little history" of men's and women's daily lives that enraptured the princess is in fact a masterpiece that came out of an insightful witnessing of hard politics and much more. No distant bystander, she was close to the people whose lives she chronicled. Thus her book was both hers and theirs, a lively prose work that shines with unrivaled granular details of Mughal wandering life.

On that August 1997 morning, as I waited to hold the book of this adventurous woman, I did not yet know the depth of her radical thinking, her daring life story, tied intricately to one of the greatest adventures in the late sixteenth-century world. Two decades would pass before I joined together the pieces of her fascinating life.

My curiosity was piqued. I dug through the British Library's resources and discovered that it housed over eleven thousand Persian manuscripts. This vast pool included the princess's father's poetry and thousands of miniature paintings, such as the one in which he greets courtiers at 'Id, his slender face captivating the viewer. In another, Gulbadan's nephew Emperor Akbar, seated on a boulder under a tree, instructs his courtiers that the slaughter of animals must cease. Scores of breathtaking Mughal works and others from the wider Islamic world can also be found in this collection—folktales, allegories, so-called morals for the heart, human, animal, vegetal terrestrial worlds, both pictorial and written. Much later, I would find a magnificent miniature drawing in which Gulbadan stands in profile holding her book. The artist captured the special status that the princess clearly enjoyed by placing her at the edge of the central frame, which immediately attracts the viewer's attention.[2]

In 1868, the British Museum purchased Gulbadan's manuscript from the widow of Colonel William Hamilton, who had collected nearly a thousand manuscripts from Lucknow and Delhi. The Delhi collection, which includes 1,957 Arabic, 1,550 Persian, and 157 Urdu manuscripts, represents what remained in 1858 of the famed Mughal Imperial Library—those items that had not been gifted, sold, or seized during constant raids and incursions, beginning with Nadir Shah's invasion of Delhi in 1739. India's British colonial government acquired the collection, estimated at 4,700 volumes, at a sale in 1859. In 1867 another 1,120 less valuable items were sold. The remainder was to be given to the newly completed Indian Museum in Calcutta, but instead everything ended up in the India Office Library in London in 1876.[3] Gulbadan's book was in one of the trunks holding the lesser items from the Delhi collection.

As I stood by the catalogues and open shelves, I looked beyond the service desk, imagining a secret crypt that held prized books and manuscripts. "Or. 166—Ruby Lal": my musings were interrupted by a gentle call from an Englishwoman in her fifties. I gave her the counterfoil of the library request slip, and she instructed, "Please take it to the special collections table." I barely listened to her; my eyes were on her hands. She opened the gray cloth folded over the manuscript. The princess's book! Bound in faded wine-red leather with gold rim, it evoked the splendor of another age.

Taking it to my table and placing it atop a wooden book stand, I began turning the pages very slowly, as if seeking blessings from a sacred text. A little book with no frontispieces or margins. The pages, which included blank flyleaves, were impossibly thin. Later I found out the exact dimensions: 229 by 140 millimeters (9 by 5½ inches) per leaf. There were eighty-three folios with approximately fifteen lines on each page. Although there was no colophon or date, based on the state of the paper and the writing style the British Library dated the text to the seventeenth century.

Each day as I returned to Gulbadan's writing, I experienced a deeper affinity with the soft texture of the book, the light golden pages dotted with faint coffee-colored blemishes, the aging inside and outside, the words penned in coal black ink, and the cursive, or *nasta'liq*, script. As I touched Gulbadan's book, its contents, familiar from the Beveridge translation, felt new. I felt a direct communication with the woody aroma of the pages, which brought the scenes Gulbadan described to life. Amid the Persian sentences, I spotted a few Turkish words as well as Hindavi ones—the language from which modern Hindi evolved. I could hear Gulbadan speak thus, heir that she was to intermingled languages. A word here, a phrase there making its way into a sentence in another language, like humans moving from one place to another, establishing homes in foreign lands.

Gulbadan was sixty-four when she wrote this unique book, the *Ahval-i Humayun Badshah* or Conditions in the Age of Humayun Badshah, popularly called the *Humayun-nama*.[4] Like that of her migratory ancestors, Timur (Tamerlane) and Chingiz Khan through Babur, the landscape of her childhood was fluid, dynamic, and flooded with awe-inspiring ancestresses. Arriving in India in 1529 at age six, Gulbadan was the first Mughal girl to travel in a royal caravan across the dangerous Khyber Pass and the massive river Indus on the way to be reunited with the militarily victorious Babur. As she came of age in mansions by the river Yamuna, strong women peopled her world.

Her poised and reserved Aunt Khanzada had been captured by her father's ardent foe and kept as booty in war, married to the enemy for over a decade. Her mother, Dildar, who had given birth to five children, generously shared her daughter the princess, with her co-wife, the woman of Babur's affection. Gulbadan thus grew up with both a biological and a guardian mother in a big clan with multiple generations and many staff members. There were no splendid permanent palaces then. Rather, it was a garden society: much of life and its activities, including get-togethers and strategic discussions, took place outdoors.

Perennial warfare was part of young Gulbadan's environment. She witnessed the turbulent exile of her brother Humayun, the second Mughal emperor and father of Akbar. She was married during this period to her second cousin, Khizr Khwaja Khan, a grandee of Humayun's court. She tells nothing about her husband except for relating a couple of difficult conversations with him in the context of momentous political events. With Khizr she had a son. When her family was routed from Agra in the late 1540s, she escaped to Kabul. From the splendor of the Afghan mountains, she returned a decade later to Hindustan, the land of her girlhood and youth.

As the weeks passed, I became increasingly immersed in the sheer physicality of Gulbadan's book. Is this her handwriting, I wondered, or that of a male or female scribe? I touched her lines, her words, intimate with the tactility of the paper that she likely once held. Her writing felt direct, as if it were speaking to me. I was looking *in* it, not *at* it. I saw her immersed in chronicling courtly life. Each page conveyed the physicality of the cross-section of humanity she lived with. A visual, visceral world: brocade tents; rhubarb picnics; gifts to be distributed in a set of nine; matriarchs putting pressure on young wives to populate their mansions with children; women arguing with kings over their visits to the elderly aunts; sour-faced men and grim-eyed women, kind eunuchs, children dying in war; Afghans and Iranians looking longingly to Al-Hind, the land beyond the river Indus.

By the end of the month, I had reached folio 83, nearly the end of Gulbadan's manuscript. Humayun, the princess's half brother and the second Mughal emperor, was having a difficult conversation with his courtiers, military and civilian officers, about the younger Prince Kamran. Those assembled unanimously agreed that "when one is an emperor and ruler, one cannot be a brother." "If you want to give special treatment to your brother," they said, "you must abdicate." The courtiers urged the emperor to give orders to blind his half brother. The charges were serious: Kamran had wounded Humayun at a pivotal moment in his career. Kamran had murdered the youngest prince, Hindal. Kamran had imprisoned people and terrorized families, disgraced and defamed people. "This is no brother; he is the emperor's enemy," the men said. Humayun listened to their arguments and asked those present to sign a document stating their views. Kamran was sentenced to be blinded. "The order was executed at once," wrote Gulbadan. I read on. "After the blinding, His Majesty the emperor . . ."[5]

I turned the folio of the Persian manuscript. There was nothing more. The sentence was incomplete. The *book* was incomplete.

I sat with it a little longer. Then took it to the desk.

"All done?" the man at the desk asked.

"Yes," I said hesitantly.

Autumn 1999
The British Library

Inside the main entrance of the British Library, readers and visitors approach the building's three floors via marble steps or steely escalators. As you move up, everything stands in your line of sight, especially the centerpiece of the library, a floor-to-ceiling black rectangle that holds prized gold-bound books and manuscripts. Centuries of splendor. The Ka'ba of books, I said to myself as I walked up.

I was back to consult Gulbadan's book one more time before putting the finishing touches to my doctoral thesis. I had been pondering an epilogue to my thesis, in which I would write that Gulbadan guided a group of harem women to the shores of the Red Sea. In the mid-1570s, along with other Mughal women, Gulbadan came to live behind the red sandstone walls of the newly built harem in Fatehpur-Sikri. New regulations, including the elevation and confinement of generations of Mughal and non-Mughal women, were put in place by her nephew Akbar, the third Mughal emperor. Unaccustomed to such grand seclusion, the princess, a highly influential matriarch by this time, devised a plan to travel to western Arabia for the annual Muslim pilgrimage, the hajj. She organized older and younger women and led them across the waters of the Indian Ocean and the Red Sea.

From behind the red sandstone walls to the Prophet's land in Arabia, it was the first collective hajj of royal women from a sixteenth-century Muslim court, a momentous event recorded in the official history, the *Akbarnama,* and those of other court historians such as Badauni and Nizam al-Din Ahmad. I knew nothing more about that journey. But the little I knew was startling. I could visualize how it took place.

Early 1576
Fatehpur-Sikri

The fifty-two-year-old Princess Gulbadan sat across from her nephew Emperor Akbar, waiting for her turn to speak. She was of average height, somewhat stocky in build, with distinctive straight eyebrows shading her penetrating kohl-lined eyes. She was dressed in a long flowing shirt over loose trousers, a scarf thrown over her chest and shoulders, her face exposed. Ruby and pearl necklaces adorned her.

The emperor was fully cognizant of Gulbadan's status as a powerful elder, a key dynastic witness, and a memory holder. Bearing the wisdom of the migratory decades she spent in Afghanistan and India with her father and brother, the first two Mughal kings, she was now a matriarch in her nephew's harem.

Elder and younger Mughal women, Hindu Rajput wives of the emperor, princes and princesses of many generations, sons and daughters of wives and concubines, eunuchs and midwives—all lived in different sections of the harem, which was studded with domes and cupolas raised on columns, tucked behind the walls that parted it from the imperial court. Gulbadan had spent much of her life on the move, in open country. Living behind dauntingly high harem walls was part of a recent state policy. Akbar, the mighty and all-powerful emperor, had built secluded quarters for the women of his dynasty and instituted elaborate regulations for their routine and welfare. Housing them in the splendid isolation of the new harem, he declared these peripatetic ladies to be sacred and untouchable, and hence to be kept strictly out of public view. Unapproachable women enhanced the emperor's strength and allure. Akbar publicly dubbed them *the veiled ones.* By the mid-

1570s, a few years into the building of Fatehpur-Sikri, all of the women had moved into their designated harem apartments. The Mughal harem was fundamental to Akbar's plan to broadcast his image as a strong and invincible sovereign: the head of the empire, whose revered women couldn't be seen. No longer able to travel as they had in the time of Akbar's forefathers, the women were now harem-bound. Thus Akbar advertised his own grandeur.

The emperor hadn't agreed to the meeting with his aunt just to pay his respects to her. Nor was it an occasion to discuss senior women's intervention in cases relating to princely disaffections or rebellions, disagreements with near or distant kin, or scandals such as the recent case of bribery implicating the chief judge of the court.

Clad in a knee-length gold-embroidered silk cloak tied at the waist with a delicately embroidered *kamarband,* the imperial dagger at his side, the broad-shouldered thirty-four-year-old Akbar sat beside his aunt, his head bent toward his right shoulder as was his wont, his eyes bright, his small nostrils wide open. On the left, between his nose and upper lip, was a dark mole.

It is likely that his mother Hamida, the dowager empress, was there, along with the astute and vivacious Salima, the emperor's second wife (who was more like a mother-wife, having been previously married to Akbar's boyhood mentor Bairam Khan), and Ruqayya, his first wife, also older than he. The women sat atop a soft Persian carpet with intricate red, green, and blue floral patterns, lilies and roses etched on a soft lemon-yellow background, and round bolsters to support their backs, as were popular in the Mughal world. Women attendants stood ready for any command.

The emperor listened intently as Gulbadan spelled out an idea. Long ago, she told him, she had made a vow to visit the Holy Places. Now she wished to travel across the seas to Mecca and Medina to fulfill her pledge to God.[6] Akbar knew that Gulbadan had traversed the vast, dangerous roads linking Afghanistan and northern India, had seen settlements and resettlements, had been part of caravans traveling amid welcome news as well as news of devastation, exile, and migration. Lately, living in her nephew's harem, she had counseled the young monarch and his associates on key domestic and political affairs. It would serve Akbar's interests if he had such an experienced and esteemed senior as an ally.

While the aunt and nephew sat talking about the hajj, the annual Muslim pilgrimage, each embodied a different perspective. The vagabond princess Gulbadan was inquisitive. Born into a long line of peripatetic rulers, she valued movement as beneficial to freedom and to the flowering of mind and body. For most of her life, she had not known the comfort that Akbar's stately residences provided. She had lived happily enough in tents, citadels, and gardens. Her relocation to Agra brought her to a new land, new languages, and new relationships. Rich and wondrous as Al-Hind was, it was difficult at times, especially in the exile and confinement of Akbar's new capital Fatehpur-Sikri.

In contrast, Akbar had established the unquestioned grandeur of the Mughal Empire and tested the bounds of inherited religion and politics. A curious mix of ambition and ferocity, he was also an ardent seeker of truth and religion. Massive tension arose between the experimental emperor and the orthodox Sunni clergy. He was the first to marry numerous Hindu Rajput women to strengthen political networks. Those strategic marriages were key to his expansionist projects. His Sunni advisers, suspicious of Akbar's eclectic inclinations, in their disapproval were insulting to Shi'a migrants from Persia and other parts of the Islamic world. Clerics weren't the only critics. Historian 'Abd al-Qadir Badauni, who served in the emperor's court, secretly wrote a huffy counter-narrative to the official (emperor-sanctioned) history the *Akbarnama*. "Hindustan is a wide place," Badauni observed, "where there is an open field for all manner of licentiousness, and no one interferes in another's business, so that everyone can do as he pleases."[7] This was not meant as a compliment.

Rumors spread that the emperor had turned against Islam. Reports that he had committed sacrilege, claiming to be the new Prophet, traveled to Persia, Central Asia, Portugal, and Spain. His true motivation was perhaps more spectacular. According to scriptural predictions, in 1591 an Islamic messiah would inaugurate a new epoch of peace and prosperity. Like the Ottoman Turkish sultan and many other Islamic monarchs and saints, Akbar dreamed of being declared the long-awaited *Mahdi,* the Renewer who would banish evil and usher in a just world order. Whichever philosophical basis for his sovereignty appealed to Akbar the most—the "Perfect Man" of philosopher Al-Arabi, the scriptural notion of the Mahdi, or the concept of divine light—all converged in the belief that he was an agent of God who would maintain the "rhythm and balance of the cosmos."[8]

By 1577 Akbar was getting closer to his Infallibility Decree, the pronouncement that made him the supreme arbitrator in civil and ecclesiastical matters. As a godlike king, he would be the final authority on any opposition to his imperial dictates and commands. In these audacious times, he needed the blessings and support of elders like Gulbadan.

And so, when Gulbadan proposed her voyage to western Arabia, Akbar accepted the idea. He knew that navigating the waters to the Holy Cities nestled upon the Red Sea was a mammoth undertaking. Pirates regularly attacked pilgrim ships. No Mughal emperor or other Muslim monarch of the time made the pilgrimage. As heads of their respective domains, they had to stay away from such risky adventures to safeguard their lands and peoples. It was the women of royal families who often went on the pilgrimage, thus accruing blessings for the entire dynasty. A royal Mughal women's visit would consolidate Akbar's standing as a great and blessed Muslim emperor.

The Muslim world would take note of the fact that a large, well-mannered group of women from Akbar's grand harem undertook the extensive journey. Over centuries, royal and aristocratic women had traveled to the Hijaz: Mecca, Medina, and other Holy Cities, accompanied by staff and attendants. A fourteenth-century matriarch based in northwestern Iran (not directly related to Gulbadan but of the same ancestral pedigree) traveled to the revered Muslim cities on a palanquin fastened atop a camel. Princess El-Qutlugh changed transport over the course of her travel, completing her journey on a horse, a quiver fastened on her waist and a parasol raised above her head.

Gulbadan would be the first royal Muslim woman in the history of Islamic courts to initiate a group pilgrimage for women. She knew that although the majority of pilgrims were devout, the hajj was not just about piety. Trade, politics, and religion intertwined in Mecca, a mercantile republic, precursor to Venice, Pisa, and Genoa. Seekers and mystics traveled there simply to wander and absorb the aura of the desert land where many prophets were given revelations. Sojourners, or *mujawirs,* spent years learning, wandering, and living in the sacred Arabian cosmos. Scholars went to gain expertise in the traditions (*hadith*) of the life and times of Prophet Muhammad in some of the finest schools in the Holy Cities.

Gulbadan's idea bore fruit. Once she had Akbar's consent, she began to work on the details. Her party would consist of eleven close female relatives and associates as well as reliable servants. The dowager empress was not to be one of the group. Once a dynamic woman, Hamida had lately grown accustomed to the pomp and ceremony of the royal court, relishing the adoration Akbar lavished upon her. The court leader of the hajj and three other men were to accompany the convoy, along with a Turkish artillery officer, who would serve as an interpreter, and scores of soldiers, attendants, cooks, and other staff.

Autumn 1999
The British Library, London

Back in the British Library, I had Gulbadan's book in my hands again. After rereading parts, I reached the end of the manuscript. I turned its pages again and again, hoping the missing pages had somehow miraculously returned. Perhaps I had overlooked something. Most of the official records of the court had references to Gulbadan's hajj trip. She must surely have written about her Arabian domicile. But there was no sign that she had.

Earlier I had focused on the singular detail that she guided her harem companions across the seas to the Muslim Holy Cities. Now I noted the striking fact that the princess and her companions stayed in the Arabian Desert for four years. What had they been doing? At the time I had no idea of the veritable scandal that erupted while Gulbadan was in Arabia.

Since I first had held the fragile pages of Gulbadan's chronicle, the mystery of the missing pages had never left me. Beveridge had made a cursory remark about the void, having searched in vain for a possible second copy of the work, given the standard Mughal court practice of having several copies of every important work, including any by persons of royal or high rank.

I was the first scholar to work closely with the princess's rarely consulted chronicle. While I gleaned unparalleled details from Gulbadan's writing, it was really the incomplete manuscript that struck me as magical. Five years after Gulbadan returned from the hajj, around 1587, Akbar made an important announcement. In keeping with his world-conquering ambitions, he commissioned the writing of a comprehensive history of his empire. It would be *the* official history, a state-sponsored record of Mughal glory unmatched in scope.

For this first-time history, the emperor asked servants of the state and old members of the family to record their memories of the Mughal dynasty. There was one woman among the invited contributors: not Hamida, a learned elder and an impressive library owner whom he adored. Rather, Akbar selected the enormously accomplished Gulbadan, now sixty-three. She had spent her life as a royal witness, partaking in the ventures of her kith and kin along with her own magnificent initiatives. She was one of the best sources whom Akbar could have asked about their dynasty—a direct witness, family member and, like Hamida, an erudite library owner, astute and highly regarded. Gulbadan noticed people, things, and happenings, and had a fantastic memory. While it was normal for aristocratic women to be literate, she was revered as a learned elder.

Once back inside the harem, Gulbadan launched into another unprecedented adventure, writing the book I was holding in my hands. Although the emperor expected his aunt to write about the grand achievements and epic moments in the career of the Mughal dynasty, and Gulbadan's writing is indeed expansive, she chose to call her work the *Ahval-i Humayun Badshah*, or Conditions in the Age of Humayun Badshah. Thus she emphasized the wider itinerant life force of Mughal kingship.

What she delivered was no simple memoir of an elderly lady—she penned in exceptional detail the ragged and robust lives of the people of her dynasty. Her writing is effortless, written as if it were being spoken, animating people and their actions in vivid characterization. Her genre is unclassifiable—not at all like her father's poetic memoir, the *Baburnama*, which she had read and admired, or the hagiographies of kings that others had written.

Her book is unique also as the only prose work written by a woman of the Muslim courts, including Ottoman Turkey, Safavid Iran, and Mughal India, where women mostly wrote poetry. A recent translator noted, "It is one of the first [prose] works ever written by a woman."[9] Not surprisingly, it yields information otherwise effaced from the official Mughal record. Her work informed my first book, a feminist history that brought to the fore the deeply embedded politics in the creation of the stone-walled Mughal harem whose dynamic denizens engaged in the advancement of the grand empire.[10]

Atlanta, Georgia
December 2022

Two decades later and three books on, I continue to wonder what happened to the rest of Gulbadan's manuscript. What was in the missing pages? During national and international promotional events for *Empress*, my biography of Mughal co-sovereign Nur Jahan, readers repeatedly asked me about Gulbadan, who appeared in the early pages of the book getting ready to go to Mecca as baby Nur was making her way to Akbar's India. I shared with listeners my ongoing obsession with the missing pages. When I told them that she had stayed in Arabia for four years, they wanted more.

And so I found myself gazing simultaneously at two facts: the four years of Gulbadan's stay in Arabia and the lost pages of her manuscript. The more I dug, the more I was persuaded that a biography of Gulbadan would demand that I probe closely the challenge involved in writing a history of disappearances and the story of a scandal.

Within a year of the princess's arrival in Mecca in 1578, Sultan Murad III of Turkey, the sovereign of the Holy Land (the Ottomans had been masters of Egypt and the Hijaz area since 1517), issued an imperial order to evict Gulbadan and her companions. He did so again two years later, in 1580. Five such orders are preserved in the National Archives in Istanbul, Turkey.[11] There may have been more.

The Mughal women had become a prominent spectacle in public places, a circumstance, according to Murad, that was throwing the area into chaos. The matriarchs became the talk of the town. Around the Great Mosque, in places such as markets and fountains, and in other cities, ordinary folk stared at and crowded around Gulbadan and her companions. The hubbub spread to areas far beyond the sacrosanct Ka'ba. According to Badauni, Gulbadan and her party also went overland to the Holy Iranian cities, such as Mashhad, and to other cities in Arabia.

The problem, as Murad saw it, was that Gulbadan and her group had surpassed the permissible boundary and propriety of being in the Holy Places. Their presence was indecorous. They violated the very source of the authority of Sultan Murad. They created *fitna* (chaos). (I will discuss in greater detail in later pages of this book what Murad dubbed the "un-Islamic" activities of Mughal ladies.) Among those he warned in his orders about the women, asking them to ensure that the ladies left the sacred area, was the sherif of Mecca, who wielded considerable prestige and political and diplomatic authority.

There was not a word from Akbar in response to Murad's charges, even though the Red Sea and the Indian coast were closely knit and in constant contact. Tradesmen and pilgrims went to and fro, and news traveled with them. Although there are no surviving records of any exchange between Akbar and Murad, it is noteworthy that soon after Murad's 1580 eviction edict, Akbar appointed Khwaja Yahya, a venerable courtier, as the next head of pilgrimage, commissioning him to escort Gulbadan and the other royal women back to India.

In March 1580 the princess, Yahya, and the women boarded the *Tezrav*, or Swift One, and headed south from Jeddah. But near the port of Aden, the ship was wrecked. Gulbadan, other Mughal women, and officers stayed in Aden for over seven perilous months. To top it all, the governor of Aden did not behave well toward the royal guests. Yet all of Murad's edicts as well as a stray entry in the imperial history of Akbar record the women's reluctance to leave Aden. Despite the rough conditions, they lived as a community amid natural surroundings in open country. By all accounts, they felt free and happy.

That Murad labeled the Mughal women's activities "un-Islamic" and directed them to leave was nothing short of a disgrace for the Mughals. No wonder Akbar and his historians refused to record the details of what Mughal women did. Instead, the chroniclers wrote sanitized descriptions celebrating the homecoming of the royal aunt, a hajji back from her pilgrimage—not someone who had infuriated a contemporary Islamic monarch ruling in that region.

Thus four extraordinary years vanished from Mughal history. In this fading, many things disappear: the lush worlds that Mughal men and women inhabited, made, and lived; networks, explorations, and wonders that pilgrims and sojourners experienced. The lost years take with them the rich experiences of Mughal women—the history of half of humanity, as is now often said. Moreover, we lose the traces of inimitable experiences and the sense of the vast terrains, people, animals, and sacred geographies of Mughal India, the Red Sea, and the desert land of Arabia.

Were the latter pages of Gulbadan's manuscript lost or deliberately removed? Were they *disappeared*? Why aren't there more copies of her work? If "disappeared" history is not a scandal, what is?[12]

And yet, to some extent we can restore and reanimate these spectacular moments, beginning with Gulbadan's birth in a mud citadel in Kabul. The visual, textual, architectural, and legal sources from Mughal India, Ottoman Turkey, and Ottoman Arabia—you can learn more about my method and sources in the "Note on Sources" at the end of the book—are rich with traces, fragments, and clues to Gulbadan's audacious life. And that is all we have for most of history: fragments, inklings, messages. The histories and biographies we write work with these, assembling relevant facts and surmises with meticulous care.

Unusual figures and disappeared histories require us to look, above all, where we don't habitually look. "To look afresh at, and then to describe for ourselves, the frescos of the Ice Age, the nudes of 'high art,' the Minoan seals and figurines, the moon-landscape embossed with the booted print of a male foot. . . . To do this kind of work takes a capacity for constant active presence, a naturalist attention to minute phenomena, watching closely for symbolic arrangements, decoding difficult and complex messages left to us by women of the past."[13]

That is what I intend to do here: to tell Gulbadan's life in full color and, for the very first time, to reassemble her missing history.

One

The Rose Princess
and Her Circle

⁓

THE RECTANGULAR PROVINCE OF KABUL STRETCHED FROM
east to west, surrounded by mountains that looked like rows of clover. As
far as the eye could see, there were valleys and glens with scattered tribal
settlements. If you turned north, you looked toward the icy Hindu Kush
Mountains that separated Kabul from Kunduz. To the east lay the Laghman
region and Peshawar. To the south were towns like Barmal and Bannu.

At the foothills of these mountains, impressed with shrines and spiritual
footprints, stood Bala Hisar, or the High Fort. The defensive walls around
it dated to the sixth century—the time of the Hepthalites. The solitude of
the landscape belied the fort's having stirred with action for centuries. In
the tenth century, at the base of the fort, a sultan of the Ghaznavid dynasty
examined 1,670 elephants for their readiness for military exploits. Chingiz
Khan, the Mongol warrior, wintered here with a massive encampment in
the second quarter of the thirteenth century. In the late fourteenth century,
Timur, the legendary Central Asian hero, stopped at the fort on his way to
invade India. In front of the Leather Gate, below the north side of the fort,
the Mughal king Babur conquered Kabul province in 1504. Legend had it
that he was broad-shouldered and strong enough to jump along the turrets
carrying two men under his arms.[1]

On the upper level of the Great Fort, the Mughal residential quarters
once again buzzed with action. The year was 1523. Dildar Begum, Babur's
third-oldest wife, was about to deliver her fourth child.[2] Gracious and quiet
in demeanor, she lay under soft cotton sheets, her head enveloped in a
long wrap tucked softly around her neck. Her bed was in the center of the
birth chamber, a two-tiered rectangular room somewhat elevated by two

floral-patterned carpeted steps. Outside, a courtyard with an awning would seat many more royal and non-royal women.

Those close to Dildar would sit and wait according to their rank.[3] The most intimate and high-ranking lady attendant stood immediately behind Dildar, adjusting the long silken bolster under her neck or raising her head to give her a drink of water. A *dai,* or midwife, dressed in loose clothing, stayed beside Dildar, ready for any emergency. Could she have been Bibi Fatima? A physically strong woman of Turkish origin now in her mid-thirties, Fatima had nursed the eldest prince, Humayun, son of the most senior Mughal wife, Maham, a decade earlier. Intimate with the household members and of high rank as the wet nurse of the firstborn prince, she would play decisive managerial and diplomatic roles in the years to come.

The second-ranking co-wife, the placid Gulrukh, an experienced mother of five, three of whom had died, would be in the delivery room. Of a less distinguished background, Gulrukh was always on the sidelines of domestic matters, at least in recorded history. The newest royal wife, the charming Mubarika, decked in her distinctive weighty long skirt with numerous folds and heavy silver jewelry, sat close to Dildar. The women knew how besotted Babur was with Mubarika, who had been brought to the harem four years earlier. Without question, some of them would have speculated why she did not yet have a child.

Even though the senior-most wife Maham knew that the time of delivery was fast approaching and eagerly awaited the event, a complicated history with Dildar likely made her remain in her own apartment. Dildar's four-year-old son was in Maham's care, but her two daughters, eight and twelve, would be in Dildar's apartment in a separate section away from the birth chamber.

A couple of loquacious elderly aunts of Babur's were there to give necessary advice. Sitting upon intricately carved wooden chairs, their feet on petite velvet footrests, they would share stories to calm the anxious women in the chamber. Birthing children was a notable and noble task. A male child was truly desirable. They knew all too well, however, that the chances of mother and/or infant dying during or after birth was high. Women elders, bearers of rituals of birthing and caring, alleviated fears. Although the process of delivery was familiar to Dildar, she was still anxious.

Khanzada Begum, Babur's elder sister, would closely monitor the goings-on. Of somber bearing and statuesque, with a slim face like her

brother, she would sit close to her paternal aunts. Lately she had led important dynastic events such as feasts and gift-giving. Advice on kingly matters
had increasingly become her forte too. It is possible that she had cultivated
a special bond with Dildar since the latter's arrival in the family a decade
earlier. Losses drew them close, although their injuries had rather different
histories. With great dignity, they carried the burdens that came with being
women of the Mughal lineage. Each of these women, part of a circle of
fabulous royals, played a critical role in the life of Gulbadan, the baby about
to be born.

Nurses scurried about ensuring everything was ready: hot water and
white cloth in which to wrap the new baby. They ensured that the bed on
which Dildar lay faced in the right direction. The woman attendant by the
bed held her up to assist her, and the midwife drew the drapes that hung
from the four wooden poles around the bed to enhance privacy.

Royal pantries were outside the apartments. The servants ensured that
a cauldron of water was kept boiling in the kitchen. They would relay hot
water and other necessities such as oil and ointments to be applied to Dildar's body and face. Attendants in the chamber would need a long roll of
thread with which the dai would tie the umbilical cord after cutting it as
well as rose water to purify the baby with a ritual bath before wrapping her
in a white cloth as prescribed in Islam for both male and female newborns.
Maids and attendants hurriedly went about their jobs, relaying goods from
the kitchen through the courtyard and on to the birthing chamber.[4]

Gray-haired Atun Mama, Babur's deceased mother's embroidery teacher,
would stand near the steps of the room, a border between the open outside
and the sheltered chamber. A wise chaperone, she guarded against unnec-
essary intrusions and, at the appropriate time, dispatched the news of the
arrival of the baby to the attendants outside the precincts of the women's
apartments.[5]

The circumstances of the birth of Gulbadan in 1523 would have brought
back a hoard of memories for Khanzada. She would think about the fertile
plains of the Punjab where her brother Babur was once again engaged in ar-
bitrations with dissident groups, negotiations that would change the course

of their dynasty. She would reflect on how men loved war, a constant feature of their lives, and how their dreams of conquest shaped them.

For sixteenth-century men of regal bloodlines, Khanzada knew well, warring satisfied their dynastic ambition and enabled them to play out their lust for power. Together with her grandmother and mother, Khanzada had often convoyed with Babur in his earlier campaigns, staying in tents pitched away from the battleground or in the vicinity of the cities under attack.

As she paced about, Khanzada would realize with surprise that over a decade had passed since she had left Samarkand—the vibrant Central Asian city and the seat of her forefather Timur, which his descendants had fought over. Babur had campaigned there thrice. His refusal to give up defined him and the dynasty as a whole, affecting the lives of women like Khanzada. During his second Samarkand campaign, in 1501, Babur had bartered Khanzada to secure safe passage out of Samarkand for himself, and she lived there for a decade, married to his lifelong enemy, the victorious Uzbek leader, Shaibani Khan.

Women living in war zones were constantly at the threshold of danger. Nothing was private, not even the birthing of children.[6] After decades of perennial war and turbulence, the Mughals had enjoyed relative stability after 1511. Babur's household and women were based mainly in Kabul and the surrounding provinces, where he was lord and master. Nonetheless, they lived amid fluid and uncertain circumstances. Babur carried on his war plans to expand his territories, his men frequently raided local tribes, and the tussle with clansmen was endless. For four years, he had been actively engaged in making inroads into Hindustan, the land beyond the river Indus or Hind. In late 1523, as Dildar birthed their fourth child in the fort of Kabul, he was afar, busy negotiating campaigns with rebel forces who contested the policies of Ibrahim Lodi, the sultan of Delhi.

For Babur as well as the women, there were no sharply distinct times of war. Rather, there was a sense of repeated, even constant, emergencies that led to war. Theirs was a universe marked by war, movement, and varied events occurring simultaneously: death, festivity, poetry recitation, adoration of nature, domestic and factional conflict, and the forging of alliances, as well as looking to the stars and sages for guidance, taking auguries, and marveling at mysteries.

Sitting in the birth chamber, Khanzada would invoke the divine. The situation was full of hope and peril. As a Persian saying of their time had it, "From the day of conception on, a woman has one foot in this world and one foot in the other."[7]

Maham was unquestionably Babur's favorite wife, though not necessarily his preferred sexual partner. At this point, she was not overly dependent on the affections of her husband. It was the authority of motherhood that mattered, as it elevated Mughal women's status and promised them a life of power. Maham's husband consulted her on important decisions such as succession. She also wielded great power over the Mughal children.

As they grew older, Mughal mothers became *vali-ni'matan,* the beneficent seniors, respected and dominant figures who could influence royal men, their decisions, and the fate of the court and household.[8] Women elders instructed younger women, urged them to have children, and intervened to protect young princes. Political ambition, intrigue, and aspirations cultivated in the households of mothers and senior women were tied intimately and intricately to courtly matters.

As the domineering Maham anxiously waited in her apartment anticipating the arrival of the new baby of her co-wife, she likely pondered the events of 1519 in Kabul. Then, as in 1523, her co-wife Dildar was pregnant, and the due date was fast approaching. Babur was away, with dreams of conquest on his mind: he had captured two forts east of Kabul and acquired the provinces of Swat and Bajaur following his marriage to Mubarika. He was about to cross the river Sind, thus setting foot in Hindustan for the first time.

Maham dispatched a letter to Babur, which reached him on January 29, 1519. Letter-carrier Yusuf 'Ali *rikabdar* served as Babur's stirrup-holder, groom, attendant, and cupbearer. The letter concerned a topic Babur and Maham had discussed earlier. Though the letter itself does not survive, Babur and his daughter Gulbadan, born in 1523 in the Bala Hisar, wrote about these events and discussed the dispatch. Whether it was a boy or a girl, wrote Maham, she would take over Dildar's child and raise it as her own. She repeated her wish with urgency. The birth was drawing near, so she implored Babur to perform the well-known rite determining whether it would be a boy or a girl and authorize her to take over the newborn.

Babur may have performed the divination rite himself or had it done by women in his camp. Two pieces of paper were inscribed, one with a boy's name and another with a girl's. The pieces were wrapped in clay and set in water. When the moist clay opened, the first name disclosed would reveal the gender, so it was believed. Babur opened the moist clay to find a boy's name. He communicated the prophecy to Maham in a letter, and assured her that Dildar's expected child would certainly be given to her.

Two months later, Dildar gave birth to a son in Kabul. Across the Indus, Babur successfully took the town of Bhira, his first Indian acquisition. Twenty miles north of Bhira, overlooking a reservoir named Kala Kahar, as his men dug the earth to build Bagh-i Safa', the Garden of Purity, the footman and expert matchlock man Darvish 'Ali brought Babur the auspicious news of his son's birth.

Babur took that news "as a good omen" and named his son Hindal, *of the dynasty of Hind.*[9] The next morning, on a boating excursion with his men, he drank spirits till late afternoon. Then, disgusted by the bad taste of the spirits, Babur and his men switched to *ma'jun,* a mild narcotic concoction made into a chewable pellet.

In Kabul the baby boy was named 'Abdul Nasir but given the sobriquet Hindal, by which he is known in history. Three days after his birth, Maham took the infant from his mother and brought him to her quarters. That was in 1519.

Now, in 1523, as Maham eagerly awaited the birth of her co-wife's new baby, the four-year-old Prince Hindal was by her side.

Dildar brought her fourth child, a baby girl with rose-hued skin, into the world. They named her Gulbadan. Her older sisters had also been named for roses, which symbolized the beloved, and elegance and beauty: Gulrang, "rose-hued," and Gulchihra, "rose-cheeked."

Women singers and dancers sitting under the tented awning outside the birth chamber sang songs of birth as Gulbadan was delivered. Atun Mama asked an attendant to relay the news to the doorkeeper outside the women's premises. The doorkeeper would announce that a new flower had appeared in the "fortunate quarters."[10] When the news reached the city and the mosque, the mullah or cleric would read verses from the Qur'an and glorify Babur. Perhaps an encomiast recited celebratory verses for Gulbadan's birth. A royal retainer gave alms to the poor and the needy.

Babur did not see the newest Rose immediately. As she came into the world, he was busy planning his next full-blown campaign in the Indian territories. Before long, the princess's little eyes would get used to the constant comings and goings of her father and his armies.

Mughal records establish that two years after Gulbadan's birth, Maham went to Dildar's apartment and took the little princess, exactly as she had her brother four years earlier. She would raise Gulbadan as her own.

We have no way of knowing what specifically made her claim custody of the princess. From time immemorial, becoming guardians of children who were not one's own ran in the royal family. Five generations earlier, Saray Khanum, a powerful (childless) wife of Babur's paternal ancestor and hero Timur, fostered her stepsons and grandsons. Later, a daughter-in-law presented Saray with her two-month-old son in a festive setting, the occasion marked by exchange of gifts. In-house adoption and fostering were frequent among the Mughals.[11]

In the absence of any record, we do not know how Dildar felt about this. Maham's higher status obviously enabled her to secure the right to raise her co-wife's children. In the lives of premodern chieftains and kings, marriages were not meant primarily to serve the modern ideals of a comfortable home or the pleasures of conjugal love. Rather, the desire for children was at the heart of royal matrimony. This desire became even more urgent in the case of peripatetic dynasties such as the Mughals. Infant deaths, which haunted Mughal women, occurred frequently; Mughal documents are laden with lists of childless women and dead children.[12] Heirs were so critical that Babur preserved the memory of Mubarika, whom he adored, not as his beloved but as a childless woman.

As a young mother, Maham had lost four children in their infancy. Her only surviving son was Humayun, fifteen at the time of Gulbadan's birth and in charge of important provinces. Overseeing royal children meant significant maneuverability and decision-making influence, which in turn would enhance Maham's power and claim to the children's long-term loyalty.

Even though physical separation was not total in circumstances where blood and guardian mothers were part of the same large household, it is to be expected that Dildar would be disconcerted to have her children taken from her. Her distant personality and subdued presence in Mughal chronicles speak of sadness.

What we know from Gulbadan's later writings is that she experienced joyful times with Maham, her guardian mother, before returning to live with Dildar when she was ten.[13] As she came of age, she and Dildar had lively conversations. She wrote of trips to the Kabul hills, wondrous gatherings and festivities in imperial tents, picnics, splendid poetry, as well as the magnificent storytelling of adventurous Mughal women. We also know that Dildar lived with Hindal later in life when she became a widow.

Two

The Rose Garden

～

IN THE *ROSE GARDEN*, EVERYONE WAS WELCOME: THE GOOD, the bad, the weak, the strong, the pious, the impious, the honest, the craftiest of cheats, stupid kings, clever vazirs, and spiteful courtiers. There were dervishes, hermits, and wandering and poor sages seeking spiritual enlightenment. There were lovers, friends, and charmers, adorable young boys, captivating aunts, a girl studying Arabic grammar in a mosque, a jurist who fell in love with a blacksmith's boy, a kindhearted vazir who advised his king not to kill a prisoner, and a beggar who amassed tremendous wealth from begging. The *Rose Garden* was not a real garden with tender, sweet-smelling blooms, but one of the most widely read books, its pages animated by enticing figures, influential characters adorned with fragrance and thorns like roses.

Written in Persian in 1258 by Shaykh Sa'di of Shiraz, the *Gulistan* is a collection of stories offering moral and practical wisdom—akin to *Aesop's Fables*. From Constantinople to Delhi, and from Central Asia to East Africa, aristocratic children read it well into the eighteenth century. Adults used its parables to guide children in appropriate courses of action. The ideals embedded in these stories included a wide range of subjects: the merits of silence, the treatment of elderly, and the arts of governance and love, for example. Sometimes people used the *Gulistan* like poetry, to facilitate conversation.[1]

Stories were the earliest components of Gulbadan's education—literary, ethical, and practical. As her plump baby cheeks gave way to higher cheekbones, and sharp black eyes appeared under straight eyebrows, a Mongol facial feature, she listened with great curiosity. Along with the stories in the *Gulistan,* Mughal women shared the delights of the sagacious storyteller

Scheherazade in the *Thousand and One Nights,* and verses from famous poets such as Mir 'Ali Sher Nava'i. The female teacher, or *mu'allima,* who may have lived in the fort or visited from the city of Kabul, taught the girls the required Qur'an and possibly arithmetic. Male tutors taught Mughal boys martial arts, archery, swordsmanship, riding, and managing horses. Royal girls and boys learned in separate spaces, but some content was shared: the craft of calligraphy, polished discourse, memorizing orations, proverbs, poems, anecdotes, dialogues, elegant stories, and witticisms, along with music, polo, and the arts of personal cultivation.

As in any imperial house of that era, Gulbadan and her older sisters spent time mainly in the company of women in their multiple and neighboring compounds. Built of lime and mortar, only the upper section of the historic Bala Hisar citadel—described as a citadel because it was a fortified residence as well as a military base—was in existence then. When in the fort, Gulbadan heard the din and clamor of marching men, the synchronized clicks of horses' hooves, the almost symphonic firearms, and victory bugles.

Dressed in a silken tunic and trousers gathered near her ankles, she ran along the ramparts with her siblings, watching men come and go, or hid behind walls decorated with blue and white diamond- and star-shaped tessellated bands. Accompanied by adults, the girls walked down the mud pathways to the ground below, where the ceremonial courtyard and the garden spread out. Beyond the walls was the city of Kabul.[2]

The news of her father's battles beyond the river Indus dominated Gulbadan's Kabul years. In 1523, at the time of her birth, Babur had been engaged in an attempt to conquer Hindustan. He succeeded when she was nearly three years old. For a year in between, from late 1524 on, Babur was based in the province of Kabul but fully involved in planning the fulfillment of his dreams of gaining the land across the river Indus. Although Babur ruled the province of Kabul and bordering regions, he had no luxurious palaces, Peacock throne, or Kohinoor diamond. The Mughals were not yet the magnificent dynasty of popular lore and memory. They still had the nomadic inheritance of Timur and Chingiz Khan, even as they inhabited the urbanity of Persian culture. Babur lived mostly in imperial tents with a coterie of close confidants, attendants, advisers, and servants. An ardent lover of the outdoors, he built a series of gardens in and around Kabul.

Often the Mughal household moved and lodged in tents spread for miles near the gardens and amid high mountain valleys, dashing streams, and trees ablaze in autumn. Embroidered awnings, many worked in gold thread, shaded the entrances to the trellis tents—round, arched, and rectangular—erected on supple wooden frames covered with waxed cloth and hung with silk or velvet. Screens of carved wood and felt pieced in ornamental patterns separated one section of the encampment from another.

At the main tent entrance, the arrivals and departures of important people were announced by the beating of drums. Outside the entrance to the left were open-air enclosures for horses and tents for the supervisors and staff of the stables. To the right was the *daftar*, the imperial office, where Babur's men managed accounts of the booty collected after raids upon the local tribes, daily expenses, and pay. Next to the daftar were tents for storing palanquins, carts, and artillery—including the early cannons that Babur began using.

Khwaja Kalan, a longtime confidant whom Babur fondly called *musahib*, or companion, and the *aichkildar*, a term that embraced his closest associates, such as the chief scribe and paymaster, often came to the tented hall. So too did the members of the *khasa-tabin*, who were in Babur's immediate command and in close physical proximity to him during his numerous battles. These men, as well as the chief equerry, the stirrup-holder, and the Lord of the Gate were important, intimate members of what Babur called "my household."[3]

Babur and his men planned military and political moves, received important news from near and far, welcomed emissaries, and made new appointments. They drank wine, and Babur wrote poems to celebrate Nawroz, the Persian New Year's Day, remarking on the beauty of the crops of Koh Daman (north of Kabul) and its wondrous autumnal trees. He finished copying the great poet Mir 'Ali Sher Nava'i's collection and sent it to his nephew Pulad in Samarkand.[4] Aspiring poets regularly copied great verses to learn their form, metaphors, and allusions.

Behind the public tents and spaces was the women's area: tents for each of the royal women were pitched in this part of the royal encampment. In keeping with her status as an exalted wife, Gulbadan's guardian mother Maham had the largest tent. Next in order were those of the other wives, and then of Khanzada, the other aunts, and the great-aunts.

Babur's tent was to the right of the women, and if the older princes were present, theirs were to the left. Quite often these princes were away, serving as boy chiefs in the provinces. Gulbadan's half brother Humayun, for example, was then the governor of Badakhshan. If he came to visit, as he often did, his tent was to the left of the women. Kitchens, quarters for servants and guards, cavalrymen, foot soldiers, and artillerymen were behind the royal camp quarters. Guards protected the campsite. Gulbadan recalled fondly the night guard, a eunuch named 'Asas.[5]

When in Bala Hisar, Mughal princesses and queens lived in their own individual quarters, attended by a large staff that focused on their needs. Among them were midwives, scribes, lamplighters, pages, stewards, door-keepers, oil keepers, cooks, tasters, tailors, palanquin bearers, water carriers, perfumers, weavers, and masons. Close companions, Atun and Bibi Fatima looked after the women and their younger children—nursing, clothing, washing, and keeping the children from bodily harm—or cleaning the silver fruit trays and keeping rose water ready so that members of the household could cool their hands and faces with an invigorating splash. Under the watchful eye of Atun, managers oversaw the production and procurement of food and clothing needed by the household and distributed foodstuffs to the cooks. They lit the fire to warm the household on chilly wintry mornings. Another servant inspected storerooms and checked the goods. When senior women like Khanzada or Maham hosted important victory celebrations or ceremonial banquets, the whole family gathered in their premises.

Although officially in the hands of Maham, Gulbadan also spent time in other women's quarters. The shared concern and responsibility of raising children blunted the desires and rivalries of co-wives. Just as in the fort premises, Gulbadan, her sisters, and the little Prince Hindal went freely from one part of the women's tent to another. In sharing their children and a husband, however, there was also friction among Mughal co-wives.

Babur was constantly on the move, even when he was in Kabul. He spent much more time in the company of his men than he ever seemed to with women. Retiring to the women's quarters was hardly the theme of his life. Being amid his men, constant movement, warfare, and drink did not leave a great deal of time or space for the company of women. But when possible, or when he desired, Babur visited the premises of his wives as well as those of the elderly aunts and Khanzada.

Many elderly matriarchs sought Babur's attention. The necessity of visiting them continued when Babur was based with his household on a more regular basis in India. In Agra, duty-bound, he used to go and see his paternal aunts every Friday. Gulbadan reports that on one of those Fridays it was very hot. Maham suggested to Babur, "The wind is very hot, indeed; how would it be if you did not go this one Friday?" Babur, disturbed by Maham's proposition, responded that he was astonished that she should say such things. "The daughters of Abu Sa'id Sultan Mirza [Babur's grandfather], who have been deprived of father and brothers! If I do not cheer them, how will it be done?"[6]

On those occasions, when Babur spent time with his women and children, his offspring looked at him with both awe and fondness. Gulbadan addressed him as "*my Baba*," dear father. Even though the get-togethers with her father were infrequent, the stories about him captivated the little princess. When Gulbadan was growing up in Kabul, news of Babur's victories and difficulties abroad dominated all conversation. Baba was fond of war and poetry alike, she learned. A skillful archer and excellent swordsman, he always wore double-soled boots. Even as he wandered as a throneless warrior, he dreamed of conquest and glory. Later on, writing about his ventures and difficulties, Gulbadan noted sympathetically that his exploits were such that the "tongue of the pen is too feeble to recount them."[7]

The Mughal household's excursions were joyous occasions. The river Baran, lined with rosebuds, was heavenly. North of Kabul, in Gulbahar, the Spring Flower hills, wildflowers crept up the hills. Forty-nine miles east of Kabul was Adinapur, and nearby Pamghan was the best place in Kabul province, according to Babur. The Garden of Fidelity, *Bagh-i Wafa*, near the Fort of Adinapur, had a stream flowing through its center. Pomegranate and orange trees filled the garden. Bananas and sugarcane abounded in the meadows. Few villages matched Istalif, a special favorite of the Mughals. As they wandered through the orchards of plane trees along both sides of the river that ran through the village, the older women may have recalled the violets, roses, and tulips in Andijan in the Valley of Ferghaneh, their ancestral home in western Central Asia.[8]

Sitting together or in their own apartments, with their children running and playing around them, women shared stories, recited poems in Turkish and Persian, read the verses of the Qur'an in Arabic, and pondered political news. Impromptu gatherings of this kind were open platforms in the

Mughal domestic world. A few women sat together, others joined in, and conversation flowed. News from afar might turn the gathering festive or somber depending on the fortune of the moment.

Gulbadan came of age in this semi-settled, outdoor-oriented royal world filled with magical tales and structured by the rhythms of homosocial lives. In the fort and tents of Kabul, she took her first steps and wrote the first letter of the Turkish script, gradually etching alphabets from right to left, as in the related Arabic and Persian scripts. Opportunities for curiosity, learning, and growth were rich. Gulbadan and her sisters shared many of the same stories and experiences, while the boys, who had greater leeway and opportunities, grew up to become warriors and governors. For most royal and aristocratic girls, despite all the cultivation of their minds and their literary sophistication, marriage and having children were their destiny. They were expected to be at the epicenter of caring. Even though they wandered the countryside and lived for long periods in tents, they were bound by the constraints of the royal household.

Babur relied heavily on the advice of his elder relatives, including his mother and grandmother. The women expressed their views in private meetings, never in public quarters. From the powerful women of her family Gulbadan learned how wars, dreams of conquests, and ancient lands shaped her father's career as well as how war and misfortune determined the fate of the brave Mughal women who accompanied them. Farsighted and judicious, her great-grandmother Isan Daulat was seized four times in wars, the first in late 1472 during a dearth of barley in Mughulistan (modern-day Mongolia).[9]

While Yunas Khan, Isan's husband and the Great Khan of the Mongols, was away to secure more grain for the household, a man named Shaikh Jamal attacked the estate and took Isan captive. She offered no objection when she was told that she would have a new husband—not Jamal, her captor, but someone else. When the chosen groom came into her quarters, Isan had the doors locked behind him. Her women servants were ready. As soon as the man entered, they stabbed him to death and threw his body into the street. Jamal sent a messenger to inquire what was happening. Isan retorted that she killed the man because giving her in marriage to another man while her husband was alive was against the law. Jamal was free to do as he wished, she added. Jamal, respecting her action, restored the brave Isan to her husband Yunas.[10]

Heir to the courage and determination of women like Isan, Gulbadan learned how impressive and dynamic ancestresses dealt with perilous situations and preserved their honor. From such stories, Gulbadan began to gather a rich sense of her Mughal heritage.

An attachment to the regions associated with their ancestors persisted in Gulbadan's family amid their movement from one land to another. For a long time, one such ancestral place, the seat of their venerable forefather Timur, dominated her father's thoughts: the thriving city of Samarkand, perched between two rivers and the richest cultural and historical city of western Central Asia.

Hearing that at age eleven her father had ascended to the throne of the lush Ferghaneh valley piqued Gulbadan's curiosity. Babur loved the natural bounties of his valley, especially the melons and the autumnal gardens of Ush where cattle browsed in rich clover meadows and among apricots and pomegranates. Her father's first sovereign seat was rich, but not as rich as Samarkand. Like many rulers of the Timurid line, Babur wanted Samarkand.

He won it for short periods on two occasions, only to lose it the third time. During the second siege of Samarkand, after agreeing to give Khanzada in marriage to Shaibani Khan to ensure safe exit, a panic-stricken Babur left behind his grandmother, mother, and the household head, Bachaka. He sped on ahead. The women eventually joined Babur's retinue after a miserable winter week spent barefoot in the hills. The old servant Atun Mama, left without a horse, journeyed on foot to join Babur and the ladies. With approximately three hundred men, brave women, and only two tents, they went south through the Hisar Mountains. After his third failed attempt to conquer Samarkand, Babur finally accepted his fate. He now sought to consolidate his hold on Kabul and its surroundings. Instead of looking north, he turned his gaze southeast across the river Indus.

The elders' whispered conversation would provoke Gulbadan's curiosity even more. Was she fascinated by the fate of Shaibani? In time Aunt Khanzada would reveal the full story, telling Gulbadan why she stayed behind, or rather was left behind, as the royal family withdrew from the gates of Samarkand. Much later, Gulbadan would write in granular detail about the bartering of her aunt.

Gulbadan grasped the allusions to the earthly and the divine in poetry and fables, and the torments and travails of Qur'anic characters. Her reading followed other prescriptions and guidance. She and her sisters were expected to read aloud the elegant lyrical prose of the *Rose Garden*. Within Sa'di's parables lay instruction for the future—allegories of the challenges of youth and adulthood as well as guidelines for wise leadership.

Contemporary works such as those of the fifteenth-century poet Jami and his friend Mir 'Ali Sher Nava'i were hugely popular, famous from Istanbul to Delhi. Babur loved the art of poetry above all, and himself wrote a collection of poems that Gulbadan read.

Poetry, prosody, and lyrical enunciations were key features of women's gatherings. Verses and odes peppered conversations. Reciting verses was like supplication to the divine in moments of awe and in hardship. Poets composed works to mark births, deaths, and military victories, and recited odes at festivals like 'Id.

A few of Gulbadan's verses survive:

A beauty who is not paired with her lover
For sure she is bereft of any kind of life.[11]

The level of mystical allusion and sophistication in these lines shows how well read she was in literary and prose traditions. A book collector, she read her father's memoirs, his poetry, and other contemporary writings. Her name appears in a major Safavid collection of female poets that covers the period from the twelfth to the eighteenth centuries.[12] Did she compose a *diwan*, a collection of her own poems?[13] We do not know.

For royal children in the early modern world, Gulbadan and her siblings among them, elders set the standard and the inspiration. Their experiences, advice, books, and poetry imparted majestic morals for the heart. *Adab*, or custom, was indispensable in character formation. Adab is also suggestive of cultural enhancement, good demeanor, and chivalry. A code of comportment in Mughal society, it is the subject of numerous books.

Manuals of comportment addressed the disciplining of the senses. One of the most important of these was Nasir al-Din Tusi's *Akhlaq-i Nasiri*, first published in 1235. "Let him [the prince] . . . from time to time adopt the custom of eating dry bread," Tusi counseled. "Such manners, albeit good in poor men, are even better in rich. . . . He should be accustomed not to drink water while eating and he should on no account be given wine and intoxicating drinks before he reaches early manhood." Walking and movement, riding and exercise were necessary. They were not to boast about wealth, possessions, food, or clothing. They were also to refrain from arrogance and obstinacy. A tutor who imparted ethical guidance had to be intelligent and religious, well versed in the training of dispositions, "with a reputation for fair speech and gravity, an awe-inspiring manner, manliness and purity; he must also be aware of the characters of kings, the manners involved in associating with them and addressing them."[14]

Strength, dexterity, daring, resolution, and loyalty led to the advancement of princes, their bodies trained for campaigns and battles. Being skilled in the martial arts, archery, swordsmanship, riding, and managing elephants and horses, along with the craft of calligraphy and polished discourse, would come in handy. Tusi's prescriptions for girls were very different. In the case of daughters, he wrote, "one must employ . . . whatever is appropriate and fitting to them. They should be brought up to keep close to the house and live in seclusion (*hijab*), cultivating gravity, continence ('*iffat*), modesty and other qualities. . . . They should be prevented from learning to read or write, but allowed to acquire such accomplishments as are commendable in women."[15] In his dogmatic manual, Tusi also declared that well-bred girls and boys should keep away from "frivolous poetry, with its talk of odes and love and winebibbing . . . for poetry can only be the corruption of youth."[16]

The people of the Mughal world disagreed. Lyrical sensibilities ran deep in the family. The Mughals also acknowledged the intellectual achievements of women. Poets and compilers of biographical compendiums wrote of Muslim women who were literary stars and of those learned in religion. According to these books, thirty-two female scholars lived in Baghdad in the eleventh century, while two hundred "noteworthy" women lived in Damascus in the twelfth century. A fifteenth-century Egyptian, Al-Sakhawi, wrote *Kitab al-Nisa,* an extensive collection of the biographies of several women of his time who were transmitters of the traditions of Prophet Muhammad's words and deeds.[17]

Closer to Gulbadan's home, seven poets in the Khurasan province of Iran were well known. A woman called Afaq Begum recited verses in the court of Babur's cousin in Herat. Another important figure before Afaq was Bija Munajjima, a well-known mystic and an excellent mathematician. A bitter rival of the major male poet Jami, she considered herself his equal.[18]

Gulbadan's prose accomplishments suggest that her elders didn't follow Tusi's harsher dictates. However, even without the stern advice of authorities like Tusi or the author of a similar earlier manual called the *Qabus-Nama,* the elders would insist that all their children learn patience, discernment, and the dutiful practice of faith. Gravity and courage marked a man; gravity, tenderness, and good judgment a woman. Indelicate language was not allowed. Short and refreshing were the "watchwords of conversation."[19] The harsher prescriptions of philosophers like Tusi could not impoverish the cultural world or imagination of enterprising queens and princesses like Khanzada, Isan, or Gulbadan.

Gulbadan wouldn't forget from her Kabul years the graceful women of her family who took her under their wings and formed the dominant landscape of her girlhood, including her mother Dildar; her guardian mother Maham; and Bibi Mubarika, Babur's last wife and the princess's dear companion in play. Gulbadan's great-grandmother and grandmother died soon after her father took over Kabul in 1504, but the stories of their bravery thrived in domestic conferences.

Gulbadan would remember also visits to the river, excursions to the mountains, the tents pitched for long periods by gushing streams in the cool countryside, and the holy footprints of the mythic Khwaja Khizr in the vicinity of a spring near the mountains. Khizr was a beloved figure of peripatetic communities, a repository of the mysteries of the universe. A saint considered to be immortal by those who loved him, he was an amalgam of the prophet Elijah, who appears in the Old and New Testaments and in the Qur'an, the Mesopotamian demigod Gilgamesh, and Alexander the Great's legendary love, his cook Andreas, who accidentally fell into the fountain of youth and gained eternal life. Associated with water, fish, and rejuvenation, Khizr roamed the world, invisible at times, appearing to mortals to impart wisdom. Such mythology planted magic in Gulbadan's mind and sparked her love of literature and adventure.

Three

Curiosities of Hind

~

OUTSIDE THE CITY OF KABUL LAY THE ROYAL CAMPSITE OF Chahar Bagh, where Mughal attendants had installed scores of tented enclosures with screens made of leather, felt, and wood, pierced with delicate flowery designs. The garden, divided by walkways into four, had an audience hall with a stylish pavilion—Gulbadan's father's favorite spot for merriment, drink, and relaxation.

For three days in late June 1526, this hamlet of tents became the abode of the Mughal family. Prince Kamran, the thirteen-year-old second-eldest designated head of the Kabul household, was there along with royal women, princesses, younger princes, members of the royal establishment, and intimate staff. Court officers stationed in Kabul and their kin had their tents pitched outside the boundaries of the royal premises. The night guard, 'Asas, an aging eunuch, had a special invitation to the gathering.

The atmosphere was festive. The Kabul branch of the Mughal family had assembled to offer thanks for Babur's victory over the sultan of Delhi a couple of months earlier. His confidant and faithful general, the kindhearted Khwaja Kalan, had just arrived from Delhi. Along with other returning officers and men, he escorted a caravan of treasure chests. He carried in his pocket an important list from Babur, now the monarch of Kabul as well as Delhi and Agra.

As soon as he reached Kabul, Kalan met Maham, the senior-most Mughal wife, nearly seven months pregnant. There were important messages he wanted to deliver. Maintaining decorum and distance, senior women received court members freely. The highest-ranking wife according to Timurid practice—the bloodline that Babur upheld more than his lineage from

Chingiz Khan—was the first to receive important updates. War booty, precious stones, goblets, manuscripts, jewels, and camels went to the senior wife. She would keep the treasures secure.

Babur had sent boxes full of splendid things, several dancing girls from the court of the deceased sultan—and a list. "I shall write a list, and you will distribute the gifts according to it," His Majesty had instructed Kalan.[1] Elder relations, royal sisters and wives, heads of households, servants, and children were on it. Babur wrote out detailed directions for what should be given to whom and in what order. He made clear to Kalan that the assembly was to take place in Chahar Bagh—hence the excursion outdoors.[2]

Under a summer sky, with the hills in the distance, the women and children, including Gulbadan, set out in palanquins, covered carts hung upon poles and carried by strong men. Her small figure attired in silken clothes, the princess huddled close to Mubarika. The pregnant Maham would travel in a separate palanquin, attended by Nanacha, an older household intimate. At two and a half years, Gulbadan would charm her relatives, lisping endearing childlike Turki sentences: dearest Aunt Khanzada, or *Aka Janam;* my dear mother *Acam*, as she called Dildar; *Mama*, her caretaker Fakhr-un-Nisa. Mubarika was *Afghani Aghacha*, the Afghan Lady.

Princes and officers rode horses. Soldiers and male staff circled in front of and behind the royal retinue. They descended from Bala Hisar and went out the Leather Gate, briefly entering the city of Kabul. They would cross Mulla Baba's bridge to skirt the bazaars. Once they passed a small building called the Bear-house, they were in the open country. When the gate with a picture hall placed prominently above it came into view, they had reached their destination.[3]

Although Babur frequently sent word about his triumphs and defeats, there was still so much to ask Kalan. Members of the Mughal household would not forget their last glimpse of Babur when he set out with his army amid the hustle and bustle of armed men, horses, and trumpets. The emperor's three paternal aunts, expecting to go to Hindustan soon, would want to know what it was like. Everyone was concerned about Babur's health. The battle with the Delhi sultan would interest Princes Kamran and 'Askari, both sons of Gulrukh, the second-in-rank wife. Seven-year-old Prince Hindal, living with his custodian mother and little sister Gulbadan, would brim with curiosity.

When Babur left Kabul in late 1525, Gulbadan had just turned two. Her guardian mother was again pregnant. Though the household was used to Babur's frequent comings and goings, this time they had been uneasy. He was going to a remote land unfamiliar to them. They'd heard that Hindustan had vast rivers, intense periods of heat and rain, and vast fertile plains. Hindustanis were not people of the Book, they had been told.

Although this was Babur's fifth expedition to Hind, it was not a small foray, as the earlier ones had been. He had set out to attack the formidable Lodi king. The northern two-thirds of the Indian subcontinent were in the hands of independent kingdoms. In its heartland, where Babur was headed, Ibrahim Lodi ruled. Ibrahim was a powerful ruler and master of the territories to the east and south, including the Punjab, Northwest provinces, Bihar in the east, and a part of western Rajasthan. He had a sizable and disciplined army. Babur was counting on the increasing dissatisfaction among Ibrahim's local chieftains. He had forged significant alliances and had the backing of large forces and men, such as the uncle of Sultan Ibrahim and the governor of Punjab. Even though Babur was confident, the women in Kabul were uneasy.

Immediately after Babur left Kabul and headed north toward Badakhshan, where Humayun joined him, the women received news that the emperor was alarmingly ill. The ailment was temporary. Babur was paying a price for drinking too much and taking drugs. His sickness was divine chastisement, he ruefully noted in his diary.

Once recovered, Babur advanced further. In the fort of Milawat, which he captured on his way to Badakhshan, he found a stack of prized manuscripts, mainly theological in content. He gave some books to Humayun when they met and sent some to his other son Kamran. Books were rare then. As the head of the Kabul household, Kamran would invite women and children for the ritual of viewing the valuable books.

Accompanied by the slim and delicate-featured Humayun, now in active service, Babur turned to the territories of Hind. Humayun's mother was elated when he secured his first victory, over the town of Hisar-Firoza in Punjab. Babur bestowed the captured town and district on Humayun, gave him a large sum of money, and immediately dispatched a courier to Kabul. The prince had his servants trim his beard, emulating his father, who had done the same after conquering Kabul in 1504. The ritual marked the launch of victory celebrations.

And so it went—good and bad news, gains and losses, the estrangement or alliance of nobles, and the web of alignments that Babur fashioned with chiefs and landlords. It was hard to keep track of the constantly shifting loyalties and numerous desertions. Until late May 1526, no one knew what the outcome would be. Then, the swiftest of runners, covering the distance in less than a month, brought joyous tidings from Delhi. Babur had overthrown and killed the sultan of Delhi. The inhabitants of Bala Hisar were elated.

His generalship was historic, Kalan told them. Babur had expertly implemented Mongol flanking maneuvers and used them to his advantage. Kalan told the assembly how His Majesty supported each section of his army any time they wavered, how he roused his soldiers, and how he inspired them and reminded them why they were on the battlefield.

"By God's grace, he [Babur] was victorious," Gulbadan later wrote. "His victory was won purely by Divine grace, for Sultan Ibrahim had 180,000 horses, and as many as 1,500 fierce heads of elephants, while His Majesty's army with the traders and goods and all was 12,000 persons, and he had at the outside 6,000 or 7,000 serviceable men."[4] A key factor in Babur's victory was the use of gunpowder, a recent invention. His army skillfully used the *tufang*, or matchlock musket. Babur also used Ottoman-inspired cannon chained together to hold his center while his cavalry swept around the Lodi army's flanks.

Kalan spoke over the three days and nights of the challenges Babur faced and the constant loneliness he felt in the new land. He recalled evocatively and with pride the day of the Friday prayer in the mosque of Delhi when the mullah read a sublime *khutba* and pronounced Babur the sovereign of Delhi. *Bismillah!* The reverberating cry ascended in the garden. A vital endorsement, the khutba was a legal ratification of kingship and one of the three emblems of kingship in Islam. The other two would soon emerge: coins and imperial orders with the ruler's name and signature.

It was exceptionally hot when Babur entered Agra, recalled Kalan. A pestilential wind blew through the city, and many local people had grown sick and died. As soon as Babur's forces came into view peasants fled, and the populace in the city and its vicinity refused to follow orders to surrender. Those peasants and villagers who stayed in the area surrounding Agra made it difficult for Babur's men to acquire grain for soldiers or straw for their horses.

Mughal nobles and warriors soon lost heart, continued Kalan, and wanted to leave. Babur summoned them for a council. Addressing them with measured yet inspiring words, he tried to assuage their fears. "What now compels us to throw away for no reason all the realms we have taken at such cost?" he asked. "Shall we go back to Kabul and remain poverty-stricken?"[5] Kalan confessed that he was not happy staying on since he hated the heat. His constitution was poor. In the end the emperor relented, and Kalan left for Kabul.

The emperor's kinfolk couldn't get enough of Kalan's reports. News of events, strange happenings in places that Babur had conquered, would be repeated afterward and discussed animatedly in women's assemblies. Gulbadan later recalled the victories and massive difficulties "of my royal father," suggestive of the impressions created on her mind. Her elders fine-tuned the story of the Mughal dynasty in Hindustan and beyond.

After hearing Kalan, the three paternal aunts of Babur, Fakhr-jahan Begum, Bakht-Sultan Begum, and Khadija, who would be among the first elders to join their nephew after his victory in Hindustan, would wonder whether their upcoming trip was safe. Babur had close relatives by his side in Delhi and Agra, including his eldest son Humayun and the loyal fiscal minister, Nizam al-Din Barlas. Nevertheless, he was dejected when Kalan left. Gulbadan would remark in her book on her father's distress, noting the half-heartedness with which he granted Kalan leave: "His Majesty was not at all willing for him to go, but at last gave permission because he saw it [as] so very urgent."[6]

After his conquest of Delhi, Babur had moved into Sultan Ibrahim's palace. A close coterie of advisers and soldiers remained in attendance on him. He asked Buwa Begum, the deceased sultan's mother, to continue residing in her establishment in one section of the palace. If Kalan shared this information with those gathered in the garden, it is likely that they wondered whether it was secure to let Buwa stay in the palace. The move was not without its risks. Babur was an enemy, the man who had hacked Buwa's son to pieces.

Despite the challenges, Babur's Kabul family was told he was determined to stay on in Hindustan. The province of Kabul was already his; he now had a foothold in a rich territory from which he aspired to build a grand empire. Every ritual and practical step he took showed his desire to settle in the newly conquered areas. After his officers made inventories of the treasures in Delhi, he awarded territories and goods to everyone in the army according to their station: Afghans, Hazaras, Arabs, and Baluch as well as those "on the other side," as Babur put it, that is, the ones not still in Hindustan.[7]

Before Kalan's departure, Babur granted him the province of Ghazni in southeastern Afghanistan. He also gave Kalan the district of Guram in Hindustan to ensure that he returned. He sent gifts to all his relatives and kinsfolk as far away as Samarkand, Khurasan, and Iraq, and gave offerings for benediction to the Holy Cities Mecca and Medina.

By the time the Mughal household assembled in Chahar Bagh in June 1526, Babur had already sent invitations to his relatives to relocate to his new kingdom. Gulbadan recalls the words of the first imperial summons: "We shall take into full favor all who enter our service, especially those who served our father and grandfather and ancestors. . . . They will receive fitting benefits. Whoever there may be of the families [of Timur and Chingiz Khan] . . . let them turn towards our court. The most High has given us sovereignty in Hindustan; let them come that we may see prosperity together."[8] The senior aunts assembled in the garden planned their visit to their nephew after receiving this invitation.

In preparation for the gift-giving ceremony, the benevolent ladies and other members of the Mughal circle sat upon a comfortable dais in the pavilion amid soft rugs, cushions, and pillows. An embroidered awning directly above them was held in place by gilded tent poles. Family members such as senior aunts, royal wives, and princes and princesses with their nurses sat together; near them were Khanzada and her half sisters. Key women of the royal staff, Bibi Fatima and Nanacha would sit in the row behind the Mughal family. Across from this group, on the other side, were Princes Kamran, Hindal, and 'Askari and the foster brothers of the emperor as well as senior male officers stationed in Kabul.

Silver ewers with rose water, drinking vessels, and water sprinklers were placed on all sides. Several heavy wooden boxes lined with gold coating at the edges were opened. Their contents were placed on trays covered with bright silken and velvet cloths. Dressed in tight upper bodices and dark blue and shiny brown cloth belts adorned with trinkets around their waists, the dancing girls sat on one side of the assembly. Frocks with multiple folds that went as far as their knees spread around them. When they stood up, tight trousers accentuated the curves of their bodies. Circular caps decorated with beads and flowers perched above their ears. The top of each cap was slightly raised.[9]

The displayed gifts, the "curiosities of Hind," as Gulbadan dubbed them in her book, were ready for distribution.[10]

Before long, splendid Arabic voices arose in a harmonious recitation of the *Words of Praise,* the verses of the *Fatiha,* the opening chapter of the Qur'an.

> In the name of God, Most Gracious, Most Merciful
> Praise be to God,
> The Cherisher and Sustainer of the Worlds;
> Most Gracious, Most Merciful;
> Master of the day of Judgment.
> Thee do we worship,
> And thine aid we seek.
> Show us the straightway,
> The way of those on whom
> Thou hast bestowed Thy Grace,
> Those whose (portion)
> Is not wrath,
> And will not go astray.[11]

Slowly attempting to speak this Arabic verse, Gulbadan would look at Mama Fakhr-un-Nisa, her chief caretaker, for guidance.

As soon as incantations to the divine were over, Khwaja Kalan would summon attendants to bring golden trays to the royal ladies. The elderly aunts were each given four trays. There were jewels: rubies, pearls, cornelians, diamonds, emeralds, turquoise, topaz, and cat's-eye. A mound of gold and silver coins, *ashrafis* and *shahrukhis,* sat on a tray made of mother-of-pearl. The treasure also comprised luxurious fabrics, including the famed brocade from Gujarat, in sets of nine, a number considered auspicious in the Turkish world. Among the gifts, says Gulbadan, was "one special dancing-girl of the dancing-girls of Sultan Ibrahim." Attendants carried identical sets of trays, dancing girls accompanying them, to each of the Mughal women: Babur's wives, senior aunts, and sisters received the same share of the "curiosities of Hind."

Mughal princes were not on the gift list. Babur had earlier sent them gifts of varied sums from the Delhi treasury and noted their amounts in the *Baburnama:* for Kamran 17 lakhs of rupees, and for Hindal and 'Askari, 15 lakhs of rupees each (approximately $20,812 and $18,363). To all the three princes, he also sent pure gold and objects of silver, a variety of textiles, jewels, and slaves.

'Askari appears for the first time in his father's memoir in this account of gifts. Babur does not say what kind of jewels or objects he sent the princes or anything about the origins of the slaves. Again, although he gave Kalan instructions about the presents for the Kabul household and wrote out a list, he did not document the details in his *Baburnama.* It was little Gulbadan, one of the celebrants in the garden, who gave a full account of them in the prose chronicle she wrote sixty years later.

In keeping with Babur's instructions, the Mughal women distributed presents from their share to royal children, women employees, nurses, and household members. "The gifts were made according to the list," Gulbadan confirmed. She does not say what she received, or which "curiosity of Hind" caught her eye. The novel style and dress of the dancers fascinated her. She saw them dance during the feast that followed the gift-giving ceremony, their floral skirts spread out like canopies, displaying the many layers of color.

Gulbadan greatly enjoyed the joke her father played on 'Asas, the gentle night guard. Before Kalan left Delhi, Babur explained to him that if 'Asas asked what His Majesty had sent for him, "you will say one *ashrafi* [coin]." Kalan summoned the eunuch to tell him this. When he found out that he had been sent just the one coin, 'Asas was hugely disappointed. He was, after all, part of the intimate circle of the royal family as the man responsible for their protection.

Kingly associates like 'Asas performed many tasks in addition to their official responsibilities. Sometimes they fought at Babur's side, tested his food, bore his cup, groomed him, and danced for him. They guarded his wives and women. They carried news of births and adoptions. They offered solace and support in times of exile and hardship. Men like 'Asas and women like Fakhr-un-Nisa, the princess's caretaker, were great loyalists, loved and admired by the royal community. Gifts were important symbols not only to those who bestowed them—the Mughals cared deeply about precision in the preparation and the manner of presenting them—but also to the recipients. Royal gifts served as public declarations, honoring and acknowledging special people as well as praising those who served the king.

'Asas was confused at the meagerness of his gift—just a coin. What bewildered him even more was the emperor's instruction that he was to be blindfolded and the coin pierced and hung around his neck; in that fashion, he was to be sent to the women's quarters. That hardly seemed the way to treat an imperial servant. Rebels and dissidents were blindfolded.

The congregants watched closely. As soon as the coin was dangling around his neck, 'Asas realized it was an especially heavy one and thus worth a great deal. He was beside himself. Clinging to the coin with both hands, he jumped for joy and danced, exclaiming: "No one will take my ashrafi." Gulbadan laughed at 'Asas's caper. The royal ladies added to the merriment by giving him more coins.

"For three happy days," wrote Gulbadan, the party "remained together" and the revelry went on.[12]

Soon after their return to Kabul, the Mughal household received new reports about Babur's homesickness. He missed the symmetrical gardens of Kabul and found Agra disagreeable, he wrote. Scouting out land around the river Yamuna, he came upon an area that had a large well from which a bathhouse nearby drew water. In this excellent patch, surrounded by tamarind trees, he laid the foundation of the first Mughal garden. His forces, meanwhile, captured Bayana and Gwalior in central Hindustan. Though he continued building gardens and his victories bolstered him, Babur's restlessness did not lessen.

Approximately two months into the garden festivities, a letter arrived that shook Bala Hisar. Buwa Begum, the late sultan's mother, had tried to poison Babur. "The wretched Buwa . . . heard that I was eating food prepared by Hindustani cooks," wrote Babur. With the help of one of the women servants, she obtained poison, wrapped it up in a piece of paper, and then gave it to another woman servant, who took it to Ahmad, the taster. Ahmad gave it to the cook and promised him a large plot of land if he added the poison to Babur's food. The cook put the poison on the emperor's plate but not in the pot. "I had given the cooks strict instructions to supervise the Hindustanis and make them taste from the pot while the food was being prepared," Babur explained in his letter. The cook took a piece of thin bread and sprinkled less than half the poison on it. On top of the poison, he laid out slices of meat dressed in oil.

It was Friday evening, wrote Babur, providing details. He ate a lot of rabbit stew, dressed saffron meat, and "tidbits from the top of the poisoned Hindustani food.... I took the dressed meat and ate it.... I felt sick ... my stomach churned." As he felt the effects, suspicion rose in his mind. Immediately, he ordered the cook to be held. His servants fed the emperor's vomit to a dog, which collapsed at once. When they tortured the cook, he confessed. Babur ordered the taster to be hacked to pieces. The cook was skinned alive. "One of the two women I had thrown under the elephant's feet, and the other I had shot. I had Buwa put under arrest. She will pay for what she [did]." He explained that he had treated Buwa with respect, allowing her to stay in her palace as a courtesy. Her revenge, which he saw as betrayal, surprised him. "Do not worry," Babur said, reassuring his household.[13] However, Gulbadan believed that the effects of the poison were long lasting. Referring to a later bout of illness suffered by her father, Gulbadan noted that Buwa's poison was so strong that it affected His Majesty's overall health.

Neither Babur nor Gulbadan discuss Buwa's state of mind in their ruminations on this episode. Her son, Ibrahim Lodi, had been killed. It was to be expected that she was sorrowful, and was also, perhaps, afraid of being in proximity to the man who had slain her son. No honor shown to Buwa would make up for the loss of her son. Babur had murdered him, and she would avenge it. That was a mother's code of honor.

The punishment meted out to Buwa was dreadful. Babur put it matter-of-factly in the *Baburnama*. He gave Buwa to two of his officers for their use and then placed her in the custody of a trusted man for conveyance to Kabul. The women in Kabul knew what "use" meant. In the wars of the time, bartered women were part of the proceedings—as in so many wars before and since, all the way to Belgian Congo, Vietnam, Bosnia-Herzegovina, Rwanda, and Ukraine.

Buwa had other plans. Dreading the harsh treatment she knew she would receive in Kabul, she eluded her guards while crossing the river Indus, threw herself into the water, and drowned.

Mughal women now received news from Hind more frequently, thanks to the new postal system that Babur established between Agra and Kabul. The distance between the two cities was divided into several posts with resting towers and horses. Riders and grooms were ready at each junction to facilitate the quick relay of messages. The message that came in the next dispatch spread joy among the women. After weeks of fierce battle, Babur had defeated the intrepid Rana Sanga in the battle of Khanwa on the outskirts of the hill of Sikri.

A period of respite followed. Babur's soldiers and generals requested the leave promised to them. Prince Humayun had worked hard. He had been through one hot summer, and another was fast approaching. Babur gave his eldest son permission to leave Agra. On his way toward Badakhshan, Humayun went to Delhi, where he broke open the treasury and stole its contents. Among these was a great diamond that the queen of Gwalior had given the Mughals to save her honor during an attack. Distraught, Babur chided Humayun in a letter and reminded him of the lavish financial awards he had already received. Nonetheless, Humayun kept the Kohinoor diamond.

At this time, Prince 'Askari went to Hindustan. Providing him with a jeweled dagger, a belt and a royal dress of honor, the standard, horsetail and kettledrums, horses, ten elephants, mules, camels, and equipage of a royal camp, Babur deputed him to govern the eastern province of Bihar. For much of his life, 'Askari remained in the shadow of his older brother Kamran, who was in Kabul. But when he left for Bihar at age twelve, 'Askari was ready to set up his court.

In what would be the last phase of their domicile in Kabul, the Mughal women, rooted in ritual and care, continued their practice of the formalities of royal duties. Two months after the garden celebrations, Maham delivered a baby boy, Faruq, who died within a few weeks of his birth. The birth of Humayun's son gave Maham the pleasure of a first grandson and was likely a distraction from her own loss, which must have been heavy for a woman obsessed with motherhood.

As Babur settled more completely into his rich newly conquered territories, Maham and other women returned to poetry readings accompanied by the elegant sounds of a Jew's harp and a hammer dulcimer. There were more visits to the flowing streams to view the graceful fall of the weeping willows and the stunning height of the tall cypresses.

In late 1528, Babur ordered a full-scale migration of the Kabul household to Hindustan. Now that Humayun was in Badakhshan and Kamran in command of Kabul, the key territorial Afghan centers were secure. The princes would take care of family interests and deal with various men of the Timurid line who eyed His Majesty's Afghan territories. It was now Hindustan that preoccupied Babur. In order to build strong political alliances, he needed extensive settlement in this new land.

When Maham and Mubarika heard of Babur's order, Gulbadan asked them what the journey to Hindustan would be like. Kabul and its pleasures had made a singular impression on her mind thus far. The Avenue Garden, where water was scarce and a stream had to be diverted to hydrate the plants, had been repaired. Khwaja Kalan had planted another garden with the best regional trees. He laid out its lawns with sweet herbs and flowers of beautiful color and scent. The construction of a mosque in Kabul was advanced.

The princess had heard about the elephant with a long trunk and tusks and the rhinoceros, which was "the size of three Oxen," in the words of her father.[14] Did she ask repeatedly about these animals and other unseen ones: the captivating, slender Nilgai, or Indigo cow; the colorful and ornamental peacock; trickster monkeys; and other curiosities? Did she ask when she would get to see Baba across the Indus? She was excited to visit her father, she later wrote, not having seen him in three years—half her life.

When she sat in the palanquin, perhaps what excited Gulbadan above all else was the long journey itself, for adventure awaited.

Four

The First *Kafila*

⌢

COMING DOWN THE SNOW-LADEN TRAIL OF THE BALA HISAR fort, Gulbadan saw numerous strong, long-necked Turkish horses. Nearly a hundred of His Majesty's officers and servants gathered on the fort premises. Hindu Beg Quchin, the sturdy and steadfast officer who had valiantly assisted Babur in the recent battle of Panipat, was appointed to escort the Mughal family, including the six-year-old Gulbadan, the first Mughal girl to venture from Kabul to Agra.

In late 1528, Babur issued a sweeping order that the Mughal women and children in Kabul migrate to Hindustan to cultivate deeper relations in the area. He had earlier sent invitations to his kith and kin to visit or settle in the newly conquered territories across the river Indus, following which his three elderly great-aunts went on an eleven-month visit to Agra. But now the emperor added the urgency that a full-scale Mughal migration held great prospects for the dynasty. This was a strategic move, sparked by his increasing loneliness.

Under the command of Hindu Beg, the first *kafila*, or caravan, that departed from Kabul held Maham, her harem associate Nanacha, Afghan Lady Mubarika, Princess Gulbadan, and her nurse, Mama Fakhr-un-Nisa. Over a hundred retainers accompanied the royals.[1] They went in advance of Gulbadan's mother and sisters, aunts, and other household women, who would leave in succeeding waves when their transport and groups were ready. Prince 'Askari was by then in Hindustan. Based in Kabul, Prince Kamran would continue to govern the Afghan territories.

In sixteenth-century Hindustan and throughout the Islamic world, comprising modern-day Central Asia, Afghanistan, Iran, Turkey, and beyond, caravans were a common mode of travel. Traders usually carried goods in groups; ordinary travelers joined the trading convoys. But the Mughal cavalcade bound for Agra was exclusive since it had royal persons traveling to join the emperor.

They departed from Kabul on January 21, 1529, leaving behind the dark winter scenery, snow-capped clover mountains, and roads burdened with thick slabs of snow. The princess and her family were carried part of the way in palanquins, covered berths padded with soft mattresses and thick draperies hung from poles, borne by strong bearers. They were thus sheltered from extremes of chill, rain, or heat. Clad in heavy wool shawls that went atop and around their conical hats, the women would switch to horses or boats when necessary.

Horses and mules carried saddlebags stuffed with cloth, goods, grain, tents, and additional supplies. Servants refilled water along the way, wherever natural water sources were found or when the caravan stopped in inhabited areas. They would travel nearly nine hundred miles, and it would take them five months to reach their destination. While their migration was necessary, the journey was not an easy one. The trip was long and rough in many parts and the facilities on the road far from adequate. In the absence of inns where the Mughal party could rest after days of travel, the retainers installed tents in halting places.

In the decades that followed, the Mughals would build spectacular inns along the route that the princess's caravan took. Babur was aware of the inadequacy of roadside lodgings. A month into the departure of his family, he asked Khwaja Kalan to spend the profits realized in land revenue on repairs of the *karwan-sarai* in Kabul.[2] Babur knew the importance of the sarais, inns that lined the trade routes in Western and Central Asia. Asking for improved facilities, the tenth-century Arab geographer and traveler al-Muqaddasi had noted that it was better to spend money on roads and caravanserais than on mosques.[3]

The six-year-old Gulbadan now came onto the center stage of Mughal history. A great deal of information about the migration of the first group of the Mughal household would come from her future writings and those of

her father and of his cousin Mirza Dughlat. Gulbadan did not map the in-
itial part of their travel. Her account becomes lively with its description of
the long-awaited meetings with her father and courtiers after they crossed
the river Indus on February 18, 1529. The route they took from Kabul to the
banks of the river Indus and on to Agra was the Kabul-Agra road, an ancient
and well-traveled route.[4]

Babur's account shows that he had ridden this road several times with
his forces. With an impulse for recording, he evocatively noted the natural
features, the lush flora and fauna, and the character of the tribes and popu-
lations that lived in these regions. Traders, travelers, and Sufis had long been
taking this route. Father Monserrate, the first Jesuit missionary at the court
of the grandson of Babur, the third Mughal emperor, Akbar, traveled from
Lahore to Kabul on the same route. Accompanying Akbar on his campaign
against his half brother in Kabul, Monserrate chronicled from the rear guard
of the army the stopovers, the location of the camps, and the surrounding
landscape, as did other explorers and wanderers.[5]

Leaving Kabul, the Mughal kafila with the princess would bear slightly
west and then south. Near the pine tree–clad town of Jugdaluk, they climbed
a lofty pass of around eighty-five hundred feet. From its summit, the Kabul
hills could be seen in the distance. Fifty-one miles south of Kabul was the
verdant Neemla Bagh and the village of Gundamak. Lined with tall cypresses, chinar, and plane trees, and with plenty of space to walk, the garden
was an excellent place for a restful stopover.

They passed several small towns and settlements. For brief halts for
relaxation they stopped in places such as Kuju, known for pomegranates,
which traders took in great quantities to Hindustan. For a longer period of
rest, the caravan halted in the mountainous, verdant town of Jalalabad. The
mountain peaks surrounding the town were snow-capped all year round, so
even in the hottest of summers, Jalalabad remained cool.

In order to maintain the privacy of the royal travelers and provide comfort in the frigid temperatures of January, Mughal retainers would pitch
tents a mile out from the town in a popular place for elite caravans. They
would secure the delivery of maize, vegetables, and firewood from the Pa-
thans, who lived by agriculture in this area. Flat stretches of land in the
recesses of the mountains received enough heat to be able to yield fruits.
Jalalabad had vineyards and gardens that in summer grew pears, mulberries,
and figs.[6] Anyone who encountered the Mughal cavalcade would know this

was a special group. The presence of several attendants, the formal dignity of the staff, and the elegant clothing of the Mughal family all indicated their station.

How fast individuals or caravans went was variable. Imperial messengers moved the fastest. A late sixteenth-century Mughal courtier remarked that a dispatch rider covered up to 372 miles in a day on a fast horse. Emperor Akbar traveled 372 miles between Lahore and Agra in 28 days.[7] The last great Mughal emperor took 303 leisurely days to return to Delhi from Kashmir in 1662.[8]

The caravan's most hazardous crossing came immediately south of Jalalabad where the Khyber Pass, an intimidating mass of black slate and limestone, opened. Its passages were constricted by endless rugged mountain passes in proximity to each other. The first half of the pass was the toughest to navigate. Always formidable, it was much more so in the rainy, icy winter.

Gulbadan's liveliness helped while away the tedium of the perilous progress through the Khyber. She would distract Maham from the sadness of losing her newborn. Mubarika and others discussed the vicissitudes of the journey, expressing faith in the divine. Daughter of the great Yusufzai tribe that controlled areas such as Swat, Mubarika knew this landscape. The last time she traveled through the Khyber Pass was in the opposite direction when she made her way to Kabul, then newly married to Babur. The caravan headed for Agra had rough patches ahead of them, she would have reckoned. The most skilled of travelers, even with expert camels, found the Khyber Pass over a very high range terrifying. If travelers slipped, wrote the Jesuit priest Monserrate, "they and their riders would have been in imminent danger of death."[9]

Attacks and murders were common. Scottish explorer, diplomat, and author of the best seller *Travels to Bokhara,* Sir Alexander Burnes, lived in Kabul in 1836 and wrote about the immense dangers of the Khyber. A day after Burnes's camp passed near Jumrood, an area before the middle of the pass, some camel keepers were killed. Men of the Afreedee tribe "came upon them," wrote Burnes, "drove off the camels, and beheaded two of the people, whose mangled trunks" were brought to his camp.[10]

Deep rounded gorges and dense winter ice posed great danger to travelers unused to these paths. Being responsible for the emperor's little daughter in the group he led must have intensified Hindu Beg's apprehension. Although a skilled commander, he would need the assistance of experienced tribesmen to guide them through the Khyber. It was regular practice to have tribal chiefs direct the traveling parties. Different tribes often divided the responsibility of ushering travelers along the corridors of the Khyber that they controlled to avoid encroachment on one another's territory. Three hundred years later, Burnes would follow in the footsteps of Gulbadan: "A tribe of Afghans escorted us for about two miles to Kundun and then handed us over to the genuine Khyberees . . . the chief of the Kokee Khyl, who, with his numerous followers, led us to Ali Masjid."[11]

Horses were best suited for the ascent. Maham, Mubarika, Gulbadan, and the others would at this point switch conveyance, riding upon Turkish horses trained in walking carefully alongside the cliffs. The kafila became longer: expert detachments of tribal men in the front, women in the middle, and more guards and watchmen in the rear for safety. If the princess showed nervousness looking down at the canyons, the adults distracted her. When she was bored and tired, a retainer entertained her with a tale. Perched upon a horse, deft attendants and soldiers by her side, Gulbadan advanced through the tall, risky corridors like a little pilgrim inching toward a much-desired union.

Once the Mughal caravan rode past Landi Khana and reached 'Ali Masjid, a mud fort encased by rugged ranges, the most treacherous part of the Khyber was behind them. The travelers, exhausted after nearly three weeks of travel, would use garlic, onions, and dried apricots as remedies for fatigue, feeding these to their animals as well. Sometimes overburdened horses and mules suffered to such an extent that they collapsed. Spare horses traveling without loads came in as substitutes.

At the sublime 'Ali Masjid, where the melting ice from the mountains came down in a torrent nearby, jetting beautifully out of a rock, they would be showered with hospitality. Greatly needed items, such as fresh cooked food and water, were on offer. The settlements of the six Dilazak Afghan clans, supporters of Babur, spread along the foothills. When Babur went past 'Ali Masjid in late 1519, Dilazak chief Ya'qub-Khel hosted the emperor and presented him, from his modest possessions, ten sheep, two loads of rice, and eight large pieces of cheese. Babur remembered the gesture. From his treasures of Delhi, he sent the Dilazak men silver coins, robes, oxen, buffaloes, and cattle.

Ardent followers of codes of civility and aware of the changing configurations of power, the chiefs would honor the Mughal party, providing plenty of sweet water, fresh food, and warm beds. In keeping with the tribal tenets—Mubarika's culture—the Mughal women would be taken indoors to the quarters of the tribeswomen for hospitality and entertainment. Hindu Beg and his associates retired with the chiefs, as Babur had done earlier, for a wine party and a massive feast.

In the comfort of the women's quarters, trays of meat, bread, dried fruit, and cheese would be brought out. Mama would ask Gulbadan to take her seat around the warm glow of the fire where the women sat.

When Babur passed 'Ali Masjid in 1519, he had just then married Mubarika. At the wine party that the Dilazak men held in his honor, Babur shared the news that he had married a daughter of the Yusufzai clan, one of the most powerful tribes in the province of Kabul. Now the Dilazak women would get a firsthand account of the Mughal-Yusufzai alliance. Did they politely ask Mubarika about her wedding with Babur?

Can it be that this version of events leading to her marriage went through Mubarika's mind? Can it be that she shared parts of the marriage proceedings with them, but withheld others since her senior co-wife, Maham, was right beside her?

This is how the story of their courtship unfolded.

Babur had professed friendship for the Yusufzai clan but turned against them due to the overtures made by the Dilazak in whose camp Mubarika presently sat. In consort with the Dilazak clansmen, Babur invited Malik Ahmad, the Yusufzai head, to Kabul. Babur's real object was to kill Ahmad but, impressed with his courtesy and valor, Babur took off his robe and gave it to him, a sign of respect. Ahmad declined a second invitation to Kabul and sent his brother Shah Mansur, Mubarika's father, in his stead.

When Mansur came back, he advised his tribesmen that they must retire to the mountains and strengthen themselves. He feared an invasion. Soon Babur led an expedition to conquer the Yusufzai lands. He invaded the region near Swat and the adjoining areas, devastating lands as he moved along. But he could not enter the Yusufzai fort. To get more information on the Yusufzai strongholds, Babur disguised himself as a qalandar, a sufi, and went with some friends one dark night to the Mahura hills.

At the back of the Mahura hills, known then as Shah Mansur's throne, a feast was being held in honor of 'Id celebrations. Masked, Babur stood among the crowds in the courtyard. As the servants went about, Babur asked questions about the family. They responded to the seemingly casual inquiries.

In the Yusufzai women's tent that faced the courtyard where Babur and the crowd stood, Bibi Mubarika was sitting with other women. She looked out and her eye fell on the qalandar. She asked a woman servant to take him some cooked meat folded between two loaves, as people did for the holy and ascetics.

When the woman brought the food to Babur, he asked who had sent it. Bibi Mubarika, Shah Mansur's daughter, she said. As Babur looked in her direction, he was entranced by just a glimpse of Mubarika from afar. He asked the servant whether Mubarika was betrothed. She sang praises of her mistress, extolled her beauty, and said that Mubarika was not yet affianced. Babur then went behind the house, hid between two stones the food that Mubarika sent him, and left.

Overcome by longing, Babur returned to his camp, not knowing what to do. He couldn't take the fort, and he couldn't return to Kabul with nothing in hand. And so he wrote a letter to the older Yusufzai and asked for the hand of his niece. There was no daughter to give in marriage, he wrote. Babur replied, telling them about his disguised visit, and as a token of the truth of having seen Mubarika, he asked them to search for the food he had hidden. They found it. Ahmad and Mansur were not in favor of giving Mubarika in marriage to Babur, but the tribesmen reasoned with them, saying that the marital alliance would save the tribe from Babur's wrath.

The drums were beaten, and Babur's men began to make preparations to receive Mubarika. A few select men, carrying his sword, went to receive the new bride. With her father and uncle, and Runa, the head of the Mansur's household, two other women assistants, and several male and female servants, Mubarika crossed the river at Chakdara near the Khyber Pass. They took a narrow road between the hills and met Babur's escort. Mubarika went toward the royal camp, Babur's men leading the way. At the Mughal camp, the bride was welcomed with all due honor.

After the midday prayers on the second day, Babur came to her tent. When her servants announced Babur's arrival, she got up from her divan and stood in the center of the carpet with folded hands. Babur entered and she bowed. Her face was fully covered. Babur sat on the divan and said, "Come, Afghaniya, be seated." She bowed again and kept standing. A second time he asked her to be seated next to him. Again she bowed, came nearer but still stood. Then Babur removed her veil. Looking at her, he was struck again by her gorgeousness. She bowed once more and said that she had a petition to make. Babur asked her to speak. With both her hands, she took up her dress and said: "Think that the whole Yusufzai tribe is enfolded in my skirt and pardon their offenses for my sake." Babur assured her he would: "I forgive the Yusuf-zai all their offences in thy presence and cast them all into thy skirt. Hereafter I shall have no ill-feeling to the Yusuf-zai." Babur then took her hand and led her to the divan.[12]

So the tale was handed down in the *Baburnama.*

From 'Ali Masjid, there were two possible routes of roughly equal distance to Attock, then called Atak, or literally *the bar,* where the mountainous territory ended and the fertile agricultural plains began. Did the Mughal caravan go past Peshawar, a crossroads town where storytellers, travelers, townsmen, and merchants mingled, and then to Khairabad and Attock? Or did it go along the river Kabul, which went slightly west of 'Ali Masjid, flowed on its own in a semi-circular bend, and merged with the river Indus at Attock?

The curved river Kabul was lined with scores of Sanskrit inscriptions from the seventh and eighth centuries CE. In the region of Hund, an engraving celebrated a nameless hero who had defeated the "powerful flesh-eating" Turks:

> . . . blessings; whose kingly and priestly rule even among his enemies spreads. . . .
> The powerful flesh-eating Turushcas [Turks], causing alarm. . . .
> Such a prince . . . persevering in the protection of his people.[13]

Whether Gulbadan and the royal group took the arched river route and spotted the visual memorials of tussle between rulers along the way is hard to tell. But even if they went through Peshawar, they would have seen something of the martial and historical traditions and Buddhist and Indic engravings that littered this area. Gulbadan certainly caught a glimpse of agile monkeys that began to appear just past the Khyber and thrived in the territory of Hindustan.

On February 18, 1529, Gulbadan's caravan reached the banks of the Nil-ab, or Blue Waters. Having traveled 236 miles south from Kabul, the Mughal household was finally beside the splendid deep waters of the Indus that originated in the Tibetan Plateau. The river Indus runs over the Ladakh region, then toward Gilgit-Baltistan, flowing south along the entire length of modern Pakistan before it merges into the Arabian Sea near the port city of Karachi. One of the longest rivers in Asia, it stoked the imagination of many. For mystics and kings alike, Al-Hind, or the land *across* the Indus, denoted prosperity, both material and divine. In many areas around the river, people found great quantities of the best and finest gold. Just south of Attock, Kala Bagh was known for its mineral riches, rock salt, alum, and sulfur.

Babur had carefully timed the passage of his family across the river. From the middle of June to August, the Indus swelled, due not so much to heavy monsoonal rains as to the steadily melting snows. The condition in those three months was usually such that the mighty river divided the sea, "(or so it is said) and sweet water may be drawn up out of the ocean to a distance of forty miles."[14] Even though they had to depart Kabul in the thick of winter, it was the best alternative, since they could then conveniently cross the enormous river and soon be in Agra.

There were only a few fordable spots where men sometimes went down the river on rafts, as Babur did. Mostly people crossed in boats. Experts figured out in advance the shallowest and narrowest areas to cross the river. The royal caravan crossed in small groups: baggage, animals, attendants, and servants would go first, followed by the princess, women, and attendant crew. The crossing would be made in boats with covered seating. Once across the waters, they would ride horses or be carried in palanquins to their tents.

Under orders from the emperor, 'Abdul 'Aziz, master of the horse, waited across the river at the royal camp, pitched on a large plain and stocked with wood and other supplies. He would escort them on the next leg of their journey as far as the banks of the Jhelum. The neighboring woods and forests afforded respite. How long would it take before Gulbadan saw her Baba?

Will we see Baba now? she must have asked. Having traveled for a month on her first major adventure, and immensely tired, Gulbadan would be impatient to see her father.

Now in Hindustan, 'Aziz led the kafila. Veering south from Attock, but staying close to the Kabul-Agra route, they went past river-enriched lands. Once on the banks of the Jhelum, 'Aziz dutifully left, handing over the party to other imperial servants. A succession of commanders guided the family toward Agra. Hindu Beg stayed with them as far as Koil or Aligarh, north of Agra, when he took leave from Maham, in keeping with Babur's orders.

Babur received a letter from 'Aziz while he was on a campaign in the eastern territories across the river Ganges. The women had been safely brought from the banks of the Indus to the Chenab. Busy surveying lands and planning more conquests, Babur had just then defeated the Afghan forces and made substantial gains in Bihar. Two spies reported to him that a Bengali commander who was fortifying sites along the river Gandak had brought fleeing Afghans into his force. Confrontation with the ruler of Bengal was to be expected.

Keenly alive to his surroundings, wherever he was, Babur went to view lotus flowers, hunted elephants in the jungle of Chunar outside Banaras, and circumambulated the tomb of Shaikh Yahya, a Chishti Sufi. Most eagerly, he awaited the news of his household. Now that they were in Hindustan proper, the exchange of letters between Maham and Babur became frequent. Shirak, or Little Lion, was one of the fast carriers who took several messages both ways.

The Mughal caravan with Gulbadan had passed the river Chenab when Shirak brought a fresh dispatch from Babur. His letter made evident how eagerly His Majesty waited for a reunion with them. Shirak also had in his possession several pages of Babur's memoirs, written in what scholars today call Chagatai Turkish to distinguish it from modern Turkish, to which it is only distantly related. To Babur, his noblemen, Maham, Mubarika, and Gulbadan, as well as the people of Central Asia, Iran, and the Eurasian steppes, the language was simply Turki.

Kings and aristocrats typically shared their poetry, memoirs, and diaries with noblemen, princes, women, and kith and kin. Babur's cousin Mirza Dughlat read his memoir, as did Humayun and Gulbadan. Shirak was due to take the pages to Khwaja Kalan in Kabul. Which pages? Several were destroyed in Bengal, where Babur spent a lot of troubled time, determined to destroy the Afghan leaders who had eluded him. He continued to pursue these men through the monsoon season. A sudden storm blew through his camp and damaged several pages of his manuscript. Babur was reworking parts of his memoir. Were the lost sections those in which Babur wrote about the events of 1520–25, the period when Gulbadan was born?

Would the pages that Maham saw have been bound along the spine, encased in gilded leather? As she read the passages, distinctive for their unaffected and candid style, Mubarika and Gulbadan would be by her side, curious about what the precious manuscript contained.

News from His Majesty continued to arrive. Guards and guides changed as the caravan advanced. From the banks of the Chenab, they went further south, crossing towns like Wazirabad and then Shahdara on the banks of the river Ravi. Across the Ravi was Lahore, a key mercantile city in the vast agricultural region of Punjab, today the cultural capital of Pakistan.

In those days, Lahore, a budding Mughal city, was crowded with merchants from all over Asia. A citadel built of brickwork with a circumference of nearly three miles held a large bazaar for traders and buyers. Merchants also congregated outside the fort—some worked the Agra-Lahore axis, a lucrative route, and some came in caravans from the northwest, selling Iraqi horses, silk thread, and musk melons.

Much of the city spread outside the citadel, featuring crisscrossing mud streets, brick-built homes, and public buildings. Brahmins and Hindus of other castes lived in neighborhoods according to their community affiliation. The Kashmiris of Lahore were well-known bakers, sellers of secondhand goods, and keepers of eating houses. Many Persian speakers from Safavid Iran and neighboring Central Asian regions could be seen in the city. With an assortment of population groups came intermingling languages: Gwaliyari, Braj, Kashmiri, Punjabi, and other rich dialects that contributed to Hindavi, the evolving language of the time.

Whether the kafila stopped in the city or outside, within their earshot were words and metaphors from the Hindustani world being integrated into the Persian language—the sounds of Indo-Persian. Sufi centers in Hindustan played a vital role in this comingling. Nearly two centuries before Gulbadan arrived in India, a new form of poetry had emerged. The genre known as *Sabk-i Hindi*—Persian poetry in the Indian style—was more than a literary form. From its beginnings, it embodied the ongoing cultural, linguistic, and literary interaction between India and Iran, highlighting the potential benefits of fruitful coexistence.[15] Sufi poets Amir Khusraw and Hasan Sijzi of Delhi called for the transcendence of religious and sectarian differences in their Persian poetry.

By the time they reached Lahore, 450 miles from Agra, the kafila had crossed the five great rivers of Punjab: Beas, Ravi, Chenab, Jhelum, and Indus, which spread out in the lush fertile plains like the five fingers of a hand. As with the hyphen in the term "Indo-Persian," the merging waters called attention to traditions meeting, mixing, and generating new possibilities.

Yearning to see his family, Babur had planned to receive them at Aligarh, fifty-seven miles north of Agra. Back from the East, he dispatched troops and officers to welcome them. "Nine troopers, with two sets of nine horses and two extra corteges," waited on them in Aligarh.[16] In Naugram, four miles short of Agra, Nizam al-Din Barlas, imperial finance minister, and his wife Sultanam were asked to receive the arriving cortege.

The kafila reached Aligarh on the afternoon of June 27, 1529, sooner than Babur had anticipated. When she didn't see her husband, Maham left immediately for Agra, her elderly companion Nanacha by her side. Gulbadan stayed behind in the care of Fakhr-un-Nisa. "She [Maham] wanted me to come by daylight the next day and pay my respects to him [Babur]," explains the princess.[17]

Just as Babur finished his evening prayers, an attendant ran to him: "I have just passed Her Highness [Maham] on the road, four miles out," he said. The royal servants immediately began to saddle his horse, but he could not wait. Impatient to see his wife, the forty-six-year-old king rushed out on foot. Maham saw him running toward her. She "wished to alight, but he would not wait, and ran along with her all the way to his quarters."[18]

The next morning, Gulbadan went on to Agra, secure in the protection of soldiers, nurses, and royal troops. Mubarika was not with her. We do not know when the Afghan Lady reached Agra. The chances are that she followed Maham in a separate contingent.

In Naugram, east of the river Yamuna, the princess's group halted at a garden. Mama Fakhr-un-Nisa helped Gulbadan down from her palanquin.

She explained to the little princess that Nizam al-Din Barlas and his wife would receive her. The other attendants chose a spot under a shaded canopy, spread a small carpet, and asked Gulbadan to sit. They briefly coached her on the required decorum in meeting the vazir and his wife. The princess should rise and embrace him. A younger person always rose first and greeted an older honorable guest.

In private assembly or in court, in sitting down and in rising, at banquets and dinners, in death and celebration, the Mughals adhered to *Chingiz-tora,* or the code of conduct prescribed by their forefather Chingiz Khan. Though this code was not binding, in Babur's view, there were good reasons to follow it. If an ancestor established a good precedent, it was meaningful, but a bad one could be replaced, he underlined in the *Baburnama.*[19]

Rituals of courtly life were not new to the six-year-old Gulbadan. She was repeatedly reminded of courtesies and required behavior. She had to adhere to protocol with great dignity.

As instructed, Gulbadan stood up from her carpet, took a step forward, and embraced the vazir. Then she sat down, she later wrote. Soon thereafter, his wife Sultanam came in. "I, not knowing, wished to get up," remarked Gulbadan. "There is no need to rise," spoke the vazir. "Your father has exalted this old servant. . . . So be it!"[20] Calling himself *servant* was an expression of the vazir's humility. Even though he was a distant relative of the Mughals—his brother was married to the emperor's half sister—his role as Babur's court official was the most significant to him. Babur had asked him to receive his daughter, a great honor. He felt doubly honored when Gulbadan made the gesture of rising upon seeing him. Courtesy in the Mughal world was not a one-sided affair. Very much in keeping with the royal ethic of hierarchy, as the princess was after all the daughter of His Majesty, the vazir suggested that Gulbadan need not get up a second time.

Once the rituals of meeting and greeting were over, the vazir began the formal ceremonial welcome of the princess. He presented Gulbadan with six thousand gold coins and five horses; his wife Sultanam offered her three thousand gold coins and three horses. The six-year-old "accepted" the gifts. Sultanam then addressed her, saying, "Food is ready. If you would care to partake, you will do us the honor." "I consented," wrote the older Gulbadan.[21]

The couple had picked a pleasant spot in the garden, a large pavilion decorated with red *escarlate,* a rich Persian fabric, from which the word *scarlet* derives. Inside were comfortable seats with mattresses and cushions of golden brocade, Gujarat's specialty. Held upon painted poles, six canopies decorated with different colored escarlate fabric stood in the pavilion. Members of the princess's group sat under these six canopies.

Gulbadan sat with the vazir, her father's deputy. The feast began. Among the dishes were fifty roast sheep, a variety of breads, fruit, and plenty of sherbet to cool the guests. After they'd eaten, wrote Gulbadan, "I got into my litter and went on to my royal father."[22]

She had only a dim memory of him. As soon as she saw him, she wrote half a century later, she felt "happiness such that greater could not be imagined."[23] Her retrospective sense of delight and emotion is arresting. Babur took Gulbadan in his arms and held her for a long time. It is likely that she was somewhat in awe of him—her father, the victorious hero. At the same time, Babur was immensely lonely. Only a day earlier, he had rushed to see Maham. He ran by the side of her cortege, stopping only when they reached his residence. Now he looked fondly at his attractive daughter, who had traveled hundreds of miles to be with him. He asked her many questions, recalled the princess. How was her trip? Was she comfortable? Did he ask her if she had seen any monkeys? At long last, she was happy in the arms of her equally happy father.

A new chapter in Gulbadan's life began. In her new home of Agra, there was a lot to learn. The majestic river Yamuna flowed near the quarters where she stayed with her kinfolk. Adjacent to the river, her father had begun building new gardens. There were trees and fruit that she had only heard about, such as the succulent mangoes that Babur rated as the best fruit of Hindustan, and the old banyan trees with their bushy knotted roots that fell like hair upon their thick trunks. There were picnics and fun times with Maham and Mubarika. Aunt Khanzada and Dildar soon arrived. But perhaps Gulbadan's favorite pastime was watching her royal father sit by a pond, diligently writing his memoirs.

Five

My Royal Father

~

GULBADAN WAS ESPECIALLY HAPPY DURING HER FIRST THREE months in Agra. She looked deferentially at her father as he proudly showed her the royal gardens and buildings that were being created. She was frequently in the company of Babur, *Babam-i Padshah,* "my royal father." They lived in a citadel mansion that stretched along the right banks of the river Yamuna. To develop the site, Babur ordered his workmen to construct huge ramparts of what later became the Agra Fort. In the open space around his residence, he built a stepwell, enclosed by rooms at three levels. The room in the middle level was linked by a passage to a domed building where a large water-lifting wheel was placed.[1] Bullocks turned the wheel.

On the other side of the river, its left bank, there were wide green spaces where Babur supervised the creation of lush gardens. The first of these was Aram Bagh, divided in quarters by walkways and waterways. He gave instructions on how water was to be channeled. In a methodical fashion, he created canals, waterfalls, and pathways. A grove of orange trees was blooming by the time Gulbadan saw Aram Bagh. She loved her outings to the gardens, enjoying the powerful scent of flowers like jasmine, *raat ki raani,* or queen of the night, and an Agra local, *morpankhi,* the peacock flower. There were groves of lemons, Ashok trees, tamarinds, guavas, oranges, almonds, pomegranates, and date palms.[2]

Gulbadan now lived in the vicinity of the bullock-powered water wheel, brick steps that took her to the cool of the well on hot summer days. Her surroundings featured large rivers and agricultural environs. Her clothes and food were altered as well. Clad in lighter cotton and linen in hot and airless summers, she returned to heavy Kabul wools in the chilly winter months.

With autumnal and spring harvests, food products were rich and varied, including wheat, barley, chickpeas, ginger, sugarcane, milk, yogurt, and ghee.

The family enjoyed many kinds of breads made of rough or coarse flour, large and small *naans* baked in the oven or made in skillets. There were many varieties of spiced-up rice and meat dishes and a wide range of fruits: mangoes, pomegranates, apples, and *amrit-phal*, mandarin oranges. Experimentation with fruits and spices in the Mughal kitchens gave birth to famous Mughlai dishes: *biryani*—rice with meat, onions, peppers, cinnamon, cumin, and other spices; or its variants *yakhni* (rice and meat cooked in gravy or broth with onions) and *yulma* (a sheep scalded in water until its wool comes off, then prepared like yakhni in potage).

Even though Gulbadan and members of the extended Mughal circle would not venture into the market and villages beyond the royal estates, strikingly heterogenous culture came to their doorsteps. Courtiers and members of domestic staff from various regions brought an assortment of languages, religions, and philosophies. In Agra, just across the river from the Mughal manors, sounds of Hindavi and Khadiboli, tongues of the region—and Persian or Bengali if traders were in the bazaar—could be heard. In the villages beyond the bazaar, sedentary, rural families reared livestock. Many of the villagers had limited resources, possessing only some grains, plows, bullocks, and maybe a few sheep and goats.

Southwest of Agra, in Sikri village, a rustic villa was nearly ready for the family. A brick-lined well and an almshouse were getting final touches. A water reservoir with an octagonal stone platform stood in the middle. Awnings shaded the platform when it was being used for festivities. Gulbadan's favorite in this Garden of Victory was the *tur khana,* a deck enclosed with a railing, where her "royal father used to sit and write his book."[3] Watching her father immersed in writing intrigued the little princess. The beauty of calligraphic script and the power of the written word likely enthralled her.

Gulbadan noticed that her father was often overtaken by dark moods. His wandering and restlessness took a toll upon his hardy constitution, and prolonged attacks of fever began to wear him out. For most of his life, he had never had the chance to enjoy the feast of Ramazan twice in the same place. Now, for the first time since the age of eleven, he was with his kith and kin. That surely enriched his domestic life, but the damage to his constitution was not easily undone.

One early October afternoon, not too hot, Gulbadan went to the Garden of Victory to be with her father, Maham, and Mubarika. Babur was in the tur khana writing his book. Gulbadan and Mubarika were playing below the railing where Babur sat. Maham had stepped behind the deck for midday prayers.

"I said to Afghani Aghacha, pull my hand," writes the princess. But when Mubarika pulled her up by hand, her wrist was dislocated. "My strength went out and I cried out," Gulbadan recalled. Mubarika was shocked, and Babur ran toward the child. Maham interrupted her prayers. The servants rushed to the village to fetch a bonesetter. After "they bound my hand," wrote Gulbadan, "the emperor went to Agra."[4]

It was the first time in her book that she called her father Babam-i Padshah, my father the emperor. Now, in Hindustan, Gulbadan was beginning to understand that her father was a monarch, the person from whom all orders came. She continued to call him Baba, but she knew that he was also an emperor—the first Mughal emperor of India. She loved this time with Babur, but soon the delightful months with her baba tailed off.

In the summer of 1529, Khanzada was preparing to leave Kabul to join the rest of her clan in Agra when she learned that Humayun was at her doorstep, en route from Badakhshan to Agra. Babur's health was declining, and he was struck by recurrent bouts of fever. Learning about this through an urgent message from his mother, Maham, Humayun set out for Agra without securing permission from the emperor. His nobles and advisers were alarmed at his decision: they reminded him that it would make the Badakhshan region vulnerable. Humayun assured them that he would use his influence to get one of his brothers to take charge. So he came to Kabul to meet his half brother Kamran. Together they persuaded the ten-year-old Prince Hindal to take up the governing of Badakhshan, even though Hindal was under orders to accompany Khanzada's convoy to Agra.

Humayun reached Agra well before Khanzada, whose cavalcade arrived in October 1529. He entered the royal quarters just when his parents were talking of him, a coincidence that Maham probably helped to bring about.

She was likely praising Humayun to his father to ease the shock of his unexpected arrival.

When Babur saw Humayun, he was livid. Humayun had placed his province in danger by withdrawing troops and princely control. In conferring Badakhshan on him, Babur had hoped that Humayun would extend Mughal territory beyond the river Oxus. He wished Humayun to return to his post. He would go if ordered, the prince responded, but it was clear from his demeanor that he was unwilling to leave. Babur was outraged, but his anger did not last long. He allowed the prince to shift to Delhi, and sent his loyal and devoted companion, whom he fondly called Khalifa, the same courtier who had welcomed Gulbadan to Agra, to oversee affairs in Badakhshan.

The Mughals did not adhere to the principle of primogeniture, whereby the throne automatically passed to the eldest son. Technically, any male Mughal descendant could claim the throne, a practice very much part of succession procedure from the time of progenitors Timur and Chingiz Khan. A prince who aspired to ascend the throne had to be militarily accomplished. He needed to have experienced and savvy noblemen by his side. And if it was thought that the reigning emperor would die soon, it was vital that the prince was at no great distance from the court. Maham had successfully ensured that her son was nearby.

Humayun's hasty arrival took place several weeks before Gulbadan's visit with her father in the Garden of Victory when her wrist was dislocated. As the bonesetter was completing his work on her twisted wrist, a messenger brought the news that Khanzada was near Agra. As soon as Gulbadan's wrist was fixed, Babur left the garden to welcome his sister and the women's cavalcade she headed. With Khanzada were Gulbadan's mother Dildar, her two daughters, and her four-year-old son Alwar, who had been conceived just before Babur left for India. There were ninety-six Mughal women in all, whom Babur received just outside Agra. Immensely pleased at their reception, the women prostrated in thanks, paid their respects to the emperor and then proceeded to Agra.[5]

By the river Yamuna, houses and manors were being built. The elder relations and women moved into dwellings near the main citadel-mansion. As before, each woman had her residence, staff, and emoluments, but they now lived in a set up different from that at Bala Hisar, where royal quarters were in closer proximity and situated on the upper level of the fort. The main domestic lodgings as well as other tents and mansions were spread out far and wide along the Yamuna. Many cousins and kinswomen lived in these households. Babur showered bounties on the women, wrote Gulbadan, and gave them "houses and lands and gifts to their heart's desire."[6]

The large Kabul household took a great deal of settling. There were new relatives in the mansions. Two Circassian women slaves, Gulnar and Nargul (Red as Rose and Pomegranate Red), gifts from the king of Persia to Babur, were already in Agra when the princess reached the city. Earlier that year, 1529, when Gulbadan left Kabul, her father gave a memorable garden feast in Agra. Representatives from Samarkand, his hometown, and Andijan as well as the ambassador of the shah of Persia attended. Gulnar and Nargul arrived in Agra with the ambassador and were taken into the Mughal household. Gulbadan took a liking for Gulnar, calling her Gulnar Aghacha. Lady Gulnar became a boon companion of the princess.

There was also a new male member of the Mughal family who is repeatedly mentioned in the records from the time the household moved to Agra: Muhammad Mahdi Khwaja, a brave, high-spirited, and generous man, but of "evil disposition."[7] This man was Khanzada's second husband. He accompanied Babur in various campaigns beginning with his forays into northern India. Neither Babur nor Gulbadan tell us when Khanzada and Mahdi married. Was it soon after she returned from her captivity, two decades before coming to Agra? Or did she marry him in Agra? What happened to the son she had with her first husband, Shaibani Khan? We do know that, dedicated to her clan, she lived with Mahdi in one of the Mughal estates.

While older rivalries, arguments, and tears persisted, there were also new bonds and ties. Babur was now the monarch of a fresh court galaxy with a mix of his loyal Turk and Mongol nobles. New recruitments were taking place, allies declaring loyalty. Babur's dominion was widespread, but not enormous in comparison with those of other Islamic rulers. Mughal princes and trusted nobles were crucial to the maintenance of faraway provinces, especially those in Afghanistan. Prince Humayun had been the governor of Badakhshan since he was twelve. Ambitious Prince Kamran presided over Kabul. Khwaja Kalan assisted Kamran in the ongoing political tensions in the province. Ghazni and Kandahar, fragile border regions, were always under threat.

In the heartland of Hindustan, Babur held Delhi, Agra, Dholpur, Gwalior, Etawah, and a small fringe of territory in Rajasthan; toward the northwest, though still east of the river Indus, he had Punjab and Multan; and among the trans-Indus regions, he controlled Bhira and Sialkot. East of Delhi and Agra, he possessed the greater part of Bihar, but the Afghans and native chiefs were still the masters of the hilly parts. The Rajput territories in western India as well as Bengal were independent. The southern provinces of the subcontinent were nowhere in the emperor's scheme of conquest.

There was no uniform court of law or system of taxation for all these territories. Babur improvised upon the existing revenue systems in the areas that he had conquered. He parceled out land and cities among officers, who levied land tax on peasant cultivators and took taxes from merchants, shopkeepers, and non-Muslims. The great landlords of these regions were nominally dependent on the court but exercised considerable autonomy.

As his extended household settled in Agra, Babur frequently spent time with his wives: Gulbadan uses the word *madran*, in Persian plural for "mothers." Even though plans for military campaigns and courtly matters took a great deal of his time, in the altered conditions of his life, Babur often returned to the domestic quarters. Gulbadan recalled with great fondness the occasions when her father visited her guardian mother Maham's residence. Sometimes her sisters came over and joined them. "He used to visit us and show us kindness and affection and favor without stint."[8]

But conflicts also arose in the mansions of Agra. Gulbadan, girl witness to the ongoing domestic dramas that had great imperial significance, writes that Maham was greatly agitated in those days after the elder ladies came to Agra.[9]

To please Maham or simply to escape emotional upheavals, Babur planned an excursion to the Gold Scattering Garden in late September 1530. The group consisted of Babur, Maham, Gulbadan, and her two sisters—a nuclear family of sorts. There was a place in the garden for ablutions before prayers. They walked toward this *vozu-khaneh*, the ablution house. Babur broke down as soon as he saw the building, wrote his daughter. He had no hope of governing or strength to rule, he said. "I shall retire to this garden. As for attendance, I shall ask only for Tahir the ewer-bearer as [a] companion. I shall grant the kingship to Humayun."[10]

His overwrought emotional state was not new to the family. The letters he wrote to his family when they were in Kabul spoke of his blues.

During the time he sent those letters, he faced financial difficulties, including a restricted treasury out of which he had to support military campaigns, procure supplies, and pay salaried soldiers, gunners, and matchlock men. Homesickness and terrible fevers took their toll. *Afsurdah* (melancholy) is the word he used in his memoirs, although it appears only once, when he had a high fever. The situation was easier now. With some victories over the Rajputs and Afghans, his heart was at peace, he wrote in his diary. Yet his sadness lingered.

After the ablutions purified his body, he was ready for prayers. He noted that he was worn out. "My esteemed Lady Maham and all the children began to cry," wrote Gulbadan. "May God most high in his mercy keep you in kingship for . . . countless decades and after you may all your children reach a distinguished old age."[11] These were the only words of solace Maham could offer.

They returned to Agra, sad but keeping the faith, relieved when this new bout of depression passed. However, a few days later, another misfortune occurred.

Gulbadan's younger brother Alwar fell ill from infection of the bowels. His condition worsened. Nothing the doctors tried worked. "At last, he passed from this transitory world to the eternal home," Gulbadan writes of the death of her little brother. Her mother Dildar "was wild with grief," and Baba "very sad and sorry."[12]

Several days passed and Dildar could not stop grieving. Babur suggested that they take an excursion to Dholpur, thirty-five miles south of Agra. Gloomy himself, Babur empathized with his wife's condition. He hoped that a visit to the Bagh-i Nilufer, a garden two miles west of Dholpur, would distract his heartbroken wife. Being in gardens and composing verses lifted his own spirits. During a serious bout of fever, Babur set in verse parts of his patron saint Khwaja Ahrar's work. He wrote ten verses each night. Usually, it took him a month to recover from a fever, but this time he recovered in a week.[13]

Dildar, Maham, Khanzada, Gulbadan, and other princesses came down from the fort. Exiting via the royal gate, they went to the banks of the Yamuna, where royal boats would take them to Dholpur. Strong boatmen sat behind the curtained rooms with awnings in the front. The oarsmen steered and began chanting river songs.

Dholpur had good sources of water. Babur hoped that the warmth of the red sandstone of the garden hammam, a bathhouse with a series of aqueducts and water channels, would restore Dildar. Once in communion with water in the intimate setting of the garden, she would be nurtured and replenished. Mughal women knew their water rituals. "A royal woman dips her feet in water: statuesque and meditative as she holds her hookah. Her chest is risen. Her attendant, bent over her, combs and takes care of her hair. They go about their job contemplatively. A quiet feel, a sense of space and leisure for the two women around water."[14]

Was Maham envious of the attention Dildar got from the emperor? After all, it was not long ago that Maham had lost her own little son, Farukh.

All seemed well with Humayun when the royal party left home to give the grieving Dildar some respite from her sorrow. However, the quiet sojourn in Dholpur was curtly interrupted. News came from Delhi that Humayun was seriously ill. "Her Highness the Begum must proceed as quickly as possible to Delhi, for the prince is quite upset." Maham was distressed to hear that her son was afflicted by a mysterious fever that refused to subside despite the court physicians' best efforts, wrote Gulbadan. Maham set out immediately for Delhi, "like a thirsty person who is far from the waters."[15] Humayun's attendants brought him to meet her at the outskirts of Agra. He appeared ten times weaker and more emaciated than she had imagined.

Growing up in Maham's charge, Gulbadan frequently saw Humayun, and she had fond feelings for this moody yet sensitive and generous half brother. As soon as the mother and son, "like Jesus and Mary," reached Agra, Gulbadan and her sisters rushed to them. "That angelic majesty" Humayun was so weak that he kept falling into unconsciousness. Each time he came to his senses, Gulbadan recalled, he would say: "Sisters, welcome. Come, let us embrace one another, for I haven't greeted you."[16] This happened three times.

Seeing him in such a weakened state, Babur became despondent. He showed concern for the prince, writes Gulbadan, such as he never had before. Maham broke down and said to Babur, "Do not be troubled about my son. You are a king. . . . You have other sons. I sorrow because I have only this one." Her words bore the weight of a Mughal mother's anxiety. Babur knew how to disarm her. "Maham! Although I have other sons, I love none as I love your Humayun," he said. "I crave that this cherished child may have his heart's desire and live long, and I desire the kingdom for him and not for the others, because he has not his equal in distinction."[17]

The prince's illness weighed heavily on Babur's mind. One day as he sat in the imperial quarters discussing Humayun's condition with his *amirs*, the wise Mir Abul Baqa, a man known for his expertise in the ancient Unani medicine, which relied on natural forms of healing by balancing the body, offered some advice. "In a case like this, when the physicians were at [a] loss, the remedy was to give alms of the most valuable thing one had and to seek [a] cure from God." Babur replied: "I am the most valuable thing Humayun possesses; he has no better thing; I should sacrifice myself for him. May God the creator accept it."[18]

It was a common belief that through the strength of prayers and the giving of alms a malady or illness could be transferred from one person to another or to an inorganic object. If someone made an offering of something precious and if the offering was accepted, heaven would heal the sick person in exchange. Babur's unparalleled heart-breaking gesture is now a staple of legend and history. He offered his life to the divine to save his son.

Khalifa, back from Badakhshan after averting a major political crisis there, was distressed by Babur's decision. He tried to dissuade him, saying that the sage meant he should offer the most valuable article of property, not himself. The courtiers suggested that the Kohinoor diamond, which was in Humayun's possession, could be sold and the sum distributed in alms. Babur found the now world-famous diamond unsatisfactory. "What value has worldly wealth?" he asked. "And how can it be a redemption for Humayun?"[19] He was adamant that he must offer his own life for his son's.

Although Mughal court histories mention the emperor's self-sacrifice, it is Gulbadan, his daughter, who takes us to the chamber where her gravely ill brother lay and where her father completed the ritual. It was customary to begin on a Wednesday, but the anxious Babur began the rites on a Tuesday.

"The weather was very hot. His Majesty's heart and liver burnt," wrote Gulbadan of her ailing father.[20] Already ill and weak, the emperor commenced his fast. Abul Baqa helped him perform the rites. Babur went into the chamber where his son lay unconscious upon a bed lined with a soft velvet sheet. Humayun's head was raised upon a floral bolster. An attendant stood behind, gently fanning him. Several other servants and companions of the prince waited in the room. A cleric sat next to the bed, eyes closed in deep meditation, rotating the rosary beads.[21] Babur walked around Humayun's bed three times, praying out loud: "O God! If a life can be exchanged for a life, I, Babur, give my life and soul to Humayun."[22]

That very day, Humayun opened his eyes. An attendant poured water on his head to cool him. As he emerged from his room, everyone was filled with joy. As the son's health improved, the father's deteriorated. "His Majesty my royal father was taken inside [to the royal chamber]," wrote Gulbadan.[23] He was bedridden for the next three months.

Gulbadan watched her father become ever sicker and more fragile, although he continued to attend to private and court matters from his sickbed. His followers could not believe what had transpired. They knew Babur as their strong *padshah* who had been wounded and poisoned but had always come out on top. Now he lay in the royal chamber, hurriedly completing tasks that he deemed urgent.

He asked to see his sister Khanzada. He ordered Gulrang and Gulchihra, Gulbadan's elder sisters, seventeen and fifteen at the time, to be married. Their weddings "must be arranged," he urged Khanzada, and suggested as suitable grooms the sons of their maternal uncle.

Dildar, the mother of the princesses, was not consulted, but she seems to have agreed with the scheme. Khanzada reported to Babur that the proposals were "very good." The wedding preparations were hasty and the ceremony simple. Gulbadan remembered that Khanzada and two great-aunts supervised the decoration of the wedding hall and had it adorned with carpets. At the fixed hour, Nanacha, the senior household associate, asked "both the princes to kneel [before His Majesty] and receive the honor of becoming imperial sons-in-law."[24]

The events that transpired in Agra at this time were overwhelming for the seven-year-old Gulbadan. The wedding of her sisters was hurried and somewhat somber. Her little brother Alwar had died. Her own wrist was dislocated. Her mother was grieving; her father incapacitated and confined indoors. There was widespread suspicion that the effects of Buwa's poisoning still lingered, seriously affecting her father's health. What did the young girl make of all this? The solemn rite her father performed to save her brother moved her. This was probably too much for a little girl in an entirely new land to absorb in a short time.

Babur's fever grew worse. A serious disorder of the bowels afflicted him. In and out of consciousness, he asked for his youngest son Hindal, who was now en route to Agra. Despite his declaration to Maham that the eldest prince would inherit the throne, Babur repeatedly asked for Hindal. While deeply fond of his eldest son, he was worried about Humayun's indulgent nature. He had expressed his concern in a letter to Humayun in late November 1528: "God willing, this is your time to risk your life and wield your sword. Do not fail to make the most of an opportunity that presents itself. Indolence and luxury do not suit kingship."[25] He did not mention his other two sons, Kamran and 'Askari.

As Babur lay dying, manipulations for the succession to the Mughal throne intensified. The supremely influential courtier Khalifa knew that Babur had favored Humayun as his heir for more than a decade: he was the eldest prince and son of the domineering Maham. Polite and refined in manner, Humayun had a cultivated mind, which Babur loved. But Khalifa had doubts about Humayun's ability to rule. Humayun's loot of the Delhi treasury and desertion of Badakhshan made Khalifa apprehensive. The two did not get along well.

Khalifa began to hatch plans to set Humayun aside in the competition for the throne.[26] The successor he had in mind was Mahdi Khwaja, the high-spirited second husband of Khanzada. The Mughal family was at the very center of Khanzada's thoughts, but there is no evidence that she had any part in Khalifa's plans. By the time her brother was dying, Khanzada was a highly regarded elder, sought out by the family for advice on major political and domestic questions. Gulbadan, her niece, idolized her aunt. Yet she has nothing to say about her aunt's second marriage—and no word about her being involved in intrigues involving Mughal succession. Khanzada and Babur may have had an inkling of Khalifa's tactics, as would Maham, although records do not clarify whether Khalifa discussed the matter of Mughal succession with Babur.[27]

Khalifa's plan to displace Humayun may have been meant to apply only for some parts of Babur's territory. In keeping with the prevalent practice in the emperor's clan, Babur's grandfather had parceled out his lands among his four sons. Provinces so varied as Babur's seemed to demand such division. Delhi and Agra were still not the center of Babur's dreams. He wanted more territory beyond the Oxus. But Khalifa's plan was not carefully thought through, and it is evident that he failed to realize that if Mahdi's succession became a reality, it would lead to a civil war because the Mughal princes would not accept his rule. The question remains that if Khalifa was suspicious of Humayun, why did he not consider the other three princes as possible successors?

Using his influence with older nobles and senior army personnel, Khalifa began to build support for Mahdi. When Mahdi learned of the growing backing for his nomination to the throne, he became arrogant. According to later Mughal court histories, he "gave himself the airs of a Padshah." His growing self-aggrandizement disgusted even his supporters. It was not long before Khalifa discovered that he was backing the wrong horse. One day, as Khalifa and an officer named Muqim were sitting with Mahdi discussing business, the ailing Babur sent for Khalifa, who went to him immediately. Forgetting that Muqim was still there, Mahdi murmured to himself, "God willing, first I'll have you [Khalifa] flayed." When he turned around and discovered that Muqim was standing right beside him, he caught hold of one of his ears and threatened him with death if he divulged what he had said.[28]

Nonetheless, Muqim hastened to Khalifa and told him what he had heard. Khalifa sent a message to Mahdi that the emperor had ordered that he should leave the imperial premises and retire to his house. He also issued an order prohibiting all persons from visiting Mahdi's house or waiting upon him. Further, he was barred from attending court. At the same time, Khalifa sent a messenger to Humayun, who had gone back to Delhi, asking him to come to Agra at once. That was the end of the Mahdi episode.

Humayun rushed back. Gulbadan writes that when Humayun saw his dying father, he summoned the royal doctors: "Think ... and find some remedy," he ordered. "Our remedies are of no avail," they said unanimously. "We hope that God the most holy will soon give one from his invisible treasures." The doctors believed that the effects of the poison Buwa Begum had given the emperor still lingered. "The ill-fated demon [Buwa] did this although His Majesty used to call her 'mother,'" wrote Gulbadan. Babur's condition worsened. The royal wives, elder relations, and staff came to the "Great House," a large tent, so as to be near Babur's chamber when he breathed his last.

On December 27, 1530, Babur summoned his chiefs and counselors. "For many years it has been on my mind to turn the rule over to Humayun Mirza and retire to a corner of Zarafshan Garden. By God's grace everything has come about, but it has not been granted me [the chance] to do this thing in good health. . . . As my last will, I charge you all to consider Humayun in my stead and not to fail in your support of him. Be steadfast and cooperative with him." Then he turned to Humayun, who was standing by his father's bed, and said: "I entrust you and your brothers and all my relatives and people to God, and I turn them over to you." All those in the chamber began to weep, and his "blessed eyes" too filled with tears.[29]

Three days later, Gulbadan's royal father passed away. He was forty-eight. He had spent thirty-six of those years in kingship and governance—twenty-six in Kabul province and five in parts of Hindustan. When the messenger brought the news of his death to the Great House, the women and children wailed in lament. "Black fell the day for children and kinsfolk and all," wrote Gulbadan decades later. "Voices rose in weeping. Each passed that black, ill-fated day hidden in a corner."[30]

Babur had wanted his body carried to Kabul and buried at a beautiful spot that he had selected on a hill near the city. But first he was laid in Aram Bagh, the first garden he had dug on the green side of the Yamuna across from his residence.

Close relations gathered in Aram Bagh. Humayun arranged a large staff for the upkeep and care of the garden premises. 'Asas, the elderly eunuch, was appointed guardian of Babur's grave. Sixty Qur'an reciters read aloud the verses of the entire Qur'an in honor of the departed emperor and offered prayers "for the soul of the royal dweller in Paradise," Firdaws-Makani, in Gulbadan's words. The revenue of the entire area of Sikri, together with 5 lakhs of rupees from Biana, near Agra, were set aside as an endowment for the tomb so that men of learning and the reciters were well supported. For the two and a half years that she outlived Babur, Maham sent an allowance twice daily from her own estate: in the morning an ox, two sheep, and five goats, and at afternoon prayer time five more goats.[31] After forty days, Bibi Mubarika escorted the body to Kabul and laid it to rest in a garden where Babur had wanted. The famous tomb garden is called the Bagh-e Babur, the Garden of Babur.

On the last day of December 1530, Gulbadan's brother Humayun ascended the throne. Hindal arrived on the same day. If he had come earlier, would there have been another act in the drama of kingship? It is hard to say.

Gulbadan greatly mourned her royal father's death. Although her mothers and siblings were by her side in Agra, and Humayun, the new emperor, was loving and thoughtful, Gulbadan felt "orphaned." The memory of the year and a half that she had had with her royal father was imprinted on her mind. She would often reminisce about that wondrous year as she stepped into womanhood.

Six

Female Guardians of the Empire

~

THREE YEARS AFTER HER FATHER'S DEATH, GULBADAN'S guardian mother died of dysentery. Although she "felt lonely and helpless in great affliction," a new life for the princess began.[1] At age ten, she went to live with her birth mother in her Agra mansion. The stately residences that lined the river Yamuna were now at the center of Mughal life. Each Mughal woman of rank was in charge of her own establishment, her domestic structure not that different from that at Bala Hisar, but systemic changes were quietly occurring.

The *harem of Humayun,* the *harem of such-and-such* prince is how records describe the Mughal households. The harem indicated the women's location and referred to *haraman,* or women of the king or princes. Whereas multiple generations had once lived collectively, now they were split into households, and extended family ties became ceremonial. A focus on close blood and marriage relatives did not efface the wider clan, but the constant company of distant kith and kin shrank. Even with the changes, mothers remained ubiquitous, and respect for elders was marked.[2]

Gulbadan was content to be among relatives she looked up to. Dearest Lady Khanzada, Acam—an appellation for mother Dildar—Afghan Lady, and concubines Nargul and Gulnar were steady presences. She was greatly attached to her half brother Humayun. His first wife, Bega Begum, arrived from Badakhshan. The couple had earlier lost their first child, an infant son. A year after her arrival in Agra, Bega gave birth to 'Aqiqa, a niece whom Gulbadan dearly loved. Just before 'Aqiqa's birth, Maham, longing for a grandson, coaxed Humayun into another marriage. Whenever she found "a good-looking and nice girl," Maham would bring up the name as a possible match. When she mentioned Miva-jan, daughter of the ebullient master of horse, Humayun "married and took her that very night."[3] But despite the hopes raised by the marriage, Miva couldn't have a child and never rose in wifely rank.[4] Then there were long-standing loyalists like Atun Mama, the former caretaker of the princess's grandmother, an esteemed member of the family. Bibi Fatima, a wet nurse since Humayun's infancy, was a prized presence and was appointed *Sadr-i Anas,* superintendent of Humayun's household.

Women interacted with other women, and men with other men. The homosocial arrangement at the heart of Mughal life persisted in Agra. Gulbadan's universe was peopled by busy women, brilliant strategists, and peacemakers advising princes as well as younger women on law, the politics of marriage, and the ethical principles of the dynasty. In the still evolving imperial practices and institutions, royal women upheld Mughal majesty and grandeur. They invoked legal principles, cited examples of great men and women of the past, and urged dissenters to follow dynastic principles. They ensured that dynastic mores remained in place in the ongoing so-cial-political adjustments. They made certain that princely squabbles didn't destroy the unity of the Mughals and the ambitions of Babur. The women did not routinely pick up weapons in war zones, but responsibility for the sustenance and longevity of the empire fell upon their shoulders. These women had frequently dealt with death and devastation relayed from the war front and would do so again.

Gulbadan would hear about Mughal women's actions and decisions, big and small, in the interest of the dynasty. To intervene on behalf of kith and kin was not novel for Khanzada, who had agreed to sacrifice herself in an un-wanted marriage three decades earlier, thus saving her brother and the dig-nity of her dynasty. Nor was it unprecedented for Gulbadan's mother to share her children with her co-wife at a time when her husband Babur struggled to gain a territorial foothold in Hindustan. The Afghan Lady ensured that peace was established between her clan and the Mughals through her mar-riage with Babur. In Mubarika's tribal world, to be honorable was the highest virtue. Honor entailed camaraderie, courage, and loyalty to one's commit-ments. Atun Mama, Bibi Fatima, and scores of other stalwarts stepped into the most hazardous situations to honor their family commitments.

Negotiation, tact, conciliation, and domestic enterprise were thought to be women's *fitrat,* natural gifts or intrinsic qualities. Gulbadan likely heard this word in her home assemblies. She brought it into play in her writing on more than one occasion. She discerned layers of female investment—the richly complex ways in which the female guardians of the empire preserved the Mughal line.

As she came of age, Gulbadan saw the relations among her brothers become fraught. Humayun was very conciliatory. He honored his father's will and allocated Punjab to his half brother Kamran, making him the governor of Kabul and Kandahar, northwest of Punjab. Multan went to the younger 'Askari. Hindal received parts of western India. Humayun imagined the distribution would ensure brotherly concord. Gulbadan, writing later, certainly understood the sharing among the princes as fair. But peace was far from realized. Princely tussles marked the times. Treacheries and rebellions came to the fore, even as Humayun placed emphasis on order in both the court and the castles.

Many things were imprinted on Gulbadan's mind from the years she lived in her mother's mansion. She never forgot the meticulous way the matriarchs held up Mughal power and grandeur, later writing about the cultural life of her dynasty embedded in feasts and the ritual around gifts—luminous codes of the privileges of seniority. She participated in the banquets and festivities that the elder haraman arranged, noticing carefully who sat where in the ritual hierarchy, the significance of the numbers of gifts, and the dazzle of the gold throne, the jewel-embroidered divan, and the cushions. A banquet that Khanzada planned left a lasting impression on her.[5] Held in the Mystic House, or Talismanic Palace, with several octagonal halls, it was a dual feast commemorating Humayun's accession and her blood brother Hindal's wedding.

A jeweled throne placed in the forecourt of one of the large octagonal halls was the centerpiece of the occasion. Humayun and Khanzada sat together on a gold-embroidered divan. On the aunt's right side were several paternal aunts and cousins. On her left, Dildar, Gulbadan, and her sisters sat upon a soft couch. Next to them were the illustrious wives of Humayun as well as Nargul, Gulnar, Atun Mama, and Bibi Fatima. Altogether, ninety-six esteemed women were in attendance, wrote Gulbadan—all loyal observers of the dynasty from its small beginnings to its stately and luxurious power. Atun never forgot her barefoot walk in the dead of winter as she made her way back to safe ground after Babur had lost Samarkand. And here she was, beholding a ceremony she couldn't have imagined then.

The courtiers sat according to rank across from the royal ladies. Draperies embroidered in gold and pearls, each one and a half yards in length, hung all around. Water pitchers, jeweled drinking vessels, utensils of pure gold and silver, betel boxes, and long-necked porcelain wine bottles were laid out. A second octagonal hall, the House of Pleasure, was decorated with gilded divans and chests of sandalwood and snug pillows. Containers stuffed with roasted sheep, chicken with herbs, meatballs with apricots, rice cooked in ghee, and sweetmeats were set upon gold brocade tablecloths.

After everyone settled in their ritual places, Humayun ordered the servants to bring out the *sachaq,* or offering of gifts. There were three heaps. Pointing to the first, he asked Hindu Beg, who led Gulbadan's caravan out from Kabul, to distribute jeweled scimitars, gilded armor, gold-embroidered daggers, and quivers to the princes, chiefs, and soldiers. The second heap, containing *juz-dan,* painted boxes with writing instruments, and beautiful book covers, went to the theologians and ascetics. Musicians and performers got the third lot—coverlets and sheets of brocade. Ashrafis, gold coins, were doled out to everyone. No one got fewer than a hundred of them. Even then, ten thousand silver shahrukhis and two thousand gold ashrafis remained. The emperor then stood up and scattered the rest upon the *vali-un-ni'matan,* the beneficent senior ladies. Coins fell upon women elders, jingled on the floor—the soft metallic yet magical sound lodged in the princess's memory.[6]

Some women left after the commemoration festivities, while others, including Gulbadan, changed seats and came over to Humayun's left side. The festivities went on. Twelve thousand robes of honor went to courtiers. A fancy bazaar was ready for the entertainment of the household. Decorated boats lined the banks of the Yamuna. Like floating gardens, the lower decks of the boats were dressed in lush flowers, sweet-smelling amaranths, cockscombs, larkspurs, and tulips. "Everyone was astonished and amazed."[7]

The merriment then moved. Hindal's wedding feast was "such as had not been made for any other child of my royal father," Gulbadan emphasized. Sultanam, the bride, was the younger sister of the second husband of Khanzada. She had adopted Sultanam at the age of two and took care of her as "her own."[8] Gulbadan doesn't explain why her aunt took charge of Sultanam. The fact of the adoption appears in passing in her description of the wedding feast alongside her remark that Khanzada organized a delightful banquet. She "planned it all and carried it all out."[9]

Gulbadan was struck by the gifts that her aunt gave the bride: nine jackets with jeweled buttons of ruby, cornelian, emerald, turquoise, and cat's-eye. Nine necklaces, earrings of ruby and others of pearl, short-sleeved jackets, tall lamps, household goods, three embroidered fans, a regal umbrella, gold and silver vessels, and horses with gold-embroidered saddles, as well as Turkish, Circassian, Russian, and Ethiopian slaves were also among the gifts. Mahdi Khwaja, the aunt's husband, gave the groom nine select horses with velvet saddles and bridles, and another set of nine horses meant to carry luggage. These animals had gold and silver vessels upon their backs. Sheets of brocade and Portuguese escarlate cloth as well as Turkish, Ethiopian, and Hindustani slaves were also given. An illustrative inventory, as nine was an auspicious number. Like the power of numbers, the spectacular gold stayed in Gulbadan's memory, all of it signaling the prosperity of the Mughals in Hindustan.

The cerebral Gulbadan was a book lover. The *kitab-khana*, or the imperial library, located in the House of Good Fortune, a section of the same building where banquets were held, was a prized haven for her. Books written in calligraphic Persian, leather-bound books, gold-lined portfolios, and gilded pen cases could be found there, as could the Turkish memoir that Gulbadan saw her father compose. She might remember that she had first seen the pages of her father's diary soon after crossing the Chenab. Messenger Shirak, then carrying the pages to Kabul, had stopped on the way to greet the first Mughal caravan bound for Agra. Many pages, including the ones in which Babur wrote about the events of the year Gulbadan was born, were in that lot, though they were later lost in a storm.

Was her father's diary encased in golden leather or was it wrapped in gold-lined linen cloth? What about early miniature paintings? Did she see a painter sitting on the floor holding delicate rice paper smaller than the size of the page of a book on one bent leg, meditatively sketching? Painters would have detailed the feather of a bird, the eyes of a dancer, the folds of cloth, battles, cannons, forts, mosques, elephants, horses, kings, and queens. They would use rose pink, ink blue, mud yellow, and sunny gold. In bound manuscripts, each page was adorned with a gold border. Inside the rim were twisting and winding green creepers and lilies and magnolias. Miniature pictures augmented the written word. Gulbadan would be amazed at the visual beauty of works from northern India, Persia, and Central Asia.

The wide-eyed princess saw new edifices come up in Agra and heard about others in Gwalior. She heard that foundations were being laid for a new capital in Delhi.[10] She learned about inventions at the court and noted that her brother gave gifts at his commemoration feast precisely the way he had divided the people of his court—into three groups. *Men of the State* included court officers, holy persons, religious men, literati, law officers, science persons, and poets. *The Propitious People,* or "honorable men," were officers in the Mughal domain in whose association eternal prosperity could be secured. As a young girl, Gulbadan found it easiest to recognize the *People of Pleasure or Joy,* playful musicians, singers, and composers— like the two women dancers, dressed as men, who played the lute and sang at feasts.[11]

After an abundant girlhood in Kabul and Agra, Gulbadan grew into maturity in rather different circumstances. The change from a life in a mansion along the river to being on the road would seem to Gulbadan akin to the peripatetic conditions of her girlhood. But it was much more. Much of her time and thinking was involved in the insurgencies and activities of her brothers that eventually led to the fall and exile of her favorite brother Humayun. In the personal vicissitudes that followed, she would lean on the self-confident appeal of Aunt Khanzada and on the stories of itinerant women and their unmatched wisdom.

When her brother ordered his men to pitch the advance camp, the *Peshkhana,* outside Agra in late 1537, the daily rhythms of Gulbadan's life began to shift. In order to build confidence in his kingship, Humayun had decided to extend his realm, as an ambitious king was meant to do.

Several haraman moved to the advance camp, from where Humayun would lead his forces down the river to Bengal. For three months they stayed together as armaments were organized, soldiers mustered, and plans spelled out. Dildar, Mubarika, Bega, and her daughter 'Aqiqa joined the camp. Miva-jan also went, as did the three other wives of lower status, Bachka, employed since the time of the first emperor's household, and women of rank such as the elderly 'Ayesha Begum, a cousin of the first emperor. So too did Humayun's stepsisters, musicians, and poetry and Qur'an reciters. Gulbadan, now fifteen and blooming into youth, joined the women in the camp. In those days, she used to wear an embroidered *taq*, the conical cap that added to her allure.

The women resided in tents that were set up according to rank. Gulbadan's was closest to Humayun. It seemed as though nothing had changed except that they had moved into tents with rotundas, audience pavilions, and offices. Tent living was a regular feature of Mughal life. In and out of forts and mansions, they frequently stayed in Gujarati cloth-of-gold-lined camps spread out in gardens and open country. There were ewers for rose water, candlesticks, drinking vessels, sprinklers, and other paraphernalia.

While in the advance camp, Humayun regularly visited his women relatives. At one point when he and other women were in Gulbadan's premises, the entertainment lasted late into the night. The morning after his visit, Gulbadan recalled, in the early hours, Bega woke him up for morning prayers. He ordered water for his ablutions. As they waited, Bega said to him: "For several days now you have been paying visits in this garden, and on no one day have you been to our tent. Thorns have not been planted in the way to it. . . . How long will you maintain such inattention to us? We too have a heart." Humayun did not say anything and went off to pray. After his prayers, he sent for all the women. "We all went," says Gulbadan.

He said not a word, so everyone knew he was angry. After a little while, he addressed Bega: "Bibi [wife], what ill-treatment at my hands did you complain of this morning? . . . That was not the place to make a complaint." Then, looking at the others, he said: "You all . . . know that I have been to the quarters of the elder relations. . . . It is a necessity laid on me to make them happy. . . . I am an opium eater. If there should be delay in my comings and goings, do not be angry with me. Rather, write me a letter, and say: 'Whether it please you to come or whether it please you not to come, we are content and are thankful to you.'"[12]

I am an opium eater, he added disarmingly. No one said anything. They knew it was time for the emperor to focus on the plains of the lower Ganges region that he longed to control. The Afghans in the eastern territories of Bengal and Bihar were proud of their ambitious commander with humble beginnings, Sher Shah, the son of a horse breeder and landholder. Humayun wanted to ensure that things didn't slip out of his hands as they had two years prior in his campaign in Gujarat. He hired Rumi Khan, a brilliant commander but a notorious turncoat, as chief of artillery. He enlisted the support of his younger brothers. Hindal was briefed that he would stay in Agra and 'Askari would accompany the departing army. Soon after his exchange with Bega, in late November 1537, Humayun set out with his grand army, with seven hundred ammunition cases and many Anatolian cannons, each of which could shoot a ball weighing 2.25 kilograms.[13]

Bega and 'Aqiqa joined the emperor in the flotilla of imperial boats that sailed toward Chunar, a strategically located fortress under the command of Sher Shah's son. Lower-status wives Shad Bibi and Chand Bibi and the elderly custodian Bachka were in the same barge as the emperor and Bega. Chand Bibi was four months pregnant. Aunt 'Ayesha, the elder cousin of Babur, went with them. Boats of great nobles and boon companions and assistants, aides, troopers, soldiers, and servants followed. Soldiers sailed with their wives and children. Mughal cavalry and artillery would move east along the highway as far as Allahabad, keeping pace with the royal barge that sailed on the Yamuna. After passing Allahabad and the holy Hindu city of Banaras, they would approach Chunar from the western bank of the river Ganges that circled the Chunar Fort.

For generations, Mughal women had convoyed with their men in battle zones. Amid war, elders gave advice and younger women brought solace. When the need arose, the matriarchs served as negotiators and peacemakers. Life went on in the tents in the war zone: arguments, feasts, poetry, and readings of the Qur'an. But gone were the days when sturdy ladies, in tune with outdoor traditions of the steppe, rode for long hours and endured chases. The geography of the riverine terrain and the extended use of boats were both relatively new.

Gulbadan bid farewell to the departing cortege with 'Aqiqa, her five-year-old niece. Humayun noticed his sister's taq, her conical cap.

News from Chunar reached Agra very quickly. The Chunar Fort sat concealed on a jutting rock over a low range of hills about 150 feet high, its walls defended by cannons, thanks to the gunpowder technology that had become widespread in the 1520s. Gulbadan heard about the tremendous bombardment and losses of life during the siege of the fort. But the strong Mughal artillery followed Rumi Khan's plan, mounting a battery upon three boats so high that it pounded the fortress into submission. By March 1538, Chunar was in Mughal hands.

Emboldened, Humayun directed his army to advance farther east, and successfully took wealthy Bengali territories such as Gaur—Jannatabad, or the City of Paradise, in its new Mughal name. The conquests were barely completed when Humayun shut himself off, listening to poetry and music and smoking opium.

After four months of siege of the impregnable fort of Champaner in Gujarat two years earlier, instead of fighting on and consolidating ground, the emotive emperor had dallied in one of the palaces. He hunted, feasted, drank wine, and smoked opium. As in Champaner, so in Gaur: nine months passed while officers and soldiers were anxious to return to their homes in Agra. People grew restless in the humid temperatures of the eastern belt. Humayun's generals despaired, as did the women in Agra receiving the disturbing news.

In Agra trouble brewed. Gulbadan's proud and self-confident blood brother, the nineteen-year-old Hindal, installed as caretaker, hatched a plot to take the Mughal throne. Gulbadan knew of the fiasco in Champaner. But she had a soft spot for her brother, and later justified the situation by saying that Humayun was "comfortably and safely" in Gaur. However, the events in Agra horrified her.[14]

After murdering the messenger Humayun sent him, Prince Hindal had the khutba read in his name at the sacred Friday prayers, a privilege that belonged only to the sovereign.[15] Proclaiming himself emperor, Hindal marched to see his mother. Dildar donned a blue cloth over her breast. Seeing the blue *Kabud*, a sign of mourning, he was infuriated. "What kind of dress is that [which] you have donned at such a time of rejoicing?" he asked her. "I am . . . mourning," she replied. "You are young and have . . . lost the true way; you have girded your loins for your own destruction," she angrily added.[16] There were times when even the most experienced of elder kinswomen were helpless. All Dildar could do was express her views. Nervous about the safety of her relatives in the eastern provinces, all Gulbadan could do was wait for them to return.

With missive after missive detailing Hindal's destructive actions, Humayun finally decided to make his way back to Agra. With his haraman, he began an arduous journey along the Ganges. The rains added to their misery, bridges collapsed, thundering showers made the grounds soggy, impeding the horses. As before, a large chunk of the Mughal army went along the highway, adjoining the riverbank. Being in the vicinity of Sher Shah's domains meant they were in immense danger. They crossed Patna and sailed undisturbed as far as the town of Muner.

The rains fell heavily. Soon after the Mughal army crossed Muner, Sher Shah's forces struck them at the rear. Massive exchange of arrows and musketry fire began. The Afghans seized the heavy guns that were being transported upon the river. Mughal soldiers kept on, reaching Chausa, where they camped some distance away from the riverbank. Sher Shah's army marched near Chausa and took up positions across from the Mughals. Between them were torrential waters and banks so steep that they could not be crossed except at the usual ford.

In the early hours of dawn on June 26, 1539, in the words of Gulbadan, "Sher Khan poured down" on the Mughal encampment in Chausa.[17] The Mughal camp and army were in no position to retaliate. Woken up by the attack, they had no time to put on armor or array themselves for battle. Humayun was wounded in the left arm, and his soldiers seized the reins of his horse and forced him toward the Ganges. Humayun urged his horse into the river, but the beast threw him off. A water carrier was at the time crossing the waters on his inflated buffalo leather bag. He rushed toward the emperor and safely floated him across. Thus, Jawhar, royal water carrier and future historian of the Mughal Empire, came on the imperial scene.

The debacle in Chausa broke Gulbadan's spirit. Away from the Ganges, she wrote, a terrifying scene unfolded in the women's section of the encampment. Humayun had sent his generals to escort the women to safety. The men rushed to Bega Begum's tent. At her doorstep, three of the best Mughal generals died wrestling the Afghans in order to protect the Begum. An Afghan chronicler notes that when Bega came out with a group of women, Sher Shah alighted from his horse to extend courtesy and respect to her. He ordered his army to refrain from taking the Mughal women or children captive.[18]

Nevertheless, many women and children died. Several were lost in the chaos of the marching armies. "Of those who were in that pandemonium," Gulbadan wrote, no trace was ever found. Bega was captured. By whom and where she went, the princess doesn't say. Chand Bibi and Shad Bibi were gone, likely drowned. Princess 'Aqiqa, nearly six at the time, went missing. The elderly woman servant of Babur's household, Bachka, who had lived through the harsh walk in snowy terrain, vanished in the mayhem of Chausa. Elderly 'Ayesha, forcibly married twice to Uzbek men, like Khanzada, survived the bartering but not the debacle of Chausa. No one would ever know, Gulbadan lamented, what had become of the missing.[19] Deeply anguished, she longed for her brother to come safely back to Agra.

Late in the summer of 1539, Humayun reached Agra, and Gulbadan went to see him. She had on her head a muslin *lachaq*, or coif bedecked with pearls and feathers. Folded at the corners, her coif narrowed at the bottom and was tied below her chin.

Humayun almost didn't recognize her. "When I led the army to Gaur, you wore the taq. . . . And now you wear . . . the muslin lachaq," he said, surprised.[20]

The lachaq was worn by a royal bride. Gulbadan was married.

Writing nearly twenty-five years later, Gulbadan recalled the gravity of the occasion and the dire circumstances in which Humayun returned home. Her grief was palpable even in her later recounting. *You wore the taq . . . and now you wear the muslin lachaq* is the only indication she provides that she was married. Khizr Khwaja Khan, her husband, was a court grandee of the same paternal family as hers, her second cousin. Her two sisters were married to two of his uncles. Khizr also had two brothers who lived in Agra at the time. It is not clear from her discussion if Khizr was among the intimate members who welcomed Humayun back to Agra.

Gulbadan said nothing about Khizr at the time she went to meet her brother, giving no direct word that she was married. It is intriguing to think why Gulbadan got married while Humayun, whom she dearly loved, was away. And why Khizr? Who arranged the match and organized the wedding?

In the weeks that followed, the newly married Gulbadan and the Mughal haraman spent time with the emperor. Humayun had lost his little daughter and was humiliated by a foe who had captured his wife. He was aghast that his brother had tried to usurp the Mughal throne. "Oh, my Gulbadan, very often I used to think of you," he said to her in one of the assemblies. He wished she was with him, he added, but after the disaster of Chausa he was glad that she wasn't. "I have been consumed by a hundred thousand regrets," he whispered, remembering his little daughter. "Why did I take her with the army?"[21]

His agony would have worsened when his captured wife Bega returned to Agra escorted by one of Sher Shah's leading generals. How soon she came back after Humayun's return is difficult to say. One view is that she returned soon after her husband; another is that it was after a considerable period had elapsed.[22] How did the royal couple deal with the haunting experience in Chausa, with Bega's captivity and the loss of their daughter? No one writes about Bega's homecoming, not even Gulbadan, who writes so movingly about the disaster in Chausa. However, we can picture the women gathered around her, offering words of solace, joining her in mourning little 'Aqiqa. Bega would have received great sympathy from Khanzada. With Khanzada, she now shared a sense of loss, indignity—and valor. Their unspoken and unwritten histories remain buried in accounts of male power.

In those weeks of grief and reunion, Humayun consulted the women on many major matters. What to do with the rebel Prince Hindal, who had fled to Alwar, one hundred miles west-northwest of Agra? He visited Dildar to discuss the question with her. Gulbadan, Mubarika, Gulnar, and Nargul were present in her mansion. He asked the attendants to retire so that he could be alone with the women. "Hindal is the might of my arm, the desired, the beloved," he said. "What was to be has happened. . . . Now there is no anger in my heart. . . . If you do not believe it"—as he spoke, he picked up a copy of the Qur'an. Gulbadan immediately took the Holy Book from his hand. "Let it be. Why are you talking like this?" she reprimanded her brother.[23] She knew Humayun meant every word he said and didn't see why he had to swear by the Holy Book.

It seemed as though everyone wanted to forgive Hindal, including Kamran, stationed at the time in a garden outside the city. He had come down from Kabul just before Humayun returned from the east. He pleaded with his half brother to forgive Hindal "for my sake." "For your sake," Humayun assented.[24] For her part, Gulbadan was confused by Hindal's actions. She wanted to protect her blood brother, but she also recognized his treachery.

Holding the Qur'an in his hand, Humayun asked Gulbadan, "How would it be . . . if you went yourself and brought your brother [to me]?" Before she could say anything, Dildar intervened: "She is young. She has never traveled alone." After a moment, she offered to intercede herself. "If you approve, I will go."[25] Humayun agreed, even though he saw how self-assured Gulbadan was and how effectively she could intercede. *Let it be. Why are you talking like this?* she had said forthrightly moments earlier. Humayun wanted his forceful sister's mediation in fetching Hindal. Dildar, on the other hand, wanted to shield her daughter from involvement in princely contention.

When Hindal finally came before the emperor, he begged forgiveness and Humayun exonerated him.[26]

The challenges to the Mughal throne mounted. By late 1540, everyone was fretful. Sher Shah was near Lucknow, approximately 215 miles east of Agra. As if to distract himself from the impending battle, Humayun installed Jawhar on the throne for two days. He was fulfilling a promise he had made to the water carrier who saved his life in the battle of Chausa. "Now the emperor put a slave on the throne," Gulbadan wrote. "I don't think I ever heard the slave's real name. Some said it was Nizam; others said Sumbul." Kamran chided the emperor in a letter that Gulbadan included in her account. "What is the need to put him on the throne? At such a time when Sher Khan is so near, what kind of affair is this to engage your Majesty?"[27] Humayun did not listen and fulfilled his promise.

Sher Shah steadily advanced. Humayun then took the field against his enemy near Kannauj. When leaving Agra, he asked Kamran to oversee matters on his behalf. As soon as Humayun crossed the Ganges, says Gulbadan, Kamran decided to retreat to Lahore. "We were sitting around," she remembered, when Kamran's instruction arrived. "You are ordered to accompany me to Lahore."[28] He led twelve thousand troops, who had come from Kabul, now to Lahore. He also forced many royal women and attendants and servants to join his convoy. He coerced Gulbadan into going with him, saying that he was ill and needed her.

She wept bitterly and made "a hundred complaints and laments," but Kamran paid no heed to Gulbadan's protests. Her mother implored Kamran to leave her alone. "You can come, too," he said to her and promised Dildar that he would take Gulbadan only a small part of the journey, after which she would return. Once they were halfway, Gulbadan wrote that she was "forcibly separated from all my stepmothers and sisters and from my father's people . . . with whom I had grown up from infancy and from [whom] I had never been separated." Angry, she sent a letter to Humayun saying that she never expected him to cut her off like that and give her to Kamran. Humayun wrote back that he didn't have the heart to separate himself from her, but Kamran was miserable and that was the reason he had begged her to join him. "I had to entrust you to him," he added, "because at present we are on a mission [against Sher Shah]." "God willing, when this is complete, you will be the first one I will summon."[29]

Sad, annoyed, and forced to undertake a journey against her will, Gulbadan left Agra. "There was nothing I could do," she wrote.[30] By the time she reached Lahore, Humayun had been defeated by Sher Shah in Kannauj. But he escaped. "Our other people in Agra . . . were headed for Lahore," Gulbadan recalled. Khanzada, Dildar, Sultanam, Afghan Lady, Gulnar, Nargul, and the wives and families of nobles and troops left Agra under Hindal's command.

Finally, the vanquished emperor too reached Lahore, only to receive news each day of Sher Shah's mounting victories. After he seized Agra, he declared himself Sher Shah Suri, a new monarch with a new establishment. Humayun had had enough. He dispatched one of his messengers to Agra. "I have left you the whole realm of Hindustan," he wrote to Sher Shah. "Leave Lahore alone." "I'll leave you Kabul. You'll have to go there," came Sher Shah's response.[31]

It was clear to everyone in the Mughal circles that they needed to act. But there was much strife. Humayun, his brothers, and the Mughal matriarchs and counselors tried to work out how, in what direction, and in what fashion the large Mughal clan would leave Lahore. Kamran made it clear that he would hold onto his territories in Punjab with Lahore as a key center. But if that wasn't possible, he would keep his domain of Kabul. What's more, he would keep Humayun out of it. When Humayun proposed to march to Badakhshan, his princely territory, Kamran would not hear of it. The road to Badakhshan lay through Kabul. Once there, Kamran figured, it was unlikely that Humayun would move out. Five months slipped by in arguments and discussions.

Nobles, troops, camp followers, royals: everyone was restless. Courtiers urged Humayun to put Kamran to death, but he didn't agree. Kamran's force was large, and Humayun had to take that into account. Moreover, 'Askari deserted the emperor in favor of his blood brother and added his forces to Kamran's. Gulbadan remained stuck in Kamran's camp.

On October 30, 1540, the five rivers of Punjab that spread out like five fingers of a hand were roaring with floods. As the Mughal brothers argued, Sher Shah bravely crossed the river Beas that ran parallel to the river Ravi, which ringed the mud citadel where the Mughal tents were pitched. One more crossing and Sher Shah would be in their headquarters.

"You'd have thought it was doomsday," wrote Gulbadan, recalling the uproar that ensued. The threatened arrival of Sher Shah's army in the city spread panic. Nearly two hundred thousand people sped out of Lahore, making sources of conveyance, such as horses, scarce. Taking a swift decision, Hindal readied his cavalcade and led it south to Multan, where there was a substantial Persian community. Mother Dildar, Aunt Khanzada, wife Sultanam, servants, and loyalists went with him.

Although still undecided about the direction they would take, Humayun and Kamran also left Lahore, abandoning possessions and places they called theirs. A little west of the river Jhelum, the road ran through a ravine of an outlying spur of the Salt Range. Just beyond the ravine, the road divided: northwest to Kabul and southwest to Sind. Kamran asserted that his section of the caravan would go first, clearly with the object of closing the road to Kabul. Humayun insisted on his right of precedence.

Abul Baqa, the wise old man, interceded. Ten years prior, he had led Babur to the chambers where he had performed the ritual of sacrificing his life for Humayun. Now Baqa advised Humayun to keep in mind Kamran's superior military force. And to Kamran he said that by law, Humayun had the right of precedence.

There was a fork in the road. Thousands waited. Gulbadan was seated in her palanquin on Kamran's side. His large force had blocked the passage to Kabul. As Humayun took the first step on the southern road toward Sind, Jawhar and Bibi Fatima among his followers, Gulbadan felt that the course of the Mughal dynasty had turned. At this point, commanders, nobles, and soldiers had to make a choice.

The mighty Mughals split. Women were apportioned. Gulbadan went with Kamran. She was already in his convoy, and there was no way she could change this. She does not say anything about her migration back to Kabul, nor does she mention her husband Khizr at this point. There is no mention either of Bega or which royal party she went with.

Each section of the clan went on its own singular journey. The royal litters that turned toward Sind were headed in an unknown direction, far from any of the homelands they knew. Gulbadan returned to her childhood home of Kabul.

Seven

Great Expectations

~

IN THE WINTER OF 1544, THERE WAS MUCH EXCITEMENT IN
Bala Hisar. Despite thick snow outside, the people in the citadel were jubi-
lant. Royal servants rushed about in a blaze of activity. In various corners,
they lit fires, adding a warm glow to the walls. In her apartment, Gulbadan
paced back and forth.

After a perilous time in Sind, where Humayun had married Hamida, a
descendant of an eminent sage, and soon after celebrated the birth of Prince
Akbar, the three had gone toward Kandahar in the winter of 1542.[1] Khanzada
was there, as were several Afghans who, his advisers were confident, could
be drawn to Humayun's side. In that frigid season, so cold that food froze
as soon as it was served, Humayun, Hamida, and baby Akbar reached the
outskirts of the city.[2]

Rain, snow, and wind tore the flaps of their makeshift camp. 'Askari
refused to let Humayun enter Kandahar. An informant on a scrawny horse
rushed in with news of 'Askari's likely plan, an attack on Humayun's camp.[3]
They had to leave the area immediately. With forty-two supporters, Humayun, Hamida, and a woman of the Baluchi tribe—the only two women in the
group—galloped away. Akbar was left in the care of two wet nurses, water
carrier Jawhar, and a few reliable soldiers. Khanzada was unable to persuade
'Askari to support Humayun, but she likely stirred his feelings.

'Askari's wife took charge of the infant Akbar. Leaving him behind was
a pragmatic move. The prince had been on the road since his birth a few
months earlier. He had to be protected and kept alive, not exposed to further
dangers on the long journey to Persia, where Humayun and Hamida had
decided to take refuge. And so, in the safe company of milk-mother Maham

Anaga, Jawhar, who would soon join the emperor in Persia, and Jiji-Anaga, favored wet nurse, the little prince became the ward of his uncle and aunt.[4]

Two years later, Akbar was on his way to Kabul from Kandahar. No longer a fugitive king, Humayun was advancing rapidly to Kandahar from Persia. With the massive support of the shah's army, he hoped to recover his son along with Kandahar. From Kabul, however, Kamran sent for Akbar. He intended to hold the prince hostage against his returning father. There was cause for anxiety. Even so, Gulbadan's anticipation knew no bounds.

Gulbadan disliked Kamran's overbearing manner and avoided any interaction with him, though he had treated her more kindly than he had other women, whom he refused even the basic stipends. Turning away from him was easier during her forced years in Kabul, when she gave birth to her son, Sa'adat-yar. In her distinctive fashion, she does not mention the birth and only briefly touches on the arguments she had with her husband.[5] In his greatest betrayal, Khizr had joined Kamran's court. She did not flinch from reproaching her husband, especially in the months after her migration to Kabul, when runners regularly brought news of the stark poverty and disgrace that Humayun endured. "Beware, a thousand times beware," she warned Khizr about aligning with Kamran.[6]

She was interacting more than ever with a small, intimate circle. Her brother Hindal came from Sind to Kabul in 1543, under the sharp eye of Kamran. Mother Dildar returned with him, full of stories of Hamida's negotiation before her marriage with Humayun. Aunt Khanzada was in Kabul. Bega was also there, though we do not know when or in whose company she came to Kabul, whether she was in the same convoy as Gulbadan, or why she did not accompany Humayun to Persia.

Among the fabulous royals in Kabul was also the now elderly Afghan Lady, with strands of gray in her hair, still handsome and dressed in her floral skirts and dangling jewels. Mubarika would tell Gulbadan's son the story of his mother's dislocated wrist in the garden back when she was a little girl. There were tales from Nanacha, the companion of Gulbadan's guardian mother, and any number of *kissas*, tales from Mama, the princess's girlhood caregiver.

How Hamida had seized her brother's heart was at the time Gulbadan's favorite family story. Twenty-one years of age, Gulbadan's heart pulsed with delight at the prospect of Humayun's arrival. It was five years since she had seen her beloved brother. She longed to meet Hamida and her infant daughter, born in Sabzwar shortly before the couple left Persia. She couldn't wait to hear the details of Humayun and Hamida's desert wedding.

It was a winter of great expectations.

Gulbadan met her nephew Akbar at the great assembly in Khanzada's premises. Kamran had received Akbar the previous day and brought him to Khanzada. Devoted milk-mothers, little *kokas,* milk-brothers 'Aziz and Zain, foster fathers, soldiers, and many servants surrounded the little prince. His half sister Bakhshi, nearly four, was in the princely train. The whereabouts of Bibi Gunwar, Bakhshi's mother and a lesser wife of Humayun, remain unclear in the records.

Full of emotion, Gulbadan beheld the darling son of her brother and Hamida, born amid hunger, deprivation, and exile. The moon was in Leo at his birth; she wrote that it was "a very good omen that the birth was in a fixed sign." A child so born, she noted, would be fortunate and live a long life.[7] Her brother had predicted that his son's fame, like the sweet-smelling musk that spread and filled one's senses, would sweep across the world. The prophecies were prescient. What Gulbadan couldn't have imagined at the time was that she would be the leading witness of her nephew's grandeur.

Khanzada held Akbar in her arms and kissed his little hands and feet. And then she began to sob, wrote Gulbadan. In bewilderment, the prince likely wrestled himself out of her arms, saying something in Turkish, the first language of the family. Most Mughals spoke Turkish, although they knew Persian and Hindavi, the gift of their lost territories across the Indus.

Having traveled nearly 310 miles—trudging through darkness, ice, and snow, many deadly passes, and howling winds—the baby would be distracted and worn out. Kamran was astonished to see the glow on Akbar's forehead despite his long ordeal: from it "streamed the glory of eternal dominion and success." Whether or not Kamran "beheld that true cypress of fortune's rosarium," the words of Akbar's future panegyrist courtier Abul Fazl, it is certain that Bala Hisar stirred with great delight.[8] The prince's name was on everyone's lips: the focus of hope for the long, dazzling life of their dynasty.

Akbar was in Khanzada's care while the family waited to reunite with Humayun and Hamida. Kamran was quiet, awaiting the next steps. Gulbadan watched her aunt and nephew with pleasure. Her aunt was very fond of Akbar, she wrote. She would repeatedly kiss his hands and feet and remark that they were the very hands and feet of her brother Babur. He is like him, she said.

But pressing questions dulled Gulbadan's enjoyment. On March 16, 1545, an update said that Humayun had marched right up to the walls of Kandahar. The city garrison was on alert and Humayun's troops were pushed back by gunfire and thrown into confusion. He withdrew to a safer location and strategized with Bairam Khan, a prominent loyalist who stood with the emperor through thick and thin. Bairam destroyed a body of enemy auxiliaries stationed behind a hill. Hamida's brother, also in the Mughal army, was wounded. The siege went on. The Persian forces backing Humayun grew restless.

The next dispatch from Kandahar reported that Humayun's forces had bombarded the walls of the fort. Courtiers from Kabul began abandoning Kamran. Many leading Kabuli men sent letters of support to Humayun. Desertions began from the Kandahar garrison: Gulbadan's husband was among the first to flee. He jumped down from the fort and submitted to Humayun, who pardoned Khizr for Gulbadan's sake.

In the last week of March 1545, Bairam traveled to Kabul. A welcome guest for the ladies, he came as an envoy to see what course Kamran might choose now that his brother was ready to take back the imperial posts. Bayazid Bayat, an officer and future historian of the Mughal Empire, accompanied him. Bairam stayed six weeks in Kabul. He saw Akbar, his future protégé. He described the events of the five years since Gulbadan and her brother were parted.

Bairam patiently waited to speak to Kamran the entire time he was in Kabul, but he had nothing to say to Humayun's envoy. To Gulbadan's annoyance, Kamran instead approached Khanzada and urged her to speak with Humayun. Rattled by disturbing messages from Kandahar, he implored his aunt, "Make peace between us," utterly apprehensive about what might happen to him.[9]

With no signs of a deal, Bairam decided to return to Kandahar. Though physically fragile by now, Khanzada went with him. By September 1545, Kandahar had surrendered to Humayun. Prince 'Askari and his peers emerged from the fort with their swords hung around their necks, a sign of submission. Humayun forgave his half brother. Later, the prince was exiled to Mecca. Subsequent events do not suggest that Khanzada was able to obtain forgiveness for Kamran.

Once matters were settled in Kandahar, Humayun did not want to delay his return to Kabul. While Hamida stayed back for a while to recover from the stress of birthing her baby girl, Khanzada joined her nephew's victorious convoy to Kabul. She had a high fever when they marched out of Kandahar. Although constant expeditions and intercessions had taken their toll on her health, no one imagined that the journey from Kandahar to Kabul would be the last one for this peacemaker.

The cortege with the proud, aristocratic woman marched on. As they neared the river Hilmand, around the area of Hasan Abdal, Khanzada closed her eyes forever. Humayun laid his aunt to rest on the mountain side and marched on. Her body would be brought to Kabul three months later.

Late in the night of November 12, 1545, Humayun marched into Bala Hisar. Gulbadan's joy knew no bounds. Merely looking at him uplifted her. "For five years, we had been shut out from this pleasure." At long last, "we were freed from the . . . pain of separation . . . lifted up . . . in meeting this lord of beneficence again."[10] She prostrated herself several times, giving thanks to Allah. For a little while, her profound sorrow over her aunt's death lifted.

Drums of victory were sounded. Kamran, who had never during his Kabul years hunted in the Hazara country, was now seized by the desire to hunt, and sped off. Hindal came out to greet the emperor from his chosen "dervish's corner."[11]

It was a household full of joy: Bega, Dildar, loyalists, and servants watched Akbar in his father's lap. Bala Hisar came alive with festive crowds, musicians and singers, and people praying and sitting together from dusk to dawn. Humayun generously gave pensions, rations, and land to the widows and relatives of soldiers who had served him through his exile.

The family buried Khanzada beside her brother in Babur's garden, surrounded by apricot, quince, pear, and almond trees. A fitting resting place for the wise, resilient elder who had spent her entire life making peace for the Mughal good. "She passed to the mercy of God," Gulbadan wrote.[12]

Rejoicing went on for weeks, heightened when Hamida joined the family in Kabul. Gulbadan took to Hamida, a self-possessed woman of average height, perhaps from the moment they made eye contact. The poised queen Bega would ceremonially welcome her co-wife.

A story is told that when Akbar was six, he had a bad toothache. Bega brought out a remedy from the stores of her mansion and tasted it herself before administering it to the prince, thus calming Hamida's fear that the medicine might be poisoned, a common anxiety in those days when royal children were easily poisoned to death. Akbar later spoke of Bega's large-heartedness and affection. Mughal records note her generosity and honored her with the title *hajji*—Hajji Begum, named so because of her hajj, or pilgrimage, to the Holy Cities. In late 1545, at the time when she received her co-wife, Bega's pilgrimage was more than a decade in the future.

Hamida's reunion with her son turned out to be a great spectacle. Humayun asked that all the royal women dress alike in delicate woolen robes, trousers folded at the ankles, and Turki caps. Would the prince recognize his mother? A servant came into the room with Akbar on his shoulders and seated him on a divan in the company of his identically dressed women elders. As soon as he saw Hamida, wrote Gulbadan, he rushed into his mother's arms amid cheers and applause.

Among royal dynasties in the early modern Islamic and non-Islamic world, having many wives signified the power of a king. Taken together, matrimony and power shaped political networks and facilitated the birth of future monarchs. So when Humayun married yet again, it wouldn't have surprised his wives or other Bala Hisar inmates. Mah Chuchak, Moonflower, was of the Arghun family, a Turkish-Mongol house that ruled between southern Afghanistan and Sind. Mughal relations with the Arghuns were unresolved, at times even combative, and the wedding was meant to bring stability to the region.

Wedding bells surely rang in the citadel, and merrymaking took place, but Gulbadan says nothing about her brother's new wife. The gentleness embedded in Chuchak's name was at odds with her personality. Described as an ambitious woman in the Mughal annals, this new wife would give birth to three daughters and two sons. Among them was Prince Hakim, a successful future ruler of Kabul. Chuchak would lead an army against a daunting Mughal commander, bringing him to his knees.[13]

Gulbadan knew that her slim-bodied, soft-natured brother was drawn to forceful women—stately Bega, self-assured Hamida, and now the warrior Moonflower. His non-royal wives such as Gunwar and Miva or those lost in Chausa, were also courageous. Although Gulbadan does not say much about Mah Chuchak, she comes across as playful and bold in the episodes she discusses.

The Mughal wife who interested Gulbadan most was Hamida. "Hamida Banu says . . ." is a phrase the princess uses repeatedly in her memoir.[14] A note of credit to the witness of the events in exile, the phrase is also a nod to her closeness with Hamida.

A new friend in the mid-1540s, Hamida was to become pivotal in the princess's life. Together they would help bickering relatives reconcile and astutely intervene in court matters as the future empress dowager and the princess counselor and memoirist, the longest-living memory holders of the Mughals and very powerful women.

Hamida revealed to Gulbadan the story of her own marriage. She harkened back to the time when Humayun, war-worn and disillusioned, a king without a throne or land, wandered into Paat in Sind, where Gulbadan's blood brother Hindal and their mother Dildar were encamped.[15]

Dildar had arranged a get-together to welcome Humayun to Paat. Among those present was Hamida Banu. As soon as he saw the fourteen-year-old, Humayun asked who she was and if she was betrothed. Her father, a Persian Sufi popularly called Mir Baba Dost, was well known in Mughal circles. Dost was also Hindal's spiritual instructor.[16]

In a private meeting later with his relatives, Humayun announced that he wished to marry Hamida. "I thought you came here to do me honor," said Hindal, instantly objecting to the idea, "not to look out for a young bride." Annoyed, Humayun left the assembly. Dildar tried to patch up matters. "You ought to consider him [Humayun]," she reminded her son, "the representative of your late father."[17]

Humayun then asked Dildar if she could help him marry Hamida. Hindal opposed him again, this time on the grounds that he saw Hamida like "a sister and child of my own." "Heaven forbid there should not be a proper allowance [ma'ash]," or great annoyance would arise.[18]

Under Muslim law, Humayun was expected to promise Hamida an agreed-upon sum of money, or *mahr*, as part of the marriage settlement, but there was more at stake. The word *ma'ash* that Hindal used in voicing his objection also implied a wider sense of livelihood or a means of living, including where one lives, one's income, and one's landed property.[19] Perhaps because of his closeness to Hamida, Hindal was concerned about proper maintenance for a new wife amid his brother's endless drifting.

High-spirited Hamida herself opposed the marriage. An opium eater and a much-married man, thirty-three-year-old Humayun was an exile and a king only in name, recognized by members of his court and clan on the basis of his bloodline. At one point, when Humayun insisted that Hamida pay him a visit, she told the messenger: "If it is to pay my respects, I was exalted by paying my respects the other day. . . . Why should I come again?"[20]

Humayun's interest in Hamida also stemmed from his belief in numinous powers, oracles, and visions. He was drawn to mystic orders, especially his chosen Shattari Sufis who interpreted cosmic forces by way of yogic practices. Just as he was being pushed out of Hindustan, in his darkest moment, he had a dream, he later told Gulbadan, in which he saw a venerable man dressed in green carrying a staff. The man handed his wand to Humayun and said, "Do not grieve. . . . God will give you a son who shall be named Jalaluddin Muhammad Akbar." "What's your honorable name?" asked Humayun in the dream. "Zinda-fil, the Terrible Elephant, Ahmad of Jam. . . . Your son will be of my lineage," he added.

Hamida was a descendent of a sage known by this very sobriquet, the Terrible Elephant. Obsessed with the prophesy of his dream, Humayun tried yet again to see her. "To see kings once is lawful; a second time it is forbidden. I shall not come," she said to the messenger.[21]

"To cut the story short," wrote Gulbadan, for forty days Hamida demurred. At last Dildar spoke with her. "After all, you will marry someone. Better than a king, who is there?" "Oh, yes, I shall marry someone," replied

Hamida, "but he shall be a man whose collar my hand can touch, and not one whose skirt it does not reach."[22]

Humayun brought out his astrolabe, chose a propitious hour, and summoned Abul Baqa, who had guided Babur in his decision to sacrifice his life to save his son's, and who had reiterated the laws of precedence two years earlier as the Mughal clan fragmented in Lahore. Humayun selected him for assistance in this vital Mughal marriage.

With two lakhs of rupees for the dower, Baqa went to Hamida's quarters. What he said or how the money was put together, Gulbadan does not say. But in the wintry January of 1542, Humayun and Hamida married.

While she was engrossed in the festive pleasures of music assemblies, picnics, and breathtaking art and poetry, Gulbadan knew that factional rifts lurked in the shadows of new beginnings in Bala Hisar. She focused on the pleasanter rhythms of Bala Hisar: days of amusement, nights of conversation with Hamida, and the joys of seeing their sons grow. It was a time of "great happiness and tranquillity."[23] However, Kamran, based at the time in Bhakkar, 317 miles southeast of Kabul, had not relinquished his claims on Kabul.

The Mughal household in Kabul celebrated Akbar's circumcision ceremony with great pomp. Elite neighborhoods as well as bazaars were decorated with lace, trinkets, and garlands of flowers. Hindal decorated his quarters beautifully. In Bega's garden, there was a joyous celebration for the Mughal women. People were dressed in green, the Prophet's color. There were weeks of elegant festivities, grand entertainment, and plenty of food and drink. Forty dancing girls wore green clothes and came out to the Hill of Seven Brothers, where Gulbadan spent a week with her kith and kin, the same garden where as a girl she had received the "curiosities of Hind" in the aftermath of her father's victory in Panipat. Now Humayun gave robes of honor to his courtiers to mark his son's circumcision. And to the pious and the poor, he gave lavish alms.[24]

Along with his mother and much-adored cousin Akbar, Sa'adat would share the rhythms of each new day. He would view the Mughals' favorite sport, pigeon flying, and study with tutors, as did cousin Akbar. Perhaps he looked attentively at the detail on the work of miniature art produced by the newly arrived Persian painters Mir Sayyid 'Ali and Mulla 'Abd al-Samad.

The two painters had set out the moment they got Humayun's *farman* with an invitation to join the Mughal atelier in Kabul. Art flourished with their presence and novel experimentation began. Humayun wrote in a letter to a friend that 'Abd al-Samad "has made on a grain of rice a large field on which a group is playing polo—two posts at one end and two at the other—with seven players on the field and behind them a rank of footmen who hand out mallets."[25] All on a grain of rice!

An old family custom to go toward the mountain passes and to the nearby orange gardens was revived. Gulbadan was disappointed to miss one such outing with Hamida, Bega, Chuchak, Humayun, and Hindal. "I could not go because of my son," she wrote. Sa'adat was "ill at the time."[26]

The happiness and tranquility were soon shattered. While what transpired was not entirely unexpected, it still left everyone aghast. Humayun was away on a campaign in Badakhshan to the north. At the time, in 1547, he was experiencing repeated bouts of dizziness. Spies rushed to Kamran in Bhakkar with the false news that the emperor had died. Wasting no time, Kamran set out for Kabul.

It was early morning when Kamran reached the citadel. The Kabulis were caught off guard. The gates of Bala Hisar were open and water carriers and grass cutters were going in and out. Kamran's men quickly captured the doorkeepers and imprisoned them. Kamran then rushed into the section where Maham's brother was in a hot bath. "He at once killed uncle," wrote Gulbadan. The men went indoors and plundered whatever came to hand. They captured the women one by one and shut the great begams, among them Gulbadan, in a shabby room full of bricks, plaster, and dung cakes. Kamran did not spare the wives and families of Humayun's officers. He ransacked and plundered their houses.[27]

Shocked to learn of these events, Humayun immediately rushed back. When Kamran learned that the emperor was in the vicinity of Kabul, he sent for Gulbadan and her mother. He directed Dildar to stay in the outhouse, the Qorbegi, or the Lord of the Bow house. He asked Gulbadan to stay in his lodgings. "Why should I?" she argued. "Wherever my mother is, I will be, too." Kamran also asked her to write to her turncoat husband to join him.

She refused, saying he had no way of recognizing a letter from her. She had never sent him one. When necessary, she added, they sent messages by word of mouth. "Write yourself what is in your mind," she told Kamran.[28]

Pitching tents outside Bala Hisar, Humayun laid siege to the fort for nearly seven months. He also sent for Gulbadan's husband Khizr. The two met on the Hill of Two Eagles, where Khizr pledged loyalty to the emperor. Gulbadan noted: "From the beginning, I had said to him [Khizr]" that his brothers may be on Kamran's side, but God forbid he should think of joining Kamran or 'Askari. "Beware, a thousand times beware of thinking of separating yourself from the emperor," she warned him. "Praise be to God, the Khan kept to what I said."[29]

In one instance, when Kamran was on the roof of the citadel, someone from his own camp fired a gun. The bullet missed him but, outraged, he asked his attendants to bring Prince Akbar and put him in a niche in the front wall of the fort facing his father's camp. Gulbadan recalled that someone went across and warned Humayun that his son was in the direct line of fire from the muskets. "We wept," Gulbadan wrote.[30] Then the elderly Nanacha somehow managed to reach Humayun and implored him to do whatever it was that Kamran wished.

On the night of April 27, 1547, the women were preparing to retire in the dungeon hall where they had been imprisoned. Usually there was considerable noise in the citadel, but at that time "there was no noise at all," Gulbadan recalled. As everything went still, there arose all of a sudden a clashing and clinking of armor and breastplates. "What a noise!" the women said to one another. They saw that nearly a thousand people were standing in front of the citadel. "We were in terror," wrote Gulbadan. There was a narrow passage by which people from below climbed up to the citadel. Reliable couriers informed the women that Kamran had escaped. "They opened the door that had been shut against us," explains Gulbadan. "Let's go to our houses," Bega urged. "Let's wait a bit," Gulbadan suggested. Royal eunuch Ambar Nazir warned the women not to leave till Humayun came.[31]

When Humayun arrived, the women cried and praised Allah. He greeted Dildar and Gulbadan, then Bega and Hamida. He instructed his chief eunuch and commander Turdi Beg to guard the women as they left the cramped hall. They spent the night discussing the terrors of their captivity.

Mah Chuchak was heavily pregnant when she accompanied Humayun on his march north for the operation in Badakhshan. On the night of the reunion in the citadel, three months later, she had with her a little daughter born during the campaign.

Kamran surrendered and Humayun once more forgave him. He invited all his brothers. The four of them, Humayun, Kamran, Hindal, and 'Askari, sat together on one carpet and shared a meal at the same table. Gulbadan was honored to be the only woman invitee.

A year and a half later, in 1549, the haraman reminded Humayun that it was time to view the *riwaj,* a kind of wild rhubarb that spread all along the Koh-daman. The area was on the route to Balkh, which Humayun had decided to reconquer. It was part of the family's former lands. Before the attack in 1549, he had moved out of the city and settled in the advance camp.

He followed the ladies' wishes, and they set out with him. Afghani Aghacha and Mama went on ahead. There was a stream in the lower part of the Koh-daman area where the Afghani Aghacha fell off her horse. They waited to ensure that she was not hurt. Other women arrived after the Afghan Lady, riding carefully. Chuchak's horse reared, turning from side to side, but she managed to control it. Finally, all the women gathered at the spot where the delicate, juicy, thick-stemmed rhubarb was sprouting. For Gulbadan, the most anticipated events of the trip were viewing the rhubarb and enjoying a royal picnic, followed by several nights spent together on a hill.

It was a moonlit night," wrote Gulbadan. "We talked and told stories." Reciters Zarif and Straight Cypress "sang softly, softly."[32] There was some delay in the transportation of the women's tents, but Humayun's, a tent with twelve divisions, each with a sign of the Zodiac and lattice through which the stars shone, was set up. All of them were "in company with that altar of truth [Humayun]." Way past midnight, they went to sleep wherever they were.[33]

The next morning, Humayun was agitated that the women had delayed the renewed visit to the riwaj patches. "Gulbadan, the proper hour for departing has gone," he said to her. Gulbadan hurried Bega and Mah Chuchak, who were still putting on their head-to-foot dresses. The vexed emperor relaxed. They walked to the slopes of the hills. Everywhere they looked, the riwaj was growing.

Tents and pavilions for women were now pitched. There were more collective moonlit nights filled with beauty, joy, and sociable chats.

The riwaj picnic would remain one of Gulbadan's most treasured memories, reminiscent as it was of the tents, outdoor festivities, and night assemblies of her girlhood. But the experience was to be the last of its kind.

Even though he had lost Kabul in 1547, Kamran longed for the city and hoped to conquer it. On November 20, 1551, he launched a nighttime attack on the fort. Rushing to save a screaming officer, the thirty-three-year-old Prince Hindal was killed in the skirmish. Hamida's father carried the prince back to his own apartment. "I do not know what pitiless oppressor slew that harmless youth with his tyrant sword! Would to heaven that merciless sword had [instead] touched my heart and eyes, or Sa'adat-yar, my son's, or Khizr Khwaja Khan's! Alas! A hundred regrets! Alas! A thousand times alas!"[34] Gulbadan was devastated, lamenting like Antigone at the loss of her irreplaceable brother.

By 1553, there was consensus in Humayun's court that Kamran's repeated disloyalty had become intolerable. Humayun summoned an assembly. Those gathered unanimously agreed that "when one is an emperor and [a] ruler, one cannot be a brother." "If you want to give special treatment to your brother," the courtiers candidly submitted, "you must abdicate." The counselors urged the emperor to blind his half brother. Kamran had murdered the youngest prince, Hindal. He had imprisoned royal women, terrorized families, and disgraced and defamed loyal courtiers and soldiers. "This is no brother; he is the emperor's enemy," they said. Humayun listened to their arguments and then asked those present to sign a document affirming their views. He then ordered Kamran to be blinded. "The order was executed at once," wrote Gulbadan.

"After the blinding, His Majesty the Emperor . . ."[35]

Blinded, Kamran went to Mecca. He performed the pilgrimage rites four times, and died there in 1557. His brother 'Askari was also banished to Mecca. He died in Damascus a year after Kamran. Critics and rebels were often packed off to western Arabia with the supposition that they would atone for their sins in the House of God. With the two Mughal brothers' deaths, their ambitions, opinions, rights, and wrongs were silenced. There is no Kamran- or 'Askari-nama; no court historian chronicled their points of view.

Once freed of his brothers, Humayun focused his energy on Hindustan. Sher Shah had built up an extensive administrative and revenue apparatus as well as legendary road networks. But his successors were no match for Humayun's forces when they reached Delhi in July 1555. The Mughals easily took the Afghan throne. Purana Qila, or the Old Fort of Delhi, became the new Mughal residence. Accompanying the emperor was the thirteen-year-old Prince Akbar, recently married to an older cousin, his first wife, Ruqayya. As governor of Punjab, Akbar now honed his skills under the tutelage of his father's trusted general Bairam Khan.

At what point Dildar passed away, we do not know. She is not mentioned after her incarceration by Kamran. Gulbadan, Hamida, Bega, and Mah Chuchak were among the royal ladies in Kabul, living together in an atmosphere of peace. The letters they received from Delhi were redolent with well-being and triumph.

And then, in the blink of an eye, everything changed. Humayun had taken two narrow flights of stone steps up to the roof of the tower he used as a library. After a time spent keenly studying the planet Venus, he descended the steps. Hearing the muezzin's call to prayer coming from the mosque, the emperor tried to kneel, but caught his foot in his *jama*, his long coat, and fell down the steps. Three days later, he died.

Eight

Butzaris

~

GULBADAN EMERGED FROM THE LABYRINTHINE INNER PRE-
cincts of the harem, an embroidered wrap around her shoulders and head.
Only a few months earlier, she had discussed with her nephew Emperor
Akbar a plan to travel to western Arabia. We first met Gulbadan when she
was occupied in that exchange. Now, on a fine autumn day in October 1576,
Akbar stood beside his aunt to bid farewell to her and other leading harem
women. Alongside the emperor were his sons, Princes Salim and Murad,
ages seven and six.[1]

Cameleers in bright red-and-yellow turbans were ready for any command
from the fifty-three-year-old Gulbadan. Eleven other "Holy Presences"—in
the words of Akbar's authorized history—ascended under royal canopies
atop graceful, black-eyed *uthnis* and set off. Salima, the princess's niece, and
Akbar's charming elderly wife, the widow of adviser Bairam Khan, joined
the matriarchs. Two daughters of the late Prince Kamran were in the group,
as was the kindhearted Sultanam, who had nourished Akbar when his parents were exiled. Umm-Kulsum Khanum, or Mother of Plumpness, Gulbadan's granddaughter, and another woman also named Salima were part
of the group. The *Akbarnama* notes that the second Salima was Gulbadan's
daughter, even though the princess never mentions a daughter. Elderly Gulnar, in her seventies, who came as a gift from the Persian king to Agra five
decades earlier, was in the group. So too were three aging women servants,
among them Bibi Sarv-i Sahi (Straight Cypress), whose moonlight melodies
were impressed upon Gulbadan's memory.[2]

The women had decided that Queen Mother Hamida and the former
superintendent of the royal household Bibi Fatima should remain in the cap-

ital. Akbar often relied on his mother for support and advice. Senior women were frequently called upon to conciliate, and to conduct the administration on certain occasions. Since many senior haraman were going away on the pilgrimage, and Hamida had already been to the Holy Cities, Gulbadan and she may have decided that one or two of the most important women should stay behind to support Akbar if the need arose. Independent and strong, the Hamida of bygone times had also fallen into the lure of imperial life, and into the habit of traveling to visit her son unannounced when he was away from the capital. Earlier that year, Akbar was hunting in the forests of Punjab when his attendants announced to him that his mother had arrived at the camp and was anxious to see him. Akbar was thrilled. Their devotion was mutual.

Of philosophical bent of mind, Sultan Khwaja was given the honor of serving as the *mir-i hajj,* or commander of pilgrimage. Under Islamic law, no Muslim woman could go to the Holy Cities without being escorted by a male relative. On this journey, there were two other men: Uncle 'Abdur Rahman Beg (a nephew of a cousin of Babur), and Baqi Khan, the Emperor Akbar's foster brother. Gold-lined wooden chests with numerous pieces of gold, twelve thousand dresses of honor, cash worth 600,000 rupees to be distributed at the Holy sanctuaries, large private allocations for the haraman, and a plentiful supply of additional gold and silver coins for distributing alms were kept securely by the soldiers.[3] Rumi Khan of Aleppo, an artillery officer of Babur, accompanied the group, perhaps as an interpreter.[4] Numerous officers, cooks, attendants, tent pitchers, and water and baggage carriers were among the travelers. There were also poorer pilgrims, given free passage on the Mughal ships in accordance with state policy.

Akbar suggested that his six-year-old son Prince Murad chaperone the women as far as Surat, the docking port in the western state of Gujarat, where they would board the ship. A little boy was, by virtue of his gender, lord enough to escort the matriarchs of the dynasty to lands across the seas. Gulbadan opposed the plan, arguing that he stay back precisely because of his tender age. Akbar acceded. She agreed that Prince Salim would escort the party on the first stage of the journey and extend his farewell once they were safely at the shore.

Ordinary men and women, old and young, and children lined the streets of the red sandstone Mughal capital, Fatehpur-Sikri. Gulbadan's upcoming journey was the talk of the town. The departing cortege would overshadow discussion of the fire that had ravaged a workshop known for producing the finest textiles in the country. Piles of fine wool Persian carpets and 10 million yards of velvet, silk, satin, and brocade had burned to ash.[5]

As Gulbadan commenced her most-anticipated journey, a caravan of the bygone years likely flashed in her mind—the convoy of nearly eighteen years prior in which she had returned from Kabul to Agra. She had arrived to a fresh regal life, so novel that she could barely envisage that she, a vagabond princess, would live behind harem walls with thousands of women she didn't yet know. The freedom of movement in the mansions along the Yamuna in which she came of age was lost to the past.

Barely had the soldiers hung Hemu's head on the Iron Gate of Kabul in 1556 when Hamida declared that it was time to join Akbar, her son, the third Mughal emperor. News of Akbar's latest victory had reached Kabul accompanied by the head of the vanquished Afghan leader. In the company of Hamida and Bega, Gulbadan once more set out in a caravan to Al-Hind. Co-wife Mah Chuchak stayed back.

The circumstances of the Mughal dynasty had transformed in the fifteen years since her forced migration to Kabul. Both of her beloved brothers had died. Under the eye of courageous and wise former milk-mother Maham Anaga and Bairam Khan, her nephew Akbar was on his way to prodigious accomplishments.

After arriving in Agra, Gulbadan became a dweller in a grand stone mansion, much more lavish than any other place she had lived in, and was soon fully engaged in the intricacies of a new kind of Mughal life, with the young Mughal monarch at its center. It was clear to Gulbadan that Akbar was poised to take his dynasty to great heights, fulfilling the dreams of his forebears and the hopes and ambitions of the Mughal matriarchs, who watched his progress with pride.

However, his fiercely independent stepmother Bega spurned the pleasures of the grand Agra court and went to Delhi instead. There she lived in Azim ki Sarai, an inn in close proximity to Deenpanah, the towering fort where Humayun had met with the accident that had taken his life. Bega immersed herself in planning Humayun's gravesite, which would be a paradisical garden tomb unprecedented in scale and in its distinctive use of red sandstone and white marble. It would contain 150 other Mughal graves. In the mid-1560s, Bega made a pilgrimage to Mecca and Medina. When she came back, three hundred Arab masons and scholars accompanied her and became involved in the ongoing work on her husband's tomb. The new Arab entrants built splendid residential premises, called Arab ki Sarai, on the grounds of the mausoleum. Palash, kapas, champa, and palm trees lined the central compound, and around it they built a mosque, a school, and deep wells.[6]

Meanwhile, Hamida and Gulbadan nourished Akbar's ambitions. He had been for some time captivated by the tales of the *Hamzanama,* the chronicle of Hamza, the Prophet Muhammad's uncle, who traveled the world to spread the doctrines of Islam. A man of impressive physical strength, Akbar was gripped with the idea of capturing ferocious cheetahs. His fascination with elephants and Arabian horses was well known. Hamza stimulated the physically robust Akbar, who put massive energy into conquering lands, adding to the Punjab adjoining Delhi, which he had inherited. He subjugated Malwa, of strategic and economic importance commanding the route to the plateau region of peninsular India. By the 1560s, Maham Anaga had retreated to the background, and Akbar had also disposed with the service of his boyhood mentor and adviser Bairam Khan. When he died, the emperor married his widow Salima. Hamida and Gulbadan, along with Salima and Bairam Khan's son 'Abdur Rahim—army general and famed poet and translator—were part of the powerful, influential circle that reinforced Akbar's imperial project, the supremacy of the Mughal dynasty.

Through massive and bloody military campaigns, he won Gujarat and the state of Bengal. He directed his might at the independent Hindu Rajput warriors of the rugged Rajputana. Adopting a policy of conciliation and conquest, he let the Rajputs hold onto their ancestral territories provided they acknowledged him as lord and master, paid tribute to him, and supplied troops when required. In order to earn their trust, after his victories over Rajput regions he married noble Rajput women. Women came to the harem in agreement with Rajput clan members, who offered their daughters in marriage to ensure peaceful relations.

Gulbadan proudly watched her nephew advance his empire through shrewd alliances and the recruitment of advisers, governors, and officers of various ethnic, regional, and religious backgrounds. He married the daughters of several of these men. Having both Muslim and Hindu wives allowed Akbar to create a stunning sense of diversity. Political networks helped him govern a Hindu majority region and expand intricate administrative and bureaucratic devices. No other Mughal would bring the women of Hindustan as close to the Mughal home as Akbar, a unique move, as a result of which Gulbadan and senior Mughal matriarchs now lived alongside Akbar's Hindu wives.

Harkha, the wise, quiet mother of Prince Salim, gave the Mughals a prized gift. Although several children had been born from Akbar's many marriages, none had survived. His courtiers suggested that he seek the blessings of the Sufi saint Salim Chishti in the village of Sikri. When Akbar visited Salim Chishti, the saint blessed him and foretold that he would have three sons. Prince Salim, named after the mystic, was born on August 30, 1569, to Harkha, the first of his Hindu wives. The grateful emperor announced that as a tribute to the saint, he would build the city of Fatehpur-Sikri.[7] Mentioned as one of the "Veiled Ones of the Kingdom," Harkha's name was not declared in the imperial history, which is full of encomiums on the birth of her son. But this consequential act would be recognized by all, especially Hamida, Harkha's mother-in-law, who knew firsthand the power given to a woman who birthed a coveted son.[8]

Many other Hindu women lived in the harem. They brought with them the traditions of Hindu Rajputs: sun and fire worship as well as festivals, fasts, and vegetarianism. Akbar embraced yogic practices, experimented with vegetarianism, and was so keen on understanding the power Hindus experienced in worshipping the sun that he memorized its 1,001 Sanskrit names.

The cultural heritage of Akbar's Hindu wives was at the forefront of the architectural designs of the red sandstone buildings of Fatehpur-Sikri and reflected in the court's artistic and literary endeavors. Stories from the *Mahabharata* and *Ramayana* epics were also illustrated in the royal atelier.[9]

Used to looking at the world with open-mindedness, Akbar made eclectic moves that the itinerant matriarchs of his dynasty endorsed, till it so happened that his deep inquiries contributed to an imperial rebranding for the women themselves. By the end of 1571, Akbar decided to move permanently to Fatehpur-Sikri. All its buildings were made from the same red sandstone, *sang-i surkh,* and its many gardens were cooled by the leafy shade of mango and neem trees and lush henna bushes. The pinnacles of the first

Mughal red sandstone harem, its multi-level stone pavilions crowned with umbrella domes, could be seen from afar.

Akbar ordered the seclusion of all Mughal women in the harem, the so-called *fortunate place of sleep.* Also called *haram-i shabistan,* it had numerous apartments with entrances and passages that connected a series of open, paved quadrangular courtyards lined with trees and pots of plants and flowers, surrounded by verandahs. Slender, finely carved columns of red sandstone supported the roofs of the verandahs and passageways. Some split-level apartments had narrow winding staircases and densely chiseled balconies overlooking the courtyard.[10]

Motifs from Central Asia, Persia, and Rajasthan embellished the women's quarters: stucco domes, lotus domes of sandstone, and arches so intricately carved that they looked like netting. Though each passage, courtyard, and set of rooms had a distinct style—some with arches, some with protruding balconies as in the Rajput *havelis* (mansions), some with pillars in arabesque designs, and some with extra extended balconies—they formed a harmonious whole.

In the eyes of Gulbadan and the generations of peripatetic women used to free-floating movement even when they lived indoors and to constant physical relocation, their new abode was much too orderly. The Mughal gazetteer, however, lauded the arrangements: "Several chaste women have been appointed as *daroghas* and superintendents over each section, and one has been selected for the duties of writer. Thus, as in the imperial offices, everything is here also in proper order."[11]

By the early 1570s, even as Akbar rejected religious orthodoxy and built a new philosophy that he called "Universal Peace," he began casting himself as a sacred figure, an infallible spiritual authority. Drawn to the ideas of the great Sufi thinker Ibn 'Arabi (d. 1240), especially his opinion that a king who fulfilled the obligations of divine regency was a "Perfect Man," Akbar, the self-styled "Chosen One of God," felt called to initiate a policy of tolerance. He took part in Muslim rites and practices, sent money to Mecca, and swept the floor of the great mosque in Fatehpur-Sikri. He admired the liberal philosophy of the Nuqtavis, a Persian Sufi sect, and held the New Testament in high regard.

As if to enhance the emperor's perfection, his favorite chronicler Abul Fazl, author of the sanctioned history the *Akbarnama,* amplified Akbar's illustrious genealogy, hinting at divine roots. The inviolability of the royal harem, penetrable only by the emperor—housing glorious and untouchable women, fitting consorts of a godlike king—was meant to be proof of his near divinity. The terms used by Abul Fazl to describe the harem and its inhabitants, for example—*cupolas of chastity* and *chaste secluded ladies*—were meant to make clear that Akbar's was an unpolluted line. The harem also served as a symbol of the emperor's strength and virility. Fazl's assertion in the *Akbarnama* that the harem held five thousand women was vital proof of the emperor's power.[12]

Gulbadan's ancestors adhered to codes of modesty and separation, but peripatetic reality and recurrent migration made the complete segregation of the sexes impossible. Her nephew carried the process much further by permanently secluding his women, whom he called *the veiled ones*.

The factions and fissures in Akbar's court were continually shifting. The comfortable coexistence of Hindu rajas and Mughals, of Hindavi and Persian, of the Bible and the Qur'an, and of the orthodox and the heterodox—in sum, the diversity of beliefs and practices that made Akbar's India a charmed place—was difficult to maintain.

So was Akbar's goal of completely confining the chaste ladies in the harem. In some ways, the harem offered women surprising opportunities—wide horizons behind high walls. Senior women were called upon by the emperor and court officials for counsel on matters of diplomacy. These matriarchs also instructed younger royal women and intervened to protect young princes. Political ambition, intrigue, and aspirations cultivated in the harem were tightly entwined with courtly matters. Here, unruly brothers could hide, as happened with Akbar's foster brother Adham Khan, who killed the *vakil,* the grand vazir or the emperor's lieutenant, at the instigation of another aspirant, and stole treasures from war booty. Here plots were hatched, such as Adham's—and sometimes botched, as when Akbar flung Adham from the steps of the harem walls.[13]

Even the treasured manuscripts celebrating the empire were retained in the harem's guarded confines. Royal women read them and enjoyed the sublime illustrations. Some even inscribed their names on manuscripts as signs of ownership. They wrote poetry and prose; they discussed matters personal and political. They made the harem a diverse and dynamic place engaged in the affairs of the world in a deeply personal way—the women lively and complex human beings with strong interests and desires. The harem was not a space meant to enhance the individual ambitions of women, especially not those of innovative younger women. But it was a place where women could take pleasure in everyday exchanges, in watching the stars, in gazing at the flow of the Yamuna below, in smoking a hookah as they dipped their feet in water in a cooling fountain.

In spite of the potentials of harem life and the unprecedented elevation it accorded, at her core, Gulbadan longed to return to life as a royal vagabond.

From Fatehpur-Sikri, the Mughal women cut southwest toward Surat in the recently conquered Gujarat. Just as they neared Udaipur, 302 miles north of Surat, attendants came up to Gulbadan and let her know that they had received warnings that the Portuguese were not to be trusted, and it was not certain that they would deliver the promised travel pass, or *cartaz,* required for all ships to sail.

By the first quarter of the sixteenth century, the commercially and politically driven Portuguese had seized ports in the Indian Ocean and the Persian Gulf, threatening the cities along the eastern coast of the Arabian Peninsula such as Basra, which was key for Persian pilgrims. Goods from Gujarat had added to their fortune. The province was well known for its luxurious deep blue indigo dye, a much-coveted export commodity used for coloring textiles such as cotton and brocade. High-quality daggers and swords were prized Gujarati weapons. The cargoes of ships to Portugal were laden with spices, condiments, aromatic products, and pepper for the Portuguese crown. According to a 1593 customs receipt housed in Lisbon, the Portuguese earned 4 million rupees, or 27 percent of their overall trade revenue, from Gujarati cotton alone.[14]

In charge of the sea lanes to Muslim pilgrimage centers and intent on taking over the ancient trade routes that ran from India through the Persian Gulf and the Red Sea to the cities of the Levant, the Portuguese introduced the policy of the pass system in 1502. Pilgrims and merchants alike had to collectively secure a cartaz for safe passage.

Jesuit missionaries who convoyed with Portuguese entrepreneurs in much of Asia added fuel to their commercial ambitions. By common law, the seas were open to all, but according to the Portuguese argument, this applied only in Europe and only to Christians. Since Hindus and Muslims were "outside Roman Law, they were outside the law of Jesus Christ." This was the argument advanced by the official Portuguese chronicler João de Barros, implying that Hindus and Muslims had "no claim to right of passage in Asian waters."[15] As far as the Portuguese king Manuel I was concerned, the Portuguese could freely attack and destroy Muslim ships on the seas.[16]

The "worrywarts" in Gulbadan's caravan, rattled by the warnings they had heard, were not unjustified in their fears. As it turned out, getting a pass was neither easy nor clear-cut. However, Gulbadan remained confident that everything was in order, and counseled them with "words of wisdom."[17] These questions had come up during her discussions with Akbar about the trip. At first, he had spent a great deal of time debating which of the two possible routes the haraman could take to the Holy Lands. Akbar refused to let Gulbadan's group travel via the land route through Persia because of "bigoted interference" from the Shi'a militant groups operating in the Persian territories who frequently attacked travelers.[18] Sunni Muslims like them were in danger. Sporadic conflicts between the (Shi'a) Persian state and the (Sunni) Ottoman Turks, then sovereign lords of Egypt and the Holy Muslim Cities, further jeopardized the path. The second way was from Surat via sea to Jeddah, for which the Portuguese pass was obligatory.

Once the sea route was chosen, Akbar instructed "the great amirs, the officers of every territory, the guardians of the passes, the watchmen of the borders, the river police, and the harbor masters" to perform "good services" for his aunt and the other women. Gulbadan also knew of the agreement her nephew had struck with the Portuguese, whom he met for the first time in 1573 after he besieged Surat.[19]

At the time Akbar was considering the state of Indian Ocean affairs and was particularly concerned about pilgrim voyages. Vasco Da Gama, the first European admiral to sail directly to the Indian subcontinent, in 1497–98, had on one of his voyages in 1502 seized an Egyptian ship, the *Meri*, which was carrying traders and pilgrims traveling from Calicut to Mecca. Gama and his men captured and burned the ship even though the passengers offered them a large payoff not to. The captain was spared because of his naval expertise. Twenty children were also released, to be converted to Christianity. An unnamed Dutch voyager who traveled with Gama from Lisbon to Calicut wrote, "on board [the *Meri*] . . . were 380 men and many women and children. . . . We took . . . at least 12,000 ducats and at least 10,000 more worth of goods, and we burnt the ship and all the people on board with gun powder."[20] Such assaults were not uncommon, especially upon those ships going from the Malabar region to the Red Sea.

As part of his discussions with them, Akbar assured the Portuguese that he would not shelter any Malabari traders. The Portuguese could not stand the highly successful Malabaris, who operated between the famed port of Calicut in the southwest of Gujarat and Jeddah in the Red Sea. Egyptians, Arabs, and Venetians were their trading partners, and Jeddah was the place of contact and exchange as well as the entry point to Muslim pilgrimage centers. The Portuguese promised Akbar one free cartaz a year and possibly an additional one. As with other ships, outbound and inbound Mughal vessels would have to call on Portuguese ports.

For ordinary traders and pilgrims on the ships, the conditions attached to the pass were even more restrictive. Before heading into the sea waters, the ships typically halted at a port to pay duties on the cargo. The cartaz was then given to ordinary people and a cash security taken from ship officials to ensure that the ship returned to the same port and the captain paid dues and taxes. Arms and ammunition aboard were limited. Certain people—namely, Turks and Abyssinian Muslims, the "enemies of the Portuguese"—were barred.[21] Seemingly straightforward, the cartaz was a mechanism for control: "a stumbling block in the way of travelers to Hijaz," as Abul Fazl described it.[22] Mughal court critic Badauni was infuriated by what he considered the idolatrous imagery the Portuguese pass bore: a stamp with the heads of the Virgin Mary and Jesus Christ.

Aware of Akbar's growing power, the Portuguese knew that he was determined to maintain secure pilgrim routes and prosperous ports. Command over the seas was of concern to him: the gazetteer of the empire has a full section, the "'Ain-i Mir Bahri," dealing with matters of the sea. Mughal aristocrats such as Qilich Khan Andijani, the emperor's cousin, who led the successful siege of Surat, had strong shipping and commercial interests. Akbar built the first two grand Mughal ships. Named after his eldest son Salim, *Salimi* was the ship that Gulbadan would travel in. The *Ilahi*, a word Akbar was partial to because it conveyed divine benevolence, would transport many of the male members of the princess's group.

When Akbar and Gulbadan bade farewell to each other, they did so with full awareness of Portuguese naval power, and with the understanding that the cartaz was ready. In Surat, however, Gulbadan learned that there was no cartaz. The doubters in her caravan were in fact right. No one trusted the

Portuguese in making their plans for journeys to Mecca. Reservations persisted. People were apprehensive that the Portuguese would interfere with the princess's plans or even try to capture the royal women. Negotiations with the Portuguese would have to start all over again. What was unclear was how long or exactly what it would take to have clarity in this matter and a cartaz in hand to guarantee safe passage for the women.

Thus Surat, a dynamic hub perched upon the Arabian Sea but pushed inward by the Tapti River that lined the town and distanced it from the sea, became Gulbadan's temporary home. Mughal records note that she and her cohort waited nearly a year before they were able to board a ship to the Hijaz. While the reference to one year by Abul Fazl, Badauni, and others is symbolic, it does suggest a protracted waiting period.

For pilgrims heading for Mecca and Medina, Surat was the "Blessed Port" or the "Door to the House of God." The city, in the district of Cambay in the southwest corner of Gujarat, was also known as the *bandar-i mubarak,* or the Auspicious Port. A large wall encircled Surat, an irregular half moon of dwellings built along the north-south curve of the river Tapti. Up the river there was an inner wall, and immediately beyond it the castle and the customhouse. Facing the customhouse was a spacious enclosure with the imperial mint. To its left was the residence of the *mir-i bahr,* the harbor minister.

Elite officers and courtiers lived in Surat's urban center in stone mansions around the castle and customhouse complex. Wealthier merchants had secure brick-built dwellings with pleasant gardens. This select settlement up the river would be the abode of the Mughal women.

Unlike the stone mansions for the princess and her party, ordinary people—the majority of Surat's inhabitants, lived in shacks made of bamboo woven with reeds and roofed with palm leaves. Their homes spread outside the elite residential centers and were distinguished by profession: a weavers' neighborhood or a textile workers' quarter. These spaces can be imagined like the inner part of an Islamic medieval city. Here, in the crooked streets of late sixteenth-century Surat, people lived on top of one another. Garbage filled the streets and there was no sewage system apart from the monsoon rains that washed the accumulated excrement into the river.

Two years prior to Gulbadan's time in Gujarat, the entire province was hit by a devasting plague and famine. Gujaratis had not witnessed such a disaster in living memory. Cartloads of dead bodies were thrown into the waters in the city of Ahmedabad. The deadly pestilence spread fast, and food supplies and other amenities became rare. A family would be grateful for just a few pieces of bread.[23]

In addition to the pestilential tragedies, years of political instability and disorder had ravaged Gujarat. A major problem was the Portuguese, who were in control of the enclave of Daman and the island fortress of Diu across the Bay of Cambay where ships halted for levies. The Portuguese opposed "any consolidations of the power of Muslim states."[24] The valiant sultans of Gujarat had resisted them—as they did the now-ascendant Mughals—with all their might.[25]

In a note sent from three hundred miles away in Banswara in Rajasthan, Akbar urged Gulbadan to defer her voyage. He suggested that she contemplate the fact that her journey to Surat itself was equivalent to the hajj. "There is a likelihood that a party of Portuguese, thinking of the money and assemblage [accompanying her] might obstruct the passage, and so vexation and trouble might be caused," he wrote. "That would really be vexation for us." God forbid, Akbar added, that an indecorous event should occur. "It is a matter of protecting one's honor," he emphasized. Next year at the same time, she could leave for the pilgrimage.[26]

Rumors about Portuguese violations of agreements were multiplying, pilgrim leader Khwaja noted in a message to the emperor. The cartaz for the imperial ship was not ready, and the "royal highnesses" were inconvenienced.[27] Reading the contents of the message in Banswara, the emperor was annoyed. He summoned his cousin Qilich Khan, the governor of Surat, a man adept in the intricacies of local administration. Qilich proposed that the *Salimi* should sail on the planned voyage without a pass or assurance from the Portuguese. Akbar did not agree, and ordered Qilich to go to Surat to "soothe and assist the pilgrims."[28]

Gulbadan became more impatient. It had already been a long time since that "shining chaste one . . . broke the repose of her noble mind," as Abul

Fazl has it, and expressed her desire to visit the Holy Places.[29] It is possible that she wrote to Akbar stressing the urgency of her trip. It is also possible that she offered to intercede with the Portuguese. Despite the dangers, pilgrims and merchants continued to travel. Gulbadan was just as insistent about her plans.

In the discussions surrounding Gulbadan's temporary halt in Surat, Bulsar is mentioned as her *jagir,* or land grant. Father Monserrate, one of the three members of the first Jesuit mission to arrive in Akbar's court in 1580, notes that "Butzaris," the princess's property, was sixty miles south of Surat.[30] Butzaris or Bulsar was at the northern tip of coastal Daman, which was a Portuguese stronghold, as was the island fortress of Diu. The vast Arabian Sea was to its west. Rich in sugarcane, papaya, guava, banana, and the sweet but dry brown chikoo, Bulsar was also the mango capital of Gujarat. Known for the Alphonso mangoes, a hybrid Portuguese variety, it was a rich agricultural area.

Nobles with rank were assigned jagir; a jagir came with lucrative fiscal rights—to tax revenues, receive a share of profits from goods sold, and levy taxes on goods coming in. Several Mughal women, Queen Mother Hamida, for example, had large estates. Bulsar was evidently a new allotment for Gulbadan. It is intriguing to think when or why Akbar allocated a piece of land to his aunt on the border of the Portuguese properties when relations between the two parties were not entirely friendly and transparent. Did the emperor expect that a chance meeting between his aunt and Portuguese officers might soften the negotiations? The Portuguese certainly knew it was the princess's jagir.

How often did Gulbadan and the haraman visit Bulsar during the lengthy time they spent in Surat? Did she catch a glimpse of the foreigners, or *feringis,* the common name for the Portuguese? Rich and abundant histories of sixteenth-century trade and the Oceanic world of which Surat was a key port make it possible to describe life in the city. Surat had been thinned by war and famine, but it was a resilient port, its vigor brimming in the ship-lined seaboard and in the bazaars full of merchants and artisans.

Along with Rander on the right side of the Tapti, a city famous for Navayat Muslims, valued in the Western Indian Ocean as shrewd pilots and navigators, Surat was by the 1540s a prominent mercantile town, a "staging point between Sumatra and the Middle East . . . attracting merchants from both Southeast Asia and West Asia."[31] Parsi, Sunni, and Ismaili Muslims, Hindu

Bania families, artisans, tanners, weavers, and fisherfolk went about their daily lives with all their dreams, pleasures, and fears. Nearly a hundred Portuguese lived there. Many of them had no official position. Several were artisans and traders. A few worked for the Portuguese king but had come out to India as private subjects. Some of them worked as agents for Lisbon financiers.

The great blue span of water, ship-lined coast, and hustle and bustle of traders and merchants made Surat a very busy and important port. Many people ranked it as the "Queen of the East." "Others saw it as a dangerous place with resemblances to a pig-sty."[32] A dynamic city, Surat was where all sorts of people mixed. The women would be told that criminals went hand in hand with a motley crowd of Indian Ocean tradesmen that thronged the port area.

Strikingly different from the Afghan mountains through which Gulbadan had journeyed back and forth, but similar in its rhythms to the plains of the Indo-Gangetic belt, Surat was a place of mixed rites and practices. It was a town with a vital lifeline given by the river Tapti, which the locals both adored and feared. After the rains, she would come roaring into the city. No wonder, then, that to the inhabitants of Surat, the river was a deity to be respected, loved, and feared. A common name for the Bania clan of Surat was Taptidas, the servant of Tapti.[33]

The city tapestry was one of contrasts—rich and poor, pretty and ugly— but its people, no matter what class or caste, were dignified, centered on the rhythms of the sea and the monsoon. Weavers and artisans structured their lives according to seasons. They spent the rainy months working hard so that they could load their stock onto ships in autumn. Indigo would be harvested and dried, and the artisans would embark on painting and printing. Every year at the end of August, the town celebrated the festival of the end of the monsoon, the calming of the seas, and the time for ships to come home.

By the time Gulbadan and her companions started their sojourn in the city in October 1576, the streets of Surat were dry. Caravans from Gujarati towns loaded with raw and finished cloths appeared. Ships from the Red Sea that arrived in September would help ascertain the stock they could sell. Whether in the castle area or around town, there was no getting away from the spell of the river, the ships, the sea, or the mixed crowds.

The royal women would sample the delights of Gujarati vegetarian cuisine: fragrant rice, slightly sweetened lentils, and *dahi vada*, fried flour dumplings in spiced-up yogurt. Sweets were intensely sugary and the result of labor-intensive culinary work: flour, sugar, and ghee mixed and spread in concentric circles upon a wok lined with scorching ghee. What came out were *jalebis,* thin and crisp. Fragrant waters and betel leaves served as palate cleansers.[34]

Major cities at the time were known for their markets. In the bazaars of Surat, stalls were arranged around a spacious square. Gulbadan would identify the open market square, the *chauk,* a distinct piece of urban architecture in northern and western India. Crowded bazaars were often adjacent to mosques, temples, or pilgrimage sites, and open to all, common and elite: distinctions of caste, wealth, and social standing dissolved. Yet markets in Surat and elsewhere were not independent bodies. Heads of temples and caretakers of mosques and tombs levied taxes and tolls, and shopkeepers were subject to their power. Certainly, the Mughal group would see the ubiquitous Hindu Bania merchant: visible in the Surat bazaars as well as on the ships carrying the much-desired cotton to the Red Sea. Known for their austere lifestyle, some of them were influential millionaires.

Gujarati traders were experts at carting the sharp and pungent pepper sacks that lined the markets to the northern Indian plains via Malwa. Ginger and the nutty nutmeg and cinnamon from the Coromandel Coast were sold in all markets. Staple Gujarati products, cotton and indigo, were everywhere. Among other commodities, Surat bustled with its horse trade. It was here that fine specimens were brought from the Arabian Peninsula. Akbar purchased scores of these Arabian horses.

There lived in Surat a thriving community of Hindu converts to Islam, the commercially active Ismaili *khojahs* and *bohrahs.* A branch of the Shi'a Muslims, they revered 'Ali, Prophet Muhammad's son-in-law. The esteemed book of the Khojahs was adorned with nine incarnations of the Hindu God Vishnu. The Khojahs adopted Vishnu as an avatar of Adam; the tenth avatar in this line was 'Ali!

For Gulbadan, such heterogenous practices were easy to identify, very much at the heart of her dynasty—layered life rituals, arts, artifacts, food, and music—in tune with the Mughal palette.

On a somewhat cool day in the spring of 1577, Gulbadan, her relatives, and the crew gathered at the north bank of the river Tapti. The princess and other haraman would shroud themselves in embroidered Kashmiri shawls, adequate for that time of the year. The heaps of sand deposits around them and scattered fishing hamlets nearby gave Surat a distinct look—a marker for approaching vessels.

They would ride in *kishti* or *ghurab*, small boats, to the village of Domus, not entirely out of view from where they stood. Beyond the village was an extensive sprawl of bush and vegetation and occasional tall trees, which had to be steered around slowly. Between Domus and Omra, the next village, was the wharf where the heavy wooden imperial ships *jahaz-i Salimi* and *jahaz-i Ilahi* waited. By the mid-seventeenth century, this was the well-recognized Mughal quay where imperial ships regularly docked, waited out rains, and equipped for the seas. *Salimi* and *Ilahi*, the earliest Mughal ships, weighed somewhere around five hundred tons and looked like *Muhammadi*, a ship that Qilich Khan owned. The *Sahebi* of Jahanara—Gulbadan's great-grand-niece—would be modeled after these early ones. The *Rahimi*, Queen Salima's ship of 1612, was the largest, weighing between twelve hundred and fifteen hundred tons.[35]

The "veiled ladies of the caliphate" boarded the *Salimi*. Sultan Khwaja and his men went aboard the *Ilahi*.[36] The *kafila-i junk*, the convoy of sea voyagers, as Akbar's history has it, set out.[37] The exact month of Gulbadan's departure from Surat is not known. But a rough estimate is possible on the basis of the monsoonal cycle that everyone followed for sea voyages, as well as from the return of Sultan Khwaja, the pilgrim leader, which is dated in a document. Ships and pilgrims went from Gujarat to Aden in the Red Sea from September to early May. A return from the Red Sea could be no later than September. The Mughal group probably set out between late January and April 1577, when ships typically sailed from Surat. In the summer of 1577, they performed the hajj rites. After escorting the Mughal women to the Holy Cities and performing the rites of pilgrimage with them, Sultan Khwaja came back to Hindustan. He sent a report to Akbar dated early 1578.

The heavy wooden top of the deck of *Salimi* was designed like the face of an uthni, a large-eyed female camel. Immediately behind it was the sailors' compartment. The weighty sail, red-colored on the inner flap and white on the outer one, was moored with heavy ropes. There were two levels of cabins. Lined with thick and rich wine-red fabric embroidered with golden flowers, the *dabusa*, or special cabins, were for the royals.[38]

The *nakhuda,* the ship's captain, the navigators, and staff such as the *tandil,* the head sailor, the *khallasis,* usually workers accompanying sailors, and the *bhandari,* the storekeeper, were on board in their designated places. Navigationally skilled, the *panjri* was in charge of the lookout and the *gunamti* would bail out the water. Sometimes several *sukangars* had to be ready to set the course of the ship under the direction of the navigator. To alter the junk's direction was a difficult task.[39]

There is no estimate of the number of merchants and pilgrims who went on the two Mughal ships. Ordinary pilgrims traveled often and in large numbers on royal ships, which often gave them free passage. Although Gulbadan's grand-niece never went to the Holy Cities, in 1643, Jahanara's *Sahebi,* built and operated from Surat, her estate, was used with an eye to profit as well as to assist ordinary pilgrims by exempting them from paying the fare. "From the dervishes, they should not charge the fare," Jahanara clarified in her imperial order. But she warned the pilgrims that they were not to carry the goods of merchants.[40]

The ships obtained income from charging prosperous customers as well as from freight. Based upon the profits, a certain number of pilgrims were given free passage. Two surviving *dastaks,* official certificates for the cargo of merchants that were loaded aboard the Mughal ship *Ganjawar* in 1643, elucidate the financial provisions. The freight was to be deposited in the treasury of the ship's steward. Goods were sold in Mecca. Profits were distributed in charity to the poor and destitute, and only the principal sum was kept out of the intake from the sales.[41]

Leaving Surat, the *Salimi* and *Ilahi* would halt at Daman. With the help of the *nagarsheth,* the head of Surat's socioeconomic collective, Governor Qilich Khan had chosen a politically powerful Cambay merchant, a man named Kalyan Rai of the Bania clan, to hold discussions with the Portuguese. Rai used plenty of tact. According to Abul Fazl, Mughal authorities offered a considerable (unnamed) inducement to secure the *qaul,* or pass.

Barely had the Mughal ships anchored in Daman than a drama began as a heated discussion arose between the Portuguese and Mughal officers and sailors. Father Monserrate recorded in his *Commentary* that one bargain still had to be completed. There would be no cartaz until then. What was the cause of the dispute? Nothing explicit is mentioned in the documentation, except that there was some uncertainty around the free passes, which always left plenty of room for blackmail. What transpired as the Mughal ships sailed into Daman would be no different from the commotion that occurred three years later, when Mughal officer Bayazid Bayat's ship docked there. Gulbadan first met him in Bala Hisar. He had accompanied Bairam Khan, and together they had brought news of Humayun's victories and return from Persia. Since then, Bayat had performed three decades of excellent imperial service: his latest assignments were as chief confidant of the late commander of Akbar's forces in the eastern campaigns and as *darogha* of the imperial treasury. Abul Fazl included Bayazid in the Mughal gazetteer as one of the "Great ones of the Eternal Realm."[42]

Along with his wife and three sons, Bayazid set sail in 1580 on the *Muhammadi,* which belonged to Governor Qilich Khan. Bayazid wrote in detail about what happened when he stopped at Daman. The Portuguese tax collectors wanted to go on board to inspect the ship's hold, but the patrols refused to do so unless Bayazid sent ashore a hostage. Iftikhar, one of his sons, went, and the cargo was inspected, but more complications arose. The ship had an assembly of poor pilgrims and other passengers who did not have much cash in hand. Since Bayazid was the only pilgrim with the means to advance the huge sum the Portuguese demanded, he gave the money on behalf of the passengers, "intending to get it back without interest" in Jeddah. The sum demanded by the Portuguese was 10,000 muhammadis, a large figure. The captain of the Surat ships, a man named Hasan Channu, carried back the detailed document of the final arrangements to the head of the Surat port, who followed the proceedings from a distance. It was evening before Bayazid's son returned and the ship left the Daman estuary.[43]

A similar scenario likely transpired when the *Salimi* and *Ilahi* docked at Daman. The patrols that came on board would make demands of the captain and the commander of pilgrimage, a "regularized blackmail," in the words of a historian writing about the Portuguese menace.[44] It is to be expected that the men in the Mughal group explained that Governor Khan and merchant Kalyan Rai had completed all the necessary procedures to obtain the cartaz.

Royal ships always carried a certain number of ordinary pilgrims. The same would be true for the *Salimi* and the *Ilahi.* Among the ordinary passengers, the *Akbarnama* notes, there was also a child.[45] Did the Portuguese ask for cash on behalf of the free passengers, as on Bayazid's ship? Akbar had warned Gulbadan that the Portuguese knew of her "money and assemblage." They likely questioned the presence of free passengers. The Mughal retainers would turn to Gulbadan, designated "head of the travelers" in the *Akbarnama*.[46]

Helping poor pilgrims was part of the required imperial practice. At this time, despite threats of all kinds upon the seas, Mughal support for annual trips to the Holy Cities was state policy. Gulbadan would confer with Salima. The two had often dealt together with matters that required sensitive intervention. Gulbadan knew she had to offer the Portuguese a final inducement. She gave them her jagir of Bulsar, which was next to Daman. The princess went so far as to give them the town of Butzaris, wrote Father Monserrate, documenting what clinched the deal.[47]

As soon as Gulbadan handed over Butzaris, her jagir, the captains got the cartaz embossed with the faces of the Virgin Mary and Jesus. With the mandatory document declaring the size of the ships and their crews, the captains steered the *Salimi* and *Ilahi* out of the estuary and into the broad blue stretch of the Arabian Sea.

Bala Hisar fortress, Kabul

View of a section of the Bagh-e Babur where Babur and his sister Khanzada Begum are buried

Panch Mahal, the pleasure pavilion in the harem quarters of Fatehpur-Sikri

Jodha Bai Palace, a section of the Fatehpur-Sikri harem complex

Akbar with Lion and Calf, folio from the Shah Jahan Album, painting by Govardhan (active ca. 1596–1645)

Ottoman Sultan Murad III

Quarters in the older part of Jeddah

Fête du tapis sacré, 1907 postcard showing the procession of the mahmal in Port Said

A magnificent image of the Ka'ba from the *Ta'rikh-i Alfi*, written in the time of Mughal emperor Akbar and Princess Gulbadan

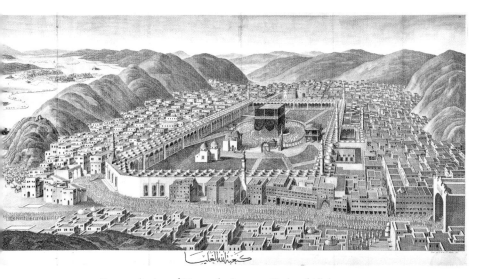

كعبة الله العليا

Panoramic view of Mecca, the Supreme Kaaba of Allah

Nineteenth-century reverse glass painting, view of Medina

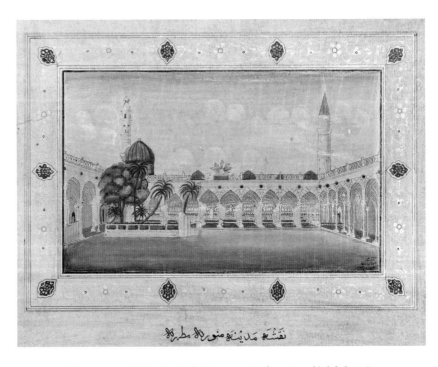

نقشه مدينة منوره مطهر

The courtyard of the Prophet's Mosque in Medina, signed 'Abd al-Basit.
Rampur, India, AH 1292 (1875 CE)

Nineteenth-century miniature painting of the Prophet's Mosque in Medina

Single-volume Qur'an, Egypt, AH 844 (1440 CE)

Celebrations in the women's quarters at the time of Akbar's circumcision
(from the *Akbarnama*). The British Library blog notes,
"One of the ladies is almost certainly Gulbadan."

Nine

The Promised Land

〜

GULBADAN AND HER CO-VOYAGERS WERE OUT OF SIGHT OF land for three weeks. Sailing out from the Gulf of Cambay, or Khambayat, which jutted into the Arabian Sea, they went south and then west on the Indian Ocean. Ancient explorers and thinkers found it trying to label these vast sea lanes. Ptolemy and Ibn Khaldun had called portions of the Indian Ocean *green ocean*, and in those days, the Red Sea was called the Coral Sea.[1]

Amid the company of other women, Gulbadan began her sacred journey. An ideal pilgrimage was one that started long before the rituals. A wayfarer needed to sever all worldly connections and extend herself to whatever she was seeking. What Gulbadan had was *intention*, a key ingredient of her upcoming journey. She longed to be in the House of God, far from the court and harem, simmering with intrigue and ambition, and from structures of confinement in Fatehpur-Sikri, so that she could direct her intention to the desert land where Prophet Muhammad had outlined a rich direction for life and being. Islamic jurists had elevated the idea of *intention* "in order to differentiate between acts of worship and customs, and the different levels of the acts of worship," wrote Ibn Faraj, a Jeddah-based sixteenth-century scholar of Islamic law and an expert in the traditions and sayings of the Prophet.[2] Intention was like a charm, an invitation to advance, to stretch oneself in the Promised Land. In this way, intention could be expanded and realized, and a vagabond was able to take on all sorts of challenges.

The travelers would pause to reckon with new forces in new lands. New adventures lay ahead, as well as fresh languages to engage with, both literally and metaphorically. The artillery officer from the time of Gulbadan's father, court-commissioned interpreter Rumi Khan, was there to assist, but Arabic was not entirely foreign to royal women's ears. What was new, and this they saw as soon as they landed in Jeddah, was a cosmos saturated in the tonality of Arabic and its many varieties. There were also scores of other linguistic sensations, including Syrian, Yemeni, Eritrean, and Bedouin dialects, as well as the Turkish of the Ottomans, the rulers of western Arabia, where the glorious Mecca and Medina, the cities of the Prophet, lay.

Traversing the seemingly infinite span of the ocean for nearly three weeks, Gulbadan and her fellow haraman advanced toward Arabia. Mentioned repeatedly in revered books, boundless ancient sea waters were born when tectonic shifts took place millions of years ago. It all began with a major rift that emerged in the Western Indian Ocean. This so-called plate divergence extended far to the north. As the Arabian and African regions parted, the Red Sea was born in the mid-Eocene epoch, which lasted approximately from 56 million to 34 million years ago. Even if those on board did not know the history of ocean formation, they certainly knew that their ultimate sea destination, the bright coral-reefed Red Sea waters, was revered.

When the winds were favorable, the two Mughal ships, each with one main mast, would glide very fast. On calm days as well as on stormier ones, buffeted by winds, the *Salimi* and the *Ilahi* cruised closely beside one another. Gulbadan and her cohort would be comfortable on these first-generation Mughal ships in their special teak cabins called *balanj*, located on the main deck. Officers' rooms and the area for kitchen supplies were below the captain's cabin. Fresh water was a much-needed commodity, yet it was difficult to store. Unlike the English ships of those days, which had boilers for water, on Mughal ships, water was kept in large vessels or tanks. The royal party would have good supplies of water brought to them in large containers.[3] As on other ships, there would be "a place for exoneration" that allowed the feces to fall directly into the ocean.[4]

The *bhandari*, or storekeeper, and the cooks provided food for the imperial ladies. Sailors usually cooked their own meals, which included salt fish, rice, lentils, and ghee.[5] The nature of general facilities aboard the *Salimi* and the *Ilahi* is not easy to establish, but as several premodern travel writers note, the conditions for ordinary pilgrims were rough and the amenities inadequate. People crowded together in corners on the deck as well as in the lower sections of the ship near the ballast and stores or even near the rudder. Many fell sick and died. A report noted that pilgrims following the coast of the Red Sea to Jeddah were crammed together "like chickens in a coop." That boat was smaller than the one Gulbadan was traveling upon. It had no nails, and the planks were sewn with cords made of coconut fiber that was sealed with palm shavings and smeared with shark oil to keep the water out. Navigation in the waters of the Red Sea was an enormous challenge, as Gulbadan and her party would later experience. Pilgrims were sometimes stranded on wild and inhospitable shores.[6]

Gulbadan's convoy was richly endowed, but whether her ship was luxuriant, we do not know. Unlike voyages by road, long voyages on the sea had limited access to certain kinds of resources. In the second quarter of the fourteenth century, royal Mamluk princesses of Egypt traveled by road to Mecca and Medina in grand style. Accompanied by a ceremonial orchestra, kingly banners, high dignitaries, and amirs, Princess Tughay's road caravan of 1321 included cows to provide her with fresh milk along the journey so that she could have her customary hot toasted cheese twice a day. Camels carried pots planted with vegetables that enabled her to maintain a healthy diet.[7] Such treats are not said to have been available for Gulbadan's party, but the essential comforts were there.

Standing upon the deck with tar, ropes, anchors, the splendid sound of water, the gentle blowing of the wind, and no land in sight constituted the daily fare of Gulbadan's sea universe. To while away the time, the Mughal women aboard would ponder the missives of women adventurers. They were familiar with Abbasid splendor, especially the celebrated travels of the ninth-century Queen Zubaida, wife of Caliph Harun-al Rashid of Baghdad. In Mecca, the well-off Zubaida spent a million golden dinars to build a canal system that supplied waters to Mecca and its vicinity. She constructed the famous Darb Zubaida, or Highway of Zubaida, a 933-mile road between Kufa in Iraq and Mecca. Hospices, cisterns, wells, and canals were among the many famous developments associated with Zubaida.[8]

Two hundred and fifty-four years before Gulbadan, in 1323, a Mongol princess left her grand dwelling in the city of Soltanieh in northwestern Iran. She rode ahead of her large cortege, a quiver fastened to her waist, a parasol with trinkets hung all around raised above her head. Dressed in a long robe held with strings upon her waist that went as far down as her knees, trousers with several folds like bangles gathering at her ankles, and Mongolian-style boots with pointed toes, she arrived in Damascus. The governor of Syria received her with the utmost respect. She stayed at the palace, her expenses all covered.

Her name was El-Qutlugh, and she descended from the line of Chingiz Khan, as did Gulbadan. Known for her sharp mind and valor, she came of age in the steppe ethic of resourcefulness and independence. When she received news that her husband had been killed in war, she accosted the killer, beheaded him, and hung his head on the collar of her horse. It stayed there for a long time. Some say that she got rid of it only when instructed by a royal decree.[9]

In 1323, the year El-Qutlugh rode out for the heartland of Islam, her dynasty negotiated a peace agreement with the sultan of Egypt. Part of the high-ranking Mongol party, she had effected reconciliation with the Egyptian Mamluks, who then also ruled Syria and the Hijaz. The negotiations brought an end to a war that had begun sixty-three years earlier when El-Qutlugh's grandfather invaded parts of Arabia. There had been many new developments in the decades since. Significantly, her family had slowly been embracing Islam. A gradual softening of relations took place between the rival empires, which now shared a common faith.[10]

The second phase of El-Qutlugh's travels from Damascus to Mecca was quite a spectacle. She took the great Syrian pilgrimage route, covering approximately a thousand miles. A major trade route, the Darb al-Hajj al-Shami was known by different names at different times in history. It linked the Mediterranean with southern Arabia in the early centuries of the Christian era. The route had in the ninth century caught the attention of Zubaida, who then funded the construction of water tanks, canals, forts, castles, mosques, bridges, and markets along the way.[11]

As El-Qutlugh moved through the desert paths, she organized traditional Mongol ring hunts employing a complex technique that involved layers of organization. Local hunters would lead the hunting party to designated spots where animals regularly appeared. Servants acting as beaters pounded the surrounding bushes with sticks to draw the game into an area encircled by the hunters. As the royal hunter, in this case El-Qutlugh, moved inward, the sound of the drums got louder, the size of the circle grew smaller, and the game was trapped. Mongol rulers were known for massive ring hunts that involved tens of thousands of men and lasted several months. These hunting campaigns, a source of amusement, were meant to discipline, train, and prepare armies for complex military maneuvers.

El-Qutlugh was very much part of Mughal women's inheritance and reflections. Ambitious about territorial expansion, Gulbadan's nephew Emperor Akbar commissioned illustrations of the *Chingiznama*, which narrated the life, progeny, and legacy of Chingiz Khan. Among the visual folios was a page that depicted El-Qutlugh's grandfather's siege in the Islamic lands.[12]

If El-Qutlugh's hunting moves came to Gulbadan's mind, they would not be new to her. Her family members ardently carried out *qamargha*, or ring hunts, a practice they took from their Mongol ancestors. When she was growing up in Kabul, Gulbadan and the Kabul household frequently accompanied Babur on such hunting expeditions, staying in tented hunting lodges.

El-Qutlugh displayed her hunting prowess en route to Mecca, but what she wanted above all was to ensure that she was seen as a royal peacemaker. Visibility was important in her itinerary. Her ring hunts in Arabia ensured that people noticed her. A century after her great-great-grandfather had ravaged Muslim-majority regions of Central Asia in his quest for world domination, El-Qutlugh, a member of that very dynasty, went out to perform the time-honored pilgrimage of Islam. She had a lot to make up for. She paraded the same roads in Arabia as her forefathers, but not as a conqueror. Registering her commitment to peace and harmony, she distributed alms in Mecca and Medina. There was no higher symbol of peace than giving alms. One of the five pillars of Islam, it affirms belief and the integrity of the faithful.

Gulbadan's close ally, Queen Mother Hamida, would have revealed tales of her pilgrimage. As we know, Bega, or Hajji Begum, as she was popularly identified by this time, had also visited the Holy Cities. Unlike Hamida's trip, for which we have no details except bulleted lines about her travel, Bega's is well recorded. She went to Mecca by road and spent three years in

Arabia, following in the tracks of *sojourners,* pilgrims who spent extended periods in the land of the Prophet. After coming back, Bega lived in Delhi and carried out her select task as a royal patron and the brain behind her husband Humayun's glorious mausoleum. Arabs from Mecca who came with her—Qur'an reciters, artisans, members of elite families, people well versed in religion, and workers of many kinds—settled in the Arab ki Sarai neighborhood that wrapped around the garden of Humayun's tomb.[13]

Islamic religious philosophers honored pilgrims who returned from the hajj with the title *hajji.* Technically, co-wives Hamida and Bega were both hajjis, but it is the latter upon whom records bestow that identity. Perhaps court chroniclers singled out Bega for this honor because she inspired them by the distance she cultivated from the court and imperial politics. Very different from Bega, the politically inclined Hamida entrenched herself in Mughal matters.

Conversations with Bega may have instilled in Gulbadan the desire to extend her once-in-a-lifetime journey. For the party of pilgrims that Gulbadan headed, there was no recorded itinerary or limit on time. The pilgrimage structured time and the very being of people. From Hamida, Gulbadan would learn another significant point: that of *return.* Once back from the voyage, renewed and uplifted, one could go about daily or exigent imperial tasks with renewed vigor, fulfilling with dedication the duties that mattered for posterity.

People's personal stories as well as intriguing and awe-inspiring waters would occupy Mughal women aboard the *Salimi.* Travelers had for centuries talked about a legendary island of Wak-Wak that lay at the edge of the world, in a sea where fish danced. On it stood a talking tree, with the heads of humans and demons growing from its branches amid leaves and flowers, and the heads of beasts sprouting from its roots—lions, tigers, dragons, cows, elephants, and mythical flying creatures called *simurghs.*

The Wak-Wak tree appears in a Qur'anic verse that calls it the Tree of Zakkum and says that its fruit was the head of a demon. (The tale may have even deeper roots; a sixth-century Chinese writer mentions a similar legend.) A great intellectual in the ninth-century court of the Abbasid dynasty described the tree as a cross between plant and animal. In tenth-century Arabic literature, it was noted that the tree grew in India, though over the centuries various writers conjectured that it could be found in the Indian Ocean on Madagascar or islands off the coast of East Africa, or on the

Pacific Rim near Japan. Alexander the Great was said to have visited the talking tree of Wak-Wak; male and female heads on the tree prophesied his death.[14]

Magic, oracles, heavenly bodies, and mythical creatures were at the core of both royal and non-royal people's lives. The Mughal court was adorned with carpets embroidered with mythic subjects. Two large wine-red carpets made for Akbar, each measuring roughly 31½ by 12½ feet, had a world of legendary creatures woven in them. These included a disproportionately elongated cheetah eating a bird larger than itself and a massive fish with a scarf around its neck emerging from a corner and gulping a long black cat.[15] Planets or heavenly bodies were brought to life with centaurs or dragons, the latter a sign of Gemini.

One subject we can be sure that everyone aboard the *Salimi* and the *Ilahi* discussed during the weeks of spring 1577 was the fear of drowning in the sea or being devoured by sea beasts. On one dark and windy night, when the ships were cruising fast due to strong gusts, a child fell off the *Salimi* into the ocean. We are not told how—only that the boy fell into deep waters. It is possible that he fell from the level below the royal cabins or from farther down the ship. The amazing thing was that people on board believed that they heard his piercing "cries [that] came for quite some time," even though the wind was pushing the ships forward at a good speed. Sultan Khwaja, the pilgrimage commander, wrote about this episode in a message he sent Emperor Akbar.[16]

"The sound of his cries came for quite some time," the Khwaja emphasized several times. The suggestion was that the child was alive, struggling in the water. Hearing about the child's cries, certainly the Mughal women would have come out of their cabins. Whether or not in consultation with Gulbadan and the captain, the Khwaja ordered the sailors to take a boat out into the ocean and search for the child. It was a practically impossible task given the gusty winds, the dark of the night, and the fast-moving ship. "The sound of the cries came still." No one believed that they could save the boy, but still they lowered the boat into the ocean. Although it seemed a hopeless effort, they lit a lamp on deck to guide the boat back. "It was not the custom" to light lamps at night, the Khwaja noted in his letter to the emperor. Light attracted sea creatures, and "in order to avoid a large beast" that could potentially chase a ship, illumination was not allowed. Navigational custom also demanded avoiding lamps to avoid fire. The child's shrieks soon stopped and miraculously, after a while the "sailors returned with the child safe and sound."[17]

The half-dead and traumatized boy would be given medicine and food. Solace from his shaken elders would calm his body and mind. Astonished that the boy was safe despite the brutal circumstances, the pilgrims would offer a thousand thanks to Allah. The return of the child would be seen as nothing short of divine intervention—a fine example of his benevolence and a sign of good fortune yet to come.

The other amazing miracle noted by Sultan Khwaja in the same letter was that for the entire trip the two Mughal ships sailed closely together. Neither the winds nor the currents over the long distance ever separated them as they closed in on their long-awaited destination. Finally, Gulbadan and her co-travelers sighted the mountains of Aden on the southern tip of the Arabian Peninsula. They entered the Red Sea via the tight and shallow Bab al-Mandab, or Gate of Lamentation, spanning nineteen miles of constricted passage. It was the most treacherous section for boats to pass. Fierce, fickle tides and abundant corals were "prime tormentors" of navigators and sailors.[18]

A sacred geography, the Arabian Peninsula to the east and the African landmass to the west, lay before Gulbadan and the Mughal party. The Sarawat mountain range ran from Jordan in the north to the Gulf of Aden on the eastern side. The Red Hills of Egypt were in the northwest, and Sudan, Eritrea, and the highlands of Ethiopia were in the southwest. The vista of water, peaks, and lands was staggeringly beautiful. The coastal plains ascended into sharp mountains on both sides of the sea. The word *Hijaz* invokes this topography: a mountainous barrier separating the coast of Arabia from the interior.

Many passengers upon the Mughal ships would envision the blessed point farther up north where it was said that the Red Sea parted. From there, *Moses led the children of Israel to safety when the Red Sea parted for them, then closed on the pursuing Egyptian Army.*[19] Gulbadan and the Mughal haraman were now in the Promised Land. It would take them seven days to reach Jeddah, situated about halfway up the east coast of the Red Sea.

At that legendary port, Gulbadan and the other pilgrims became the responsibility of the Ottoman sultan of Turkey. In the early fifteenth century, the Ottomans waged wars against the Mamluks of Egypt, who headed the Hijaz that had the prized sanctuaries, Mecca and Medina. By 1517, with masses of territorial gains in hand, the Ottomans became the uncontested masters of the region. Although far away in Istanbul, Sultan Murad III was at the time of Gulbadan's visit the sovereign of the holiest of holy Islamic lands.

After passing through the Bab al-Mandab, cruising north, Gulbadan alighted in Jeddah, a city steeped in legend and history. Oriented toward the sea, a large wall lining its three landward sides, Jeddah was said to have been established in 350 BCE, when an unknown group of fishermen came to a particular spot on the coast of the Red Sea. According to the sixteenth-century writer Ibn Faraj, Jeddah was the resting place of Eve: she was *jaddah,* or the grandmother of the world, and hence the city came to be called Jeddah. This desert hinterland was transformed with the advent of Islam in the seventh century CE. While Jeddah had no ritual significance, it eventually gained standing as a major place for traders and goods and as the main port of entry to Mecca, roughly fifty-three miles east.[20]

Lying in a bowl surrounded by barren hills, Jeddah in the olden days was not the first choice for a pilgrims' landing. That select port was the nearby Shaiba. In 646 CE, the third caliph was thinking about a harbor for pilgrims that would be safe from pirates. He happened to have bathed in the sea at Jeddah and liked it. And so the port town came into the limelight. "Praise be to God who has made the port of Jeddah the best of ports," wrote Ibn Faraj, "and who has honoured her by attaching her to the House of Good Fortune."[21]

As for the famous wall that enveloped the city on three sides, the Mughal party would learn that in the early sixteenth century, the commercially ambitious Portuguese launched a series of attacks on the city. The Arabian Bedouins also assaulted Jeddah as part of their alignment with different political and tribal groups in the region who had expansionist interests. As a safeguard, the sultans of Egypt decided to build a wall on Jeddah's landward side. This 1509 structure saved the city from attacks and ensured the preservation of Al-Balad, its historic core.

The Mughal party likely took the main road that cut straight from the harbor in the west to Mecca Gate in the east. They would have waited a while to restore and replenish themselves before heading to Mecca, where Sultan Khwaja performed one round of pilgrimage with them before returning to Hindustan.

On coming ashore in Jeddah, ordinary pilgrims and merchants who came on the Mughal ships went to the *diwan*, the customhouse, where their names and country of origin were recorded. Their belongings were thoroughly checked, and taxes taken even though they were pilgrims. However meager their possessions, these were taken out for inspection and thrown around in a chaotic way. Because of overcrowding, goods often disappeared.[22]

As Ottoman guests, the Mughal women would go with much more comfort straight to the city, where their lodgings would be ready. By 1577, when Gulbadan came to Jeddah, there was a body of works about the land of the Prophet. Curious travelers and devotees left annals of their time in the Hijaz. Mystified, shocked, impressed, alienated, and awed, they told different kinds of stories. Jeddah—or Jiddah, Jidda, Jadda, or Juddah, depending on who named it—was always part of the narrative.

A visionary dream brought the Persian poet and wine-loving bureaucrat Nasir-i Khusraw to the Hijaz in the eleventh century. In the first-ever travelogue of the area in premodern times, Khusraw gave a positive assessment of "Jidda" despite its lack of trees. Everything necessary for life was brought from surrounding villages, he wrote. Jeddah had five thousand people, good bazaars, and the Mosque of the Prophet of God. Back then, there were two gates, one facing the east and Mecca, and the other the west and the sea.[23]

Ibn Faraj chose the evocative title *Bride of the Sea* to describe the history and surroundings of his home city. Like most other commentators, he wrote about the problem of scarce water that plagued Jeddah and the cisterns that spread all over town, a sight that the Mughal ladies would not miss. What were these cisterns? Ibn Faraj explains by providing a history of Jeddah's waterworks. The Persians designed the first proper layout of the town. They built a wall that surrounded the city and four gates that were linked to four main thoroughfares. On the gate on the southern side, there was a green stone with a talisman: "If anything was stolen in the town, the name of the thief would be found [the] next morning written on the stone." All around the town, outside the gates, the Persians dug a wide and deep ditch. They fortified Jeddah as if it were an island in the middle of the sea. Fearing water shortages, they built sixty-eight reservoirs. Others estimated the number at three hundred reservoirs, according to Faraj.[24]

Ibn Jubayr arrived at Jeddah from Andalusia during his travels to the Hijaz between 1183 and 1185. Impressed by the water cisterns, he gave a full list of them, noting the places where they were installed as well as their shapes and sizes. The "antique cisterns" made an impression on the avid Moroccan traveler Ibn Battuta, too. And in the city, he wrote in his fourteenth-century *Rihla*, "are pits of water, bored in the solid rock and connected with each other in numbers beyond computation."[25] Nevertheless, the city continued to suffer from severe shortages of water; the groundwater too was of poor quality. Rarely was there a massive downpour, and water was collected in cisterns placed outside the gates of the town and underneath some of the houses.

But Jeddah captivated travelers. The first European traveler on record, Ludovico di Varthema, disguised himself as a Mamluk soldier to visit the Holy Cities in 1503. Fond of intrigue, for much of the day, he hid as a sick beggar in the vicinity of the Ebony mosque, emerging at night to get food and go about the town.[26]

Of the three main Jeddah mosques, al-'Jami al-'Atiq was the largest and the oldest. It was said that the second caliph commissioned it. Four decades before Gulbadan, an Indian merchant named Muhammad 'Ali came to Jeddah with wood and pillars with plinths and rebuilt parts of the 'Atiq mosque with "determination, producing a fine, beautiful building which pleases the beholder."[27] A number of houses and shops bordered the mosque. Dates, tamarind, goats, honey, and firewood were sold in the bazaar.

Outside the walls of the city, the tomb of Eve was the site of a recurring miracle.[28] If any ship was delayed or if there was no news, a procession with a sailor from the town, accompanied by pipes and drums, would head to the tomb. The sailor would fall near the tomb "in a faint" and then ask for news of the delayed ship. He would soon be able to tell those around him the situation of the ship, its location, and whether it was safe or wrecked. The power of Eve's tomb, where visitors came "from all directions," was well established.[29]

What vow would Gulbadan make at Eve's tomb? For the princess, life in the Mughal palaces posed a grave problem. The Arabian sacred land was known to inspire people, calming their earthly fears. Wondrous openings emerged in people's dreams. At times, grand planetary events occurred, as happened when the Black Stone was hurled from heaven to Mecca. For some, revelations continued for years.[30]

Arabian history was littered with adventurous men who left hundreds of pages cataloguing their searches. Travelers and observers read and built upon each other's works. They cited masterworks and journeyed in the footsteps of mujawirs who had gone before them. Travel chronicles as well as hajj accounts had accumulated into a large body of works.

Although there were no hugely celebrated women's books to which Gulbadan could turn, there were nevertheless stories of female adventurers. El-Qutlugh, builder Zubaida, and Bija Munajjima, the dazzling Syrian literary star, mystic, mathematician, and bitter rival of stellar poet Jami all flourished in legends and court chronicles. Struck by women roving Arabian lands, male biographers wrote about them.

A fifteenth-century Egyptian scholar produced in his *Book of Women* an extensive cluster biography of female transmitters of the traditions of the Prophet's words and deeds.[31] These brilliant women had walked onto theological ground meant to be the province of men. Breathtaking illustrations appeared in the *Ta'rikh-i Alfi*, the millennial history that Emperor Akbar commissioned, with spirited folios on the history of Arabia, on the sacred Black Ka'ba, and on the magnificence of Zubaida's dynasty.[32]

That women had not written accounts of their experiences was not a problem for Gulbadan. For centuries, women had chosen other forms of expression: poetry, for instance, which had its own power, clues, and distinct suggestiveness. In Gulbadan's inheritance, poetry was an approach, a mode of interaction. One remembered verses from the great poets, noting a line to admonish someone or reciting a verse in praise.

There was architecture: a register of statecraft, beauty, power, and a way of thinking all at once. Zubaida broadcast intentionality in the construction of her fertile thoroughfare, the Darb Zubaida, which ran southwest from Baghdad to Mecca, parts of which El-Qutlugh passed. The hundreds of miles of this road were paved, and Zubaida commissioned water storage at intervals. At its most glorious, the road had stopping places that could nourish up to forty thousand camels.

In Al-Rabadha, one of the principal cities along Zubaida's road, there lived major grammarians and reciters of the Qur'an. In its heyday, the caliphs spent time there. The city had excellent cisterns, mosques, wells, and cemeteries. Pale brown mud houses had Kufic inscriptions carved in a faded wine-red color: *In the name of God the Merciful, the Compassionate, there is no God but He.*[33]

When Zubaida saw that pilgrims had difficulty procuring water, she ordered engineers to construct tunnels to transport clean water along the road to Mecca. On her fifth pilgrimage, she found out that a drought had devastated Mecca and reduced to a trickle the legendary Zamzam Well in the precincts of the Great Mosque. She ordered the well to be deepened and spent over 2 million gold dinars improving the water supply of Mecca and the surrounding province. Every reservoir, pool, or well on the road from Mecca to Baghdad was due to her munificent bounty.

The supply of water was at the core of Zubaida's architecture. It seized her thinking, as did peace and hunting for El-Qutlugh. Water and the desert were entwined, water the vital nourishment in the desertscape. No wonder Ibn Faraj, the Jeddah scholar, went into great detail to explain the history of the waterworks of his town and the construction of cisterns that the Persians had innovated. Jeddah was not exceptional. Cisterns, reservoirs, wells, and water systems were important subjects everywhere.[34]

Water, peace, and hunts were subtle languages. Pilgrims and travelers were singly yet collectively linked in searching the universe, connected above all in the physical distance that each had created in going away from their land of origin. The idea was rooted in Judeo-Islamic traditions. God had asked Abraham to go from where he lived, from the land of his fathers and the land of his birth, to the place that God would show him. God was asking something profound: he was asking Abraham "to go out of himself so that he might make space for what God intended him to be."[35] Seek and you shall find.

Like the mujawirs before her, who took to the roads of Arabia, Gulbadan pressed on in her quest, fulfilling a vow that she had made "long ago." From Jeddah, the vagabond princess and her party of women royals were ready for the next steps.

Like other pilgrims, sojourners, and seekers, Gulbadan would exit from the gate that looked toward Mecca. It usually took between two and three days to go from Jeddah to Mecca. Nasir-i Khusraw had started out after the Friday afternoon prayers and was at the gate of the city of Mecca two days later.[36]

Perched upon a camel's back in a canopy designed for royal women, Gulbadan rode out on the same road. Like the eleventh-century Persian Nasir, as she followed the dusty track she would await the moment of arrival on the outskirts of the city of the Prophet. Like other vagabond pilgrims, she would anticipate guidance on handling the vicissitudes in her itinerant life. She would have her own way of knowing what Allah proposed for her. That her spiritual quest would lead to a rupture in the diplomatic relations between the Mughals and the Ottomans, she could not have imagined. But that too was in God's design.

Ten

The Road to Mecca

~

SEATED UPON A TENT-SHAPED PALANQUIN, ITS SILKEN COVER held firmly with clasps of gold and silver, Gulbadan was primed to take the road to Mecca. Brocade and soft linen textiles from India were spread on the single hump of her brownish-yellow dromedary, also called the Arabian camel, an elegant being with black eyes, a long body, and long hair on its neck. A red steering cord was fastened around its mouth.[1]

Gulbadan was dressed in her classic flowing attire and a finely stitched muslin stole. A pearl- and cornelian-embedded gold necklace graced her neck. When the day got hot, she could wrap her face with the soft muslin. Similarly dressed, Salima and other women would ride upon their finely decorated Arabian camels.

As royal guests, it was expected that the Mughal women would ride the *mamiyya,* the best dromedaries with excellent pacing, so smooth that "one could easily go to sleep while riding such beasts."[2] For the distinguished aunt of the Great Mughal of India, it is also certain that the special *laissez-passer*—called *yol emri* in Ottoman Turkish—was arranged. The document was an important part of Ottoman practice in easing the travel of eminent guests and ensuring that no interruption took place. Local jurists and provincial governors had instructions to provide escorts and local guides along the dangerous stretches. The governor of Jeddah, a major regional Ottoman appointee, would enable the arrangements for the Mughal convoy.[3]

Mughal court historian Nizam al-Din Ahmad says that Gulbadan's *kafila,* or cavalcade, was patterned after the style and order of the legendary Egyptian and Syrian desert caravans.[4] The Egyptians went from Cairo to Mecca via Ajrud and Aqaba, then south along the eastern shore of the Red Sea. They usually took between forty-five and fifty days to reach their hajj destination, making lengthy stops along the way. The Damascus caravan took the same time, although its route was through the desert forts such as Hasa, Tabuk, and al-Rahba, used for stopovers.[5]

The logistics of a mixed land and sea convoy with a "multitude of people," as an imperial Ottoman document remarked about the Mughal procession, were of a different nature.[6] Gulbadan had in the first leg of her journey covered approximately eight hundred miles between Fatehpur-Sikri and Surat. After spending nearly a year in Surat before securing the cartaz from the Portuguese, the group had sailed across the Arabian Sea for nearly four weeks before reaching Jeddah. Now that they were on the desert road to Mecca, it was possible to emulate the Egyptian and Syrian desert processions.

Members of the Mughal convoy assembled in designated places before exiting Jeddah from the Mecca Gate. In the Egyptian and Damascene caravans, the hajj commander's secretary was in charge of important decisions on the road, such as paying subsidies to Bedouin leaders to ensure their safety. Thieves and poor Bedouins with meager resources lurked around the ancient shrines along the Arabian roads. Attacks on caravans during the forty-mile route between Jeddah and Mecca, which typically took two to three days, were possible.[7] Bedouin guides familiar with the challenging and dangerous stretches of the desert would gallop at the head of the Mughal caravan. Water carriers would be with the party.[8]

At the epicenter of the procession, perched upon an elegant camel, Gulbadan, "the leader of the caravan," heightened the splendor of the pilgrim ensemble.[9] The Mughal haraman rode by her side, adding to the stateliness of the convoy. Encircling the royal women were Akbar's foster brother, Gulbadan's elderly uncle, and Sultan Khwaja, the commander of pilgrimage.

In close proximity behind Sultan Khwaja marched armed soldiers with lances and bows. They guarded the boxes containing cash in gold and silver, goods, and textiles. They also carried 600,000 rupees for donations and twelve thousand dresses of honor designated as gifts for the inhabitants of Mecca and Medina, as well as gifts for the Holy Sanctuaries and largesse for the sherif of Mecca. There was an unspecified but enormous amount of cash for the upkeep of the Mughal women, too. Gulbadan had a "large amount of money and goods," wrote Abul Fazl in his Akbarnama. Akbar had "poured into the lap of each [woman] the money that they wanted," Fazl added.[10]

Emperor Akbar had also set aside separate amounts for the free-passage pilgrims, such as the child who had earlier fallen into the sea.

Then there were allowances for the maintenance of staff, saddlers, cooks, tasters, tent pitchers, and torch bearers. The valuable merchandise that the Indian traders brought for sales had to be shielded: incense, prized cotton, silk, brocade, satin, linen textiles, candlesticks, pepper, ginger, indigo, and mastic. As Ludovico di Varthema saw in the 1510s, aside from the extensive traffic of jewels and spices of every kind from India, there was "wax and odoriferous substances in the greatest abundance."[11] Merchants sold their goods in the markets of Mecca and Medina and donated part of the earnings in alms, in addition to the dues owed to the Mughal state. Behind the soldiers guarding the treasured gifts, merchandise, and cash were storekeepers, cooks, and assistants, followed by merchants and common folks. At the tail end were more soldiers.

The grand Arabian caravans that inspired the Mughals had a unique feature, the *mahmal*. In the likeness of a majestic lady covered in splendid fabric and gold, an enclosed tent topped by a circular finial made of gilded silver, this insignia in procession was the star attraction of the Egyptian and Damascus processions. The color of the mahmal depended on which dynasty it represented. Yellow was the color of the Mamluk sultans, black the color of the Abbasids. The silken fabric of the mahmal was handsomely stitched in silver- or gold-plated wire with arabesques, scrollwork designs, and inscriptions from the Qur'an. The patron's name was usually embroidered in the front of the pyramid-shaped roof. Sizes varied. The height of a fifteenth-century Syrian mahmal, now housed in the Topkapi Palace Museum, is 12 feet from its base to the pyramid and the wooden tuft on the top.[12]

Grounded in ancient feminine traditions, women in history were connected with the lore of this ceremonial tent. A high-ranking lady in a gilded canopy, for instance, accompanied armies to embolden them. The Prophet Muhammad's wife 'Ayesha is said to have had that role. Noble girls rode in palanquins decorated with lavish ostrich feathers and shells. In a silver, ebony, and sandalwood palanquin draped with blue, green, yellow, and red sable and silk, Abbasid Queen Zubaida went on pilgrimage five times. Her delicate tented seat embellished with gold thread inscriptions is among the possible origins of the mahmal.[13]

By the twelfth century, the mahmal regularly appeared during the hajj as a vehicle for transporting rich pilgrims. An early twelfth-century classic and best seller, the *Maqamat,* or the Assemblies, consisting of a series of fabulous stories, was written by Al-Hariri, a poet and philologist who lived and studied in Basra. Seven hundred authorized copies of the *Maqamat* were sold by the time of his death in 1122—a large number in those days of hand-made books.

Over a hundred years later, in 1237, Yahya al-Wasiti drew glorious illustrations for the book. Accompanying the thirty-first Assembly is a double-page folio depicting a caravan accompanied by musicians, drums, trumpets, and black flags, the dynastic color of the Abbasids. A turbaned man is seated on horseback, the hajj commander and attendants on foot. And there, on the back of the camel, is a red- and gold-painted pyramid-shaped mahmal. On the left folio, pilgrims and camels sit on the ground and so does the mahmal, now a stupendous black with just a delicate gold lining like a necklace around its neck. Red to black, "from joyful to reflective."[14]

After their conquest of Egypt, the Ottomans started a second mahmal from Damascus with Syrian and Turkish pilgrims, in addition to the Egyptian one. Like the former Arab and North African sultans, the Ottomans used this luxurious sign to enhance their protective role as the rulers of the Holy Places. The ceremonies accompanying the legendary litter grew more elaborate.[15]

Many observers documented the alluring mahmal. Ibn Battuta, Moroccan traveler and writer, noted the excitement among the people of Cairo in 1326 when the mahmal came out from the imperial citadel. "All classes of the population, both men and women, assemble for this ceremony . . . camel drivers singing to their camels in the lead . . . resolves are inflamed, desires are excited, and impulses are stirred up."[16] Dervishes marched behind the camel with the ceremonial canopy. Shopkeepers along the route painted their houses and hung precious carpets. Martial exercises with lances were common. Local artists wore demonic masks to amuse the crowds and extort money.[17] Sieur Paul Lucas in 1744, Edward Lane in 1825, and Sir Richard Burton in 1853 saw the exquisite mahmal. Lane also made sketches of it. Orientalist Alfred Dehodencq likely never saw one, but he depicted it in 1853 in a painting of a procession set around the Red Sea.

Over centuries, royal women had journeyed to Mecca parading their grace and intent. Zubaida's silver and ebony palanquin and El-Qutlugh's ring hunts signified beauty and power, in pilgrimage as in daily life. In the late tenth century, a princess went to Mecca from Mosul with a cortege of four hundred mahmals, all of the same color, "so that it was impossible to recognize the one that the Princess was in."[18] Fifteenth-century Mamluk queen Fatima chose a silken palanquin embroidered with ruby, turquoise, and pearls to enhance her distinction.[19] The color or selection of jewels a woman chose heightened her persona.

Yet in the end, it was the person of the dignitary that mattered most. Gulbadan and her companions knew the mahmal's credentials and beauty. Guidebooks, histories, chronicles, and travelogues mentioning it were part of the wider Islamic milieu, including Mughal India.[20]

Gulbadan was in the innermost shielded spot amid caravan dignitaries. Like the exquisite mahmal at the center of the desert cavalcades, the princess and the Mughal matriarchs were the luminaries of Emperor Akbar's convoy. Splendidly guarded yet in full view, they created their unique pageant. Singular in composition and singular in vision, the star-studded Mughal women's convoy thus embarked on the road to Mecca. Never had a group of royal women traveled this way to Arabia. Unified in their vision of a women's cluster hajj, the haraman were also unanimous about how they wished to broadcast their arrival in the city of Mecca.

As it rode through the ancient caravan corridor from Jeddah to Mecca, the Mughal procession would pass the road that ran along the Hejaz mountain range. It was filled with igneous rocks, in some parts covered by volcanic mountains. Precambrian rocks underlie the entire Arabian Peninsula. After the alluvial sands, coralline reef rocks, and ancient petroglyph-filled rocks were the basaltic lava fields locally known as *harrats*: these extend in the north-south direction and cover approximately 111,847 miles.[21]

Many stark, bare turns, dead volcanos, and naked mountains with black basalt boulders were found along the way, and yellow gravel covered the ground. Fed on bitter velch and barley meal, the dromedaries steadily headed forward. Travel in those days involved considerable physical pain and fatigue. A hundred years after Gulbadan's visit, an anonymous Iranian woman traveled to Arabia with a couple of companions. Documenting her experience in twelve hundred verses, she wrote an unusual work, in line with the writings of mujawirs, describing the winding rivers, rough mountainous terrain, odd yet hospitable people, riches, and deprivation she saw along the way, as well as the pain of travel. She broke down from time to time and cried, she wrote. Her bones ached. Once in Mecca, at the feet of the revered Ka'ba, she nearly fainted.[22]

Slowly the plains between the open hills began to show. Memorials of holy persons whom Gulbadan worshipped appeared everywhere, like the desert sand itself. Thirty-six miles before Mecca were spring-water wells. Between two hills there was a pavement in the shape of steps with "traces of old buildings," a well attributed to 'Ali, the Prophet's son-in-law, and an ancient fort with solid stone masonry. Thirteen miles before Mecca was Wadi Fatima, a fertile valley named after the Prophet's daughter. Numerous date palm trees lined it and spring water gushed from many places.[23]

With camel bells ringing, cameleers singing songs to urge the animals on, they neared Mecca. Sitting low in the mountains, at last Mecca heaved into view. From whichever direction travelers came, they could not see the city until they were fairly close to it. The barren Hijaz was dependent on other regions for food supplies. The land was thorny and unbearably hot. Shortages of water and food often plagued the region. Wells and cisterns supplied water, but its distribution was a technical as well as a political problem. It was hard to persuade the Bedouins to share water without compensation. During periods of drought and increased food scarcity, travelers often died due to thirst, hunger, and exposure to the elements. In this delicate ecology and economy, each visitor meant an additional burden on the limited resources.

Although Mecca had done well under the long leadership of Sherif Abu Numay II, who took on the role after his father died six decades earlier, political machinations nonetheless affected the relay of supplies. If gifts to Bedouin tribes along the desert routes were omitted or not paid in full, or if there were disputes among Egyptian or Syrian officers, pilgrims' security as well as the conveyance of goods was affected. Similar problems occurred if the Bedouins and their camel population were decimated by drought. Local residents, such as merchants with no claims to pious subsidies, needed upkeep. In Medina, there were scores of sojourners, many of them elderly, who needed support.[24]

The movement of people and goods through Arabia was politically charged. After the Ottomans established hegemony over the region, Egypt continued its major grain-supplying role. Grants from Egyptian foundations were indispensable. Before the Ottoman conquest of the area, Sultan Beyezid had sent the poor of Medina 14,442 gold pieces. Later, Suleyman the Magnificent established two soup kitchens in Medina. Named after his beloved consort Roxolena, these were funded by Egyptian tax revenues. By the 1520s, the Ottoman central administration budget allocated separate expenditures for pilgrims. Merchants and well-placed artisans from Istanbul and larger Anatolian cities established foundations to help the poor.[25] Every major Muslim emperor sent bounties. Giving alms was (and is) considered the most virtuous of acts. In the late sixteenth century, when Gulbadan went to Mecca, there was an additional spark to almsgiving.

After the Ottomans became the uncontested masters of the region in 1517, for Islamic writers and thinkers who deliberated on political authority and for Arabian local rulers and upper classes, a great quandary arose. The Ottoman sultans had never claimed descent from Prophet Muhammad, and therefore lacked in Arabia "an important element of religious legitimation." What made it even trickier was that they had never controlled Islamic heartlands; for the most part they had ruled over Christian territories, the Balkans as far as Belgrade and western and central Anatolia. In 1517, when the Ottoman rule shifted from "the periphery to the center of the Islamic world," says an Ottoman historian, they began to take measures to tackle the issue of their legitimacy as rulers in Arabia. They did not and could not suddenly claim descent from the Prophet. Rather, they sought a philosophical ground within the framework of Islam to establish their legitimacy as rulers. They began a sustained policy of generosity toward pilgrims and inhabitants in Arabia. The sultans stressed their singular role as benefactors, their obligation as providers of provisions for their subjects and for pilgrims, including alms for the poor and needy.[26]

Alms were at the core of the argument supporting the legitimacy of Ottoman sultans as the Islamic sovereigns of the Holy Land. The Ottomans endeavored to support pilgrims: rich and poor, royal and ordinary, Bedouins as well as regular residents. Beneficence on a grand scale was the keystone of their rule in the Prophet's land. In keeping with the guiding principle that the sultans would take care of and protect people, and in tune with the reigning courtesies between the courts, Gulbadan and her companions were prized Ottoman guests. But even as distinguished visitors, they were on a par with other travelers and pilgrims. They would be required to follow the code of conduct established in the Holy Places. Obeying the law was not only in consonance with Ottoman values but also, in the Prophet's home, it was Islamic duty.

Even though he lived two thousand miles away in Istanbul, Sultan Murad III's image as the benefactor of the inhabitants and pilgrims of Mecca and Medina was widespread. Like his forefathers, Murad was the "Servitor of the Holy Sanctuaries," the "Protector of the Holy Cities."[27] Protection of his subjects, visitors, and pilgrims in Arabia validated his rule.

Control of far-flung lands in desert areas was difficult and expensive. Aside from close connections with the powerful local sherif of Mecca—whose authority was counterbalanced by an Ottoman governor in Jeddah—a sultan could flourish only with artful and religiously grounded statements. Murad made imperial alms key to his kingly image. He kept abreast of all of the activities in the region. He knew that Akbar the Great's hajj convoy had reached the Hijaz and that several harem women under the leadership of the emperor's aunt graced the Mughal procession.

At a fixed place before Mecca, the commoners among the pilgrims would leave the Mughal caravan. Local guides helped with the rituals and visits. The pilgrims donned the required garb, the *ihram*, marking the beginning of the ritual consecration. The ceremony had been intact since Prophet Muhammad's time. After a full body wash, the men wore two pieces of seamless white cloth around the waist and over the top of the body. Women pilgrims had no prescribed clothing. A woman could wear any color she wanted, including white. During the time of the rites, men and women could not have sex, use perfume, or cut their nails or hair. Men could not shave. There is no sign in sixteenth-century records that women covered their faces. Sir Richard Burton noted in his mid-nineteenth-century travelogue that women were required to wear veils during the rites.[28]

The dignitaries of the sherif would welcome the Mughal convoy and lead the royals into the city gate of Mecca, either from the Bab-ul Zahir or the Bab-ul ʿUmra. Still unable to see the blessed sights and spots, Gulbadan would focus on her arrival at the center of the sacred geography that Gods and the angels built. Each haraman knew that this was where Adam, Abraham, and Muhammad circled the Kaʿba seven times. From here began

Prophet Muhammad's nighttime journey—"on the magic conveyance of the buraq—a winged steed with a human face—[he] travels to the sacred mosque at the furthest sanctuary [the Temple Mount in Jerusalem], and thence upward to Heaven."[29] On this land uniting the Islamic and Abrahamic faiths, in the footprints of the great prophets, they would walk around the most ancient of ancient shrines, the Ka'ba, toward which Muslims look and pray five times a day wherever they are in the world.

Medina is the other "City of the Prophet." Back then, when hajj caravans arrived there, children came out with little baskets of palm branches and begged for alms from the pilgrims. *Praise be to God, O Pilgrims, go unhurt, and in peace!* said the Arab boys. *Praise be to God, we have arrived at the shrine of our Prophet who came as a mercy for both worlds,* the pilgrims responded.[30] As in Medina, so in Mecca, the young and the old alike welcomed the Mughal pilgrims.

Settling into her lodgings, which overlooked the compound of the Great Mosque, in close proximity to the section where Sultan Murad owned a mansion, Gulbadan would gradually unstring her burdens.[31] Now she had the time and had reached the place where she could unravel the meaning of her journey. Her exploration had just begun.

Eleven

Everyone's Mecca

~

MUD-BUILT, LATTICE-WINDOWED HOUSES WITH BALCONIES jutting out over streets, bazaar lanes jingling with goods, the scent of fragrant olives, dates, sweetmeats, sherbets, and pilafs, and throngs of rich and poor travelers, pilgrims and merchants from around the world, characterized the monumental gateways of the Great Mosque of Mecca. Gulbadan and her companions likely stayed in the vicinity of this Noble Sanctuary, where the sherif of Mecca also resided and where many well-to-do Meccans owned houses. Some of them rented these out during the pilgrimage season. A mansion was kept here in the name of the current Ottoman sultan, Murad III, even though he never came to Mecca. The four theological schools that Murad's grandfather built were used as dwellings for influential pilgrims. Quite a few hostels were situated in this part of town for ordinary and poor travelers.[1]

Slender Meccans, their "eyes like gazelles," wandered freely here. Dressed in baggy pants and long shirts made of Indian silk and cloaks of various kinds, Circassian-style shoes or slippers on their feet, they moved about.[2] When these elegantly dressed Meccans came out to buy food, orphan boys assisted them, thus getting work. Sitting with two baskets each day in ritualistic fashion, the boys took their place in the bazaar. After the buyer finished his purchases, one of the boys put grains in one basket and meat and vegetables in the other. He carried the goods to the man's home in return for a few copper coins. The man, meanwhile, headed to the mosque for prayer. A firm trust lay beneath this arrangement.[3]

Each week on the eve of the Friday congregation, musk- and ambergris-soaked women of Mecca, renowned for their love of perfume, gathered to circumambulate the Kaʻba, the House of God with the mythical Black Stone. "The sanctuary is saturated with the smell of their perfumes," wrote Ibn Battuta.[4] Their attire and aroma-laden bodies had led to a massive controversy. A ban on their nighttime visit to the Great Mosque nearly went into effect in the third quarter of the sixteenth century. Pious men and jurists argued that perfume, jewelry, and women's ululation disrupted the absorption required in the Holy Place. It was one thing to have sweet aromas of incense and scents oozing from every wall of the sanctuary, another if women wore fragrances. But they went on, undeterred and unfettered, fully present, fragranced and beautiful in the House of God. The ban did not come to pass.[5]

Mecca was after all a city for everyone in whatever quest they had—whether they were pilgrims, vagabonds, merchants, theologians, artists, musicians, lovers, rich or poor, men or women. Wandering and pilgrimage were signs of hunger, a quest, as Gulbadan's travel indicated, even as she had reasoned that she wanted to go to Mecca because she had taken a vow to do so. Visitors who wanted quiet reflection or needed to obscure themselves in spiritual flames found a home here. Thinkers came looking for stimulus. The three years that the thirteenth-century Andalusian writer Ibn ʻArabi spent in Mecca led to a body of textured, visionary works and his philosophical creation *the unity of being,* or *wahdat al-wujud,* which had at its core the idea that God and everything in his creation is indivisible. Sublime symbols of concord are manifest in each thing in the world.

Mecca was also renowned for love poetry. A new genre of *ghazal* consisting of rhyming couplets, lines sharing the same meter, came into being here. The man known to have shaped this kind of ghazal was ʻUmar ibn Abi Rabia of the Quraysh, the same tribe as Prophet Muhammad. ʻUmar was a cult figure in the seventh century. Men of Mecca were eager to follow this alluring poet, the "hero of his poems, the handsome young man no woman could resist."[6] A city of poets, virtuoso singers, performers, tricky politicians, Sufis, and sojourners, Mecca had a thriving life concentrated near the Great Mosque.

But the huddled and huddling buildings around the Great Mosque detracted from what might have been an arresting, distinct façade had it been a stand-alone monument. It was folded amid buildings, and multitudes of people were always about and around it. This was precisely why a few years before Gulbadan arrived in Mecca, Sultan Murad had launched a full-scale clearing out of the structures crowding the Holy Sanctuary. He wanted a solemn, regulated space of worship. The high houses in which royal guests like Gulbadan resided and which afforded a view into the grounds of the mosque were deemed disrespectful. The sultan had in mind a classical Ottoman mosque with an unblemished outer square. Only public institutions like the madrasas, libraries, and soup kitchens could envelop it, not any private houses. Thus, his plan was to remove all housing around the Great Mosque of Mecca and demolish the surrounding structures, pushing the poor and those in poorer lodgings to the periphery of the city. Among those driven out were the pilgrims from Mughal India. The poor and "often smelly" Indian quarter was a "prime target."[7]

Many Indians of meager means had been traveling to Mecca to fulfill their lifelong dream thanks to the subsidies they received from Emperor Akbar, including a free passage on imperial as well as commercial ships. Akbar had also built a small pilgrim shelter in Mecca. Evliya Celebi, the seventeenth-century Ottoman bureaucrat-traveler, visited this place, which has a fountain bearing Akbar's name. A key problem for all the poor, not only Indians, was that they did not have a determined place in Mecca where they could spend the night. A few places here and there were not enough. At the end of the day, many would settle in a corner of the Great Mosque. Quite apart from the "dirt and smells . . . inimical to the solemnity" of the mosque, the Ottoman bureaucrats felt that the personal use of the mosque was inappropriate, contrary to Shariah or, in Ottoman Turkish, *na-meshru*. Some Iranian families had spread cushions in the mosque courtyard, relishing the view. The officers were furious with them for such na-meshru behavior.[8]

You could not casually saunter in the courtyard of the Great Mosque. You could not soil its surroundings with bad smells, as the Indian pilgrims allegedly did. If Sultan Murad's officers had to classify the alluring, sweet-smelling Meccan women who ostensibly disrupted spiritual concentration in the mosque, what else could it be but na-meshru? Even drinking coffee, considered an intoxicant by some and not appropriate in spiritual awakening, had been a problem in the past. Any disruptive potential in anyone or anything was na-meshru. You surely could not step on the covering of the Ka'ba. Almsgiving, an act of utmost value in Muslim life, was closely monitored. The Ottomans were severe about na-meshru. It was a standard bearing immense consequences—and a word that Gulbadan would soon confront.

Discussion about revamping the Great Mosque neighborhood was still ongoing when Gulbadan, her relatives, and the accompanying officers commenced their hajj in 1577. As he had with other renovations, Sultan Murad took legal advice and brought in important theologians and influential city folk. Prosperous Meccans were not enthusiastic about the removal of the cluster of elite houses around the mosque. But the areas where people with meager resources hung on got a thorough clearing. It was not possible to expel the Indians altogether, but they were transferred outside the city where the "smells they generated would not waft into the Great Mosque."[9]

Seven slender, Ottoman-style minarets that bordered the outer periphery of the Great Mosque could be seen from afar. This Haram-i Sherif, or Noble Sanctuary, sat in the middle of Mecca running lengthwise from east to west, its breadth on a north-south axis. Eighteen arched doors supported on marble columns surrounded the mosque. They remained open at all times.

Eager for an unmatched encounter, Gulbadan, the Mughal celebrants, and the staff entered the illustrious Great Mosque. Everyone observed the age-old guidelines. Men and women took a full body bath. The women wore flowing attire and wraps over their adorned faces, while the men were clad in an unstitched two-piece white garment, with no cut, no buttons, and no shape, denoting equality and finality, the same white that wrapped a new-born baby, the simple cover in which the dead would be laid.

Where did stately women like Gulbadan or dignitaries like the hajj commander commence the state of ihram? For ordinary folks, there were the *miqat makani,* fixed places outside where they moved into the spiritual state. Then began the chant in Arabic, *Labbaik allahumma labbaik—I am present.* A more literal meaning is *Here I am, Lord, here I am, Lord [to perform the Hajj].*

They likely went in through the popular Bani Shayba Gate, also called the Gate of Peace, at the northern angle of the east wall of the mosque.[10] It usually took ten days to complete all the rites of the pilgrimage. The period for the rites was fixed according to the Muslim lunar calendar and took place in the twelfth month, Dhul-Hijjah. The hajj includes a vital visit to Mount 'Arafat. A lesser pilgrimage or *'umra,* limited to the perimeter of Mecca, can be carried out at any time.

The ancient rites and ceremonies were time bound, which meant that large numbers of people from Mali, Anatolia, Egypt, Yemen, Iraq, China,

Sumatra, and several other places undertook them together. Forty thousand Egyptians and as many Syrians and Iraqis were on a pilgrimage in 1279. Fourteenth-century Christian pilgrim Jacob of Verona met a hajj caravan in the Arabian Desert that had seventeen thousand people. An anonymous 1580 Portuguese account notes that fifty thousand participants traveled in the Egyptian caravan alone.[11]

Guards and officers of the sherif of Mecca provided security and protected avenues for Mughal women to accomplish the ceremonial steps. Yol emir, the Ottoman laissez-passer, facilitated uninterrupted movement for elite guests across the Hijaz area. Stepping into the Great Mosque, the worshippers walked below the gorgeous marble galleries with red stone columns that wrapped the inner boundary of the holy grounds. Facing them obliquely was the Ka'ba, the *qibla* or the direction that Muslims face in their five ritual prayers each day. A waft of luxurious musk and a puff of saffron and ambergris captured their senses. Passing this covered arcade with hundreds of olive oil lamps to be lit at night, they came out on the wide courtyard. No one could touch, alter, or add on to this wide space, but the domed galleries with olive oil lamps that Gulbadan passed had clear Ottoman accents.

Since occupying western Arabian and Egyptian territories, the Ottomans had spent a great deal of money on transforming local buildings. Powerful emperors and empresses in much of the Islamic world constructed buildings, employing distinctive styles. Grand structures implied statecraft. In striking alterations and aestheticizing edifices, sultans came into public view. *They* became visible. Each time citizens and visitors looked, they were reminded of the glorious sultanic endeavors, lest they forget that the Holy Places were under the aegis of the Ottomans. Small domes covered the galleries, a classic style of shielded porticoes that created a sense of enclosed rooms, a sultanic impulse. You entered the most magnificent and most powerful Islamic shrine through Ottoman doors that shaded and protected you. Members of Sultan Suleyman's council had debated building between four hundred and five hundred domes. In the end it was 172 mini cupolas that Gulbadan and her companions saw.[12]

Under the open skies with sweet scents of paradise, Gulbadan finally came face-to-face with the venerable Ka'ba. The Black Stone, Abraham's pre-Islamic gift that Muslims kissed in adoration, was embedded in the eastern corner of the outer walls of the Ka'ba. The cube-like Ka'ba was so sublime that no tongue could presume to describe its perfection. A beloved masterpiece, it was "like a bride . . . displayed upon the bridal chair of majesty . . . in the mantles of beauty."[13]

The wide-open quad with the Ka'ba where Gulbadan stood had been so for centuries, inviting everyone to step into the holy precincts and garner blessings. This was the House of God—the most ancient harem. How brilliantly Gulbadan's nephew Akbar had extracted the sacred vision of this original harem and its utter sanctity for the first red sandstone harem for his women. And yet, in creating his sacrosanct arrangements, he ended up robbing his women, notably those of Gulbadan's generation, of the vagabond nature within them. This thought likely occurred to the princess—but she would turn from the thought.

Here, before the Ka'ba, she was neither remote nor removed from the world. At long last, she would accomplish the vow she had taken. Here, blissful like Gulbadan, vivacious Queen Salima would hold in her thoughts her husband Akbar, summoning Gods for his well-being. Responsible for guiding the pilgrims, a *mutawwif* chanted prayers, many that Prophet Muhammad himself had spoken and commended. Pilgrims repeated prayers after the guides, the air filled with revered utterances. Praying among a worldwide community, taking blessings from the Ka'ba covered in black *kiswa* with a golden band below its roof, niece Salima knew that people died in the arduous travels to the Hijaz. Getting here safely for the second time was a sign that God was protecting her. Her joy was palpable.

Artists, poets, and calligraphers had illuminated guidebooks written in gold Arabic lettering with floral script containing blessed words. The attractive handbooks, often a combination of illustration and verse, delighted the sultans, to whom these were often dedicated. Readers and travelers purchased these ornamented guidebooks, "a souvenir of a journey of a lifetime."[14]

Often a mix of religious and lyric verse, astronomy, geometry, and instruction, guidebooks were loved in Mughal circles. An early fifteenth-century work was at one time in Gulbadan's paternal family. It featured the grayish blue Ka'ba on one of its folios, angels hovering over it, and a throng of male pilgrims wearing white ihram around it. On an adjacent chrome-yellow page, with shards of blue china etched in, a caravan approached Mecca. There were delicate camel figures and covered seats with incoming pilgrims.[15]

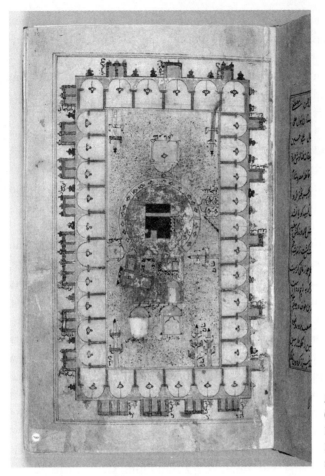

Futuh-i Haramayn
(Description of the
Holy Cities), by
Muhyi al-Din Lari,
mid-sixteenth century.

Closer to Gulbadan's era, approximately fifty years before her visit to the
Hijaz, a Persian man named Muhyi al-Din Lari composed a slender book of
verse called the *Futuh-i Haramayn,* or Revelations of the Two Sanctuaries.
Lari wrote in honor of the ruler of Gujarat, and his marvelously illustrated
book enjoyed great success and was repeatedly copied. The surviving copies
measure approximately 8½ or 9½ inches in height, 5½ or 6 inches in width
and contain forty to sixty folios. Yellow-and-red ornate Persian Qur'anic
verses and prayers are inscribed across the width of the rice paper. The *Futuh*
pages are packed with glorious miniature images of the sites in Mecca and
Medina, and the work stands out as an early guidebook. Among the copies
of *Futuh* still extant, twelve were produced in Mecca. One was signed by

scribes in front of the Black Stone, one was deposited in the collection of the Great Mosque, one was copied in Istanbul, and one in India, its painter likely an Indian.[16]

To be in awe of something that the prophets had built, to feel overcome in the very place trodden, it was believed, by Gods, angels, and celestial beings, was a common pilgrim experience. The story of the creation of the Ka'ba was well known, told and retold in home and harem circles, near shrines, and in books. When Prophet Abraham's second wife, Hagar, and his son Ishmael were cast out by Sarah, the first wife, he took them to the valley of Mecca. Abraham gave Hagar a bag of dates and some water and told her that he would return. It was the will of God, he said, and so Hagar accepted her fate and Abraham left. From time to time, he visited her.

When Ishmael grew up, it was time for an important task: rebuilding the Ka'ba. Adam had originally erected the Ka'ba, but by the time Abraham came to Mecca, it was no longer there. God showed Abraham where it had been, and so he began the sacred work. During the process of rebuilding, Abraham engraved the Black Stone into one of the walls of the Ka'ba. After the completion of his work, Abraham and his son walked seven times around the Ka'ba. This ritual, the *tawaf,* would live forever. Muhammad declared the Ka'ba as the direction of prayer, confirming its eminence.[17]

Visitors who wrote about their first glimpse of the Ka'ba often said they were transfixed and awestruck. An anonymous Iranian woman who saw it a hundred years after Gulbadan remembered that she nearly fainted. She could not open her mouth to express her thrill. It was as if she had no strength. Summoning all her energy, she finally prostrated before God.[18]

Gulbadan and the haraman would reverently step on the grounds where Adam, Abraham, and Muhammad had once walked. Originally covered with pebbles, the floor of the Great Mosque had lately been laid in marble. The reason for the change was that when poor pilgrims who had no rugs came to worship, the sharp pebbles scratched their knees during prostration. As with many other Ottoman-redesigned projects, this one ran into trouble. Just as the marble slabs were cut in 1577, Meccans began objecting that the smooth surface would give a luxurious appearance to the sacred ground. The pious-minded were particularly displeased. The matter was settled when Judge Qazi Huseyin held a conference to secure the consent of the inhabitants, clearly the more prominent citizenry.[19]

Walking on the lustrous white marble, the Mughal women circumambulated the Ka'ba, keeping to the right, the cube-shaped sanctuary to their left, roughly fifty feet high, about thirty-five by forty feet at its base. Constructed of gray stone and marble, it was oriented so its corners approximately corresponded to the points of a compass. The door of the Ka'ba was to one side and its sill rested above the ground. Delicately assembled silver-plated lintels covered the door. The bolt of the door passed through two large silver rings.[20]

The Prophet had given the keys of the Ka'ba to the family of the Bani Shayba. "Take it, O Bani Shayba," he said, "eternally up to the Day of Resurrection, it will not be taken from you unless by an unjust, oppressive tyrant."[21] Subsequent rulers designed opulent keys, steel inlaid with silver in the shape of a pillar or tower, slender and elegant. Inscribed with the patron's name and lined with Qur'anic verses, the key was enclosed in an embroidered bag, mostly in silk with silk-gilt thread, and was gifted to the Bani Shayba. To unlock the door each Friday after the midday prayer and on the anniversary of the Prophet, the "Opener of the Noble House" mounted the steps, carrying the holy key. The doorkeepers drew aside the curtains and the opener unlocked the door. He kissed the threshold, entered alone, and remained there to offer prayers. Then the rest of his clan entered and prayed. Only then did the people waiting outside go in.

Going around the Ka'ba gave the Mughal women an exalted feeling. Tears filled their eyes, and their elation filled the precincts as a wave of humans paid obeisance. Above them, pigeons flew, never alighting, even when they were level with the Ka'ba. Swerving their course from side to side, the pigeons of Mecca would not set their delicate feet on the blessed sanctuary.[22]

Gulnar Aghacha, Gulbadan's companion of nearly five decades, blessed her for this gift and thanked Allah, who had facilitated it all. They kissed the wall at the eastern corner and went on. Kissing and taking a full round designated one tawaf, or circumambulation. They encircled it seven times, three times quickly and four slowly. Each time they passed the Black Stone, they kissed it, touched it, or pointed to it, with words of prayer upon their lips: "Lord, give us good in this life and good in the hereafter and protect us from the torment of Fire."[23]

In this ritualized movement, the Mughal women went toward the next step, the Maqam-i Ibrahim, the station to the east of the Ka'ba, where Abraham began the building work. Tradition has it that he stood at this point in prayer, and as the walls of the Ka'ba went higher, the *maqam* upon which Abraham stood rose up so that he could continue building. Then it went down so that Ishmael could hand his father stones to build. Footprints appeared at the spot where Hagar stood washing Abraham's hair and where Abraham beckoned people to perform the pilgrimage to Mecca.[24] The station was originally a rock with imprints of Abraham's feet. When Nasir-i Khusraw saw it in the twelfth century, it was covered in a wooden scaffolding with silver drums on all four sides up to a man's height. By the fourteenth century, a cupola balanced on an iron grill surmounted the area.[25]

Recalling Hagar's well-known search for water, Gulbadan would slowly sip the sweet *zamzam* that all wayfarers and pilgrims longed to drink. After Abraham left Mecca, Hagar began to look for water to quench her son's thirst. Leaving her little son behind, she ran to and fro between two hillocks that later came to be called Safa and Marwa. When she returned, water was springing from the ground where she had left little Ishmael. Angels intervened, some say. Others say that when the baby kicked the sand with his heels, a miracle occurred, and water sprang up. In the fourteenth century, it was believed that the volume of the zamzam increased every Friday.[26]

After taking sips of the sacred water from a *dawraq*, a narrow-necked jar with a looped handle, Gulbadan and her companions rubbed some on their faces, gazing on their surroundings in awe. After that, the group exited the premises through the Safa gate at the south end of the mosque. They were now at a point in the ritual cycle when they ran like Hagar between Mounts Safa and Marwa. Outside the gate, they went up the steps to Safa. Once atop it, they faced the Ka'ba and prayed. Then they descended and ran north to Mount Marwa through a bazaar, a hectic business corridor that Ibn Battuta called a "torrent bed."[27]

The bazaar was full of sacks of grain of various kinds, meat, dates, and clarified butter. Barber shops, sellers of cooked sheep's heads, butchers, cloth merchants, and suppliers of goods of many kinds traded here, and thieves, pious sheikhs, and poor and rich pilgrims wandered here. The large numbers of temporary, makeshift food and coffee stalls had become such an obstacle to the movement of pilgrims that Ottoman authorities had lately prohibited the establishment of new ones.[28]

There were not many lively markets like this in Mecca, except the cloth and drugstore lanes at the Peace Gate or the Apothecaries' Market near the street between Marwa and Safa. Prophet Muhammad had resided in the apothecary area. From his house, it was said, he used to cross the Prophet's Door to go to the mosque for prayers.[29]

Scurrying back and forth, adjusting their garments, the Mughal women could scarcely get clear passage. Security guards and attendants would lead the way, then Sultan Khwaja and Mughal followers, guaranteeing safe passage for the royals as much as possible. Rumi Khan would alert wayfarers in Arabic. The pressure of the crowds around the vendors and pilgrims was immense. When they reached the gate where Prophet Muhammad had commanded the run between the two hills, they slowed down as required, now unhurriedly moving to Mount Marwa. The elderly Gulnar took a deep breath. After reciting prayers at the mount, they came down and repeated the run through the bazaar, four times from Safa to Marwa and three times from Marwa to Safa: in total, seven runs, thus completing the 1.7-mile ritual circuit.[30] This was much easier for Gulbadan's granddaughter and two nieces to accomplish than for the matriarchs in the party. Slowly or fast, they went up and down the bazaar street. Pilgrims and vendors would turn to look at the haraman of the Great Mughal of India. No person could fade into obscurity here.

As on other hajj occasions, the *qazi* (judge) of Mecca addressed the travelers and wayfarers to enlighten them about the significance of the next part, a vital custom called *wakfa,* or staying on Mount 'Arafat. That night after the hillock rituals, along with thousands of others, Gulbadan and her co-pilgrims would leave Mecca and travel three miles east to Mina. 'Arafat was another nine miles east.

Although they were in an exclusive caravan headed to 'Arafat, Gulbadan and the Mughal women were in close proximity to the enormous crowd. According to one estimate, two hundred thousand people and three hundred thousand animals were at the prayer meeting at 'Arafat in 1580.[31] Would the numbers in 1577 be radically different? All arrangements were in place, including good-quality camels. Spare camels were necessary, whether on short or long routes. Complex dealings between Ottoman officers and Bedouin elders were the norm. Official subsidies to Bedouins living along the *surre,* the hajj roads, were major incentives that helped officers procure safe passage, the overall security of travelers, and provisions for water and food supplies. Attacks could heighten during periods of food scarcity, such as in late 1577 and 1578.

Pilgrims spent a night at a regular stopover, an uninhabited locality called Muzdalifa. It had an abundant water supply thanks to the historic initiative of Queen Zubaida, who had built a network of water reservoirs. The following day, they arrived at the 'Arafat plateau, which stood out by its well-marked stone boundary. It was essential for pilgrims to arrive on time to hear the qazi's sermon. Ottoman traveler Evliya Celebi reported that his caravan was pressed to hurry forward to arrive in time. In another case in 1671–72, a time of political tension in the area, Bedouins attacked a caravan coming from Basra. Reinforcements from Mecca repelled the assault but the pilgrims nearly missed the meeting in 'Arafat. People hoped for the 'Arafat ritual to take place on a Friday. Prophet Muhammad had promised that if the rite happened on a Friday, greater blessings would ensue.[32]

Here God, here I am, Here God, here I am, chanted the gathered crowd. Gulbadan, Salima, Gulnar, the younger Mughal women, and everyone else uttered the phrase for an hour. The qazi then instructed the congregants about the course of the ritual, stressing the need for proper behavior when throwing stones at the rocks in Mina that symbolized the devil. They were on the 'Arafat plain until sunset, reading the Qur'an, glorifying God, and listening to the sermon. At sunset, the crowd dispersed. Some went back to Muzdalifa. When Celebi made the pilgrimage in the late seventeenth century, he wrote that a group from Khurasan lit hundreds of candles in Muzdalifa, illuminating the quiet, dark landscape. Human ecstasy was interupted only by the rumbling animals. Tents were spread out for miles. Nights were spent in prayer or reading the Qur'an, sleeping under the stars.

Back in Muzdalifa, Gulbadan would collect pebbles for stoning the devil. In the secure care of attendants, respectfully distanced from others, younger and older Mughal women bent over the grainy red ground gathering stones. In the morning, they would head to Mina. Keeping Abraham in mind, Gulbadan would throw seven stones against a designated rock. Niece Salima would do so for a second time; for the others it would be the first time. Sultan Khwaja would confer with Gulbadan about sacrificing an animal, its meat to be distributed among the poor. Mughal offerings were starting to be on display in line with the declaration in the Qur'an: "It is neither their meat nor blood that reaches God, but your piety."[33]

Pilgrims spent several days in Mina after the 'Arafat ceremonies. Two covered markets in Mina were well known. Caravan officers and public criers regularly announced that traders were under the protection of the Ottoman sultan. The smaller market was known as the Syrian market because of its connection with Syrian goods and merchants. The sherif owned a residence near the market and had the area illuminated during the pilgrimage season. Artisans decorated coffeehouses and tents with aromatics, and trinkets were everywhere. Mina was renowned for the sale of Bahrain pearls. Food and beverages, luxury goods, precious stones, and perfumes were sold in freestanding stalls.[34]

The Mughals loved bazaars and had made their own into an art form. It is possible that the fabled Mina bazaar, held behind the Mughal fort, was inspired by its Arabian counterpart. As the Mughal bazaars grew in fame, they continued to display how special they were. In the late seventeenth-century Mina Bazaar of Delhi, only the emperor and the royal women participated, looking at select objects presented by select merchants, a change from the sixteenth century, when many more merchants came to the royal bazaar displaying goods for royalty. Gulbadan and Salima might muse about the origins of the Mughal bazaar as nieces Salima and Gul'izar busied themselves procuring Bahrain pearls for relatives in Fatehpur-Sikri.

Sultan Khwaja, the hajj commander, due to return to Hindustan immediately after the pilgrimage, bought gifts for the emperor. In addition to a splendidly designed metal or china *zamzamiyya*, a flask containing the holy zamzam water, a must, he might have purchased some lustrous Bahrain pearls and possibly a Qur'an copied with ink made from zamzam water, which had protective powers. He may even have bought prayer beads and perfumes.[35]

Back in Mecca, the group circled the Ka'ba, and then went once more to Mina to throw stones at all the rocks, not just the targeted one as in the first instance. After the second brief trip to Mina, the hajj rites drew to a close. Gulbadan, her granddaughter, Salima, the two Mughal nieces, Gulnar, Sultan Khwaja, every person in the Mughal group, and all and sundry who had completed the rites were now the revered hajji. This age-old honorific denoted that they had fulfilled one of the five canonical obligations of Muslim practice. A large community of hajjis spread out in the Holy Land in 1577 as in other times. They declared their faith explicitly, the avowal being another pillar of the faith. Regular prayers, fasting during daylight in the month of Ramadan, and the obligatory alms, or *zakat,* were other key principles of Muslim life.

But there was an even higher principle in Islam—*sadaqa,* voluntary benevolence. Alms to the less fortunate surpassed everything. Sufis, scholars, widows, orphans, and mujawirs flocked to the areas that Gulbadan visited: the Muzdalifa grounds, the Mina bazaar, and 'Arafat, as well as the Great Mosque and Mecca neighborhoods. Food, clothes, and books were standard items for donation, as was water: at Akbar's fountain in the pilgrim house, the poor drank plentifully. In the famous Ottoman public kitchens, intellectuals, students, functionaries of the mosques, travelers, and indigents all ate together. Fully functional in the mid-sixteenth century, a hundred years after it began, one Istanbul kitchen served fifteen hundred people twice a day. After the dignitaries, students from colleges attached to the mosque, doorkeepers, guards, proctors, and kitchen staff finished eating, the remaining food was given to the poor.[36]

Sultan Khwaja had much to accomplish before leaving for Hindustan. To keep up with the rhythm of the monsoon and align with seasonal winds across the seas, he had to return no later than September 1577.

He left behind in Arabia not only the many pilgrims and merchants but also Gulbadan and the haraman. At what point the princess and her group decided to stay on in Arabia we do not know. The timing of her decision or discussions surrounding her choice are not stated in the sources. All Mughal court chroniclers, however, note that the women stayed nearly four years in Arabia. Unanimous in their decision to leave the harem, they were likewise united in their choice to be vagabonds, mujawirs in the desert lands.

Alongside making select and secure arrangements for the women, foremost among the Khwaja's jobs was to ensure that his attendants conveyed the twelve thousand precious robes of honor to the sherif of Mecca. Ornamented mules would bear the Mughal gifts. The Khwaja also had with him a large amount of cash in addition to other, unspecified gifts. "To the sharif of that land, who had always sent presentations, and the rarities of that country, there were sent a lakh of rupees and splendid goods," Akbar's historian diligently recorded.[37] Typical specialties from Hindustan included silk, linen, brocade, sandalwood, and candlesticks. It was not the first time that such lavish presents came in the Mughal emperor's name. On two previous occasions, Akbar had sent goods and cash amounts of 600,000 and 500,000 rupees to the people of Mecca and Medina.

The rulers of Bengal and Gujarat too had been sending sumptuous gifts to the Holy Cities. Sultan Muzaffar II of Gujarat transcribed with his own hands two copies of the Qur'an in gold water and sent them to Mecca. He allocated a yearly grant for the upkeep of these special books. He also constructed a school in Mecca and a place for the distribution of water to pilgrims, and set aside endowments for teachers and students. Another sultan of Gujarat reserved the revenues derived from villages near Cambay for distribution to the poor in Holy Cities. Kings of Golconda in southern India sent great quantities of rice as alms to be given to the poor.[38]

As Sultan Khwaja went about his responsibilities, Gulbadan and her cohort went about theirs. The princess began to hand out alms magnanimously—bread to the needy, donations to orphans and widows, and food and cash for scholars and dervishes. Much was possible within their means.

In addition, when delighted by a military victory, fine verse, or excellent shooting, Mughals scattered coins over the harbinger of good news. Harem women valued coins as gifts. An emperor or empress would also strew coins in public when they traveled through a village or town. Coins were distributed when royal Mughal women visited Sufi tombs. And coins were given to the needy on imperial birthdays and accession days. A Mughal king or prince sat on one side of the weighing scale, following a Hindu practice that Akbar had adopted. Imperial servants balanced the weight of the royal person against an equal weight of food (such as grain, saffron, and clarified butter) and coins. These were distributed to the poor.

The less fortunate were everywhere—near the Great Mosque, where they regularly sought shelter, near the bazaar between Marwa and Safa, and near the fountain that Gulbadan's nephew had built. To all and sundry, the highly visible Gulbadan and her companions liberally dispersed alms, coins, and necessities. There was an immense shortage of grain deliveries in Mecca, Medina, and the surrounding areas.[39] Sufis holding the *kashkul* would take with humility whatever was put in their crescent-shaped bowl, which was large enough to hold food and water. Mendicants would accept offerings in the sea coconut shells, which washed up on the shores of the Arabian Sea.[40] Beggars readily took alms; coins were special. The poor Indians, condemned to the margins of the city of Mecca, also came forward to take alms.

Twelve

Send Them Back

~

AFTER TEN DAYS ON THE ROAD, A ROUGH, PERILOUS TERRAIN of 280 miles, the Mughal haraman stopped in Kuba. A "multitude of people" convoyed with them.[1] Although the pearl-like Kuba mosque was "in ruinous condition" due to age, for Gulbadan, her relatives, staff, and caravan folk, seeing the venerable site, which had a date palm in the courtyard that the Prophet had planted with his own hands, was nothing short of viewing divinity. [2]

Local guides and reciters would remind the royal party that when deniers in Mecca had threatened Prophet Muhammad's life, he migrated to Medina in 622, taking with him his freshly emergent vision. Three miles south of Medina, it was in Kuba that he built a glorious white mosque. Archangel Gabriel enlightened him in a dream and gave him auspicious signs. Here, the Prophet established his nascent monotheistic community before making Medina his home.

As with other rites, Sherif Abu Numay II of Mecca and the local authorities in Medina enabled the Mughal women's travel to Kuba, Medina, and neighboring areas. Traveling in these parts was akin to peeling the layers of an onion: there were stark and bare hilltops, valleys with sparse villages, numerous shrines, arrival gates, and history at each step. For the curious mind and anyone with an appreciation for serendipity, the land held great promise. Whichever direction travelers took to come into Medina, there would be numerous possibilities for refreshing their tired eyes. The Mughal convoy took the customary route from Mecca, which cut through Kuba, an essential site associated with the Prophet, where travelers often stopped, and also a favorite picnic ground for Medinans.

Nothing was more soothing to the eye weary of the glaring sun than the date groves and rose gardens around Kuba. Songs of nightingales arose from the village trees. The group would eagerly wait to see the point where the Prophet had received a vision from Archangel Gabriel, and where he had built a mosque: "Such is this ancient mosque where prayers are heard by God," wrote the Ottoman traveler Evliya Celebi. Gulbadan, Salima, Gulnar, and younger and older royals quenched their parched throats with the water at the foot of the large lotus tree, reminiscent of the soothing zamzam of Mecca, still fresh in their minds. They longed to view the small prayer niche where the Prophet had regularly prayed. There was a hole in it, a window that opened in the direction of Mecca. The thought of the Prophet looking through the hole and desiring his old home would fill them with amazement. Such was the magic of this village, where they saw many sacred symbols.[3]

The schedule of visits in Kuba was straightforward: the Kuba mosque and that of 'Ali, the Prophet's cousin and the husband of Fatima, his beloved daughter. 'Ali had risked his life by sleeping in Muhammad's bed to impersonate him, thereby thwarting an assassination attempt and ensuring the Prophet's escape from Mecca. There were lush gardens as well as a famous lodge that the current Ottoman sultan, Murad, had built to house and support the pious and dervishes. Funded by the sultan's foundation, it attracted a shaikh, who was based there and who taught theological subjects.[4] Places like Kuba (and Medina) were major centers for the study of traditions pertaining to the Prophet's life and actions. Scholars were attracted to these eminent places of learning.

Hidden amid the chief sites of Kuba were wells, gardens, mosques, and edifices of the women of the Prophet. Across the street from the garden of Iram, easily missed by the visitor, was the mosque of 'Ayesha, Muhammad's favorite wife. In Iram garden was the Well of Aris that the Prophet had dug. The oxen attached to this well drew out healing water day and night. After they performed ablutions, the Mughal women would sit and converse under the lemon and orange blossoms. Inside the Prophet's date garden was yet another well, Women's Well, with its "pure life-giving" water famous for healing seventy ailments afflicting women. If she had a difficult labor, she drank this therapeutic water and her womb opened. If she sipped it during menstruation, her bleeding stopped and she could "have intercourse again." Virgins bathed here. Dedicating it to his women, the Prophet named the orchard and the well the Garden of Women.[5]

Obscured in more renowned structures, these gardens and wells had their lore and history. Like the intrepid and resolute Fatima, the Prophet's daughter, they were imperceptibly present in the land. Gulbadan and her companions would soak in the splendor of the rich yet hidden parts women played in early Islam. Fatima had nurtured her father when he was hurt during the battle of Uhud, north of Medina, where he lost his tooth. A relic, the Shrine of the Tooth, was a must-see for visitors. Untiringly, Fatima visited the graves of the martyrs of Uhud. Mughal women would again hear stories of Fatima's resilience in her poverty-stricken marriage, her dignity in scarcity, and her grief at the death of her father. She fought hard when the first caliph impeded her from inheriting property. Among the few women in Islam to hold powers of intercession in the cause of justice and forgiveness to sinners, she exemplified bounteousness.

Once you saw such grounds of sacredness, a slight shift occurred—a slender reallocation of leitmotifs. The story was still Prophetic; only now the feminine (such as the magical Women's Well) filled spaces in one's thinking. It was said that ten houris came bearing a jug of water from a river in paradise to wash the newly born Fatima.[6] Which story dominated Gulbadan's thoughts? Whose power did she muse on? Feminine power was inexhaustible. It lay tucked in sediments of virtue and duty and around and behind omnipresent gods.

Amid feminine memorials of courage and generosity, Gulbadan would see herself in a much larger framework. Punitive, restrictive orders no longer mattered. Enclosed harem life was so far from her present reality as to be nonexistent. Figures like Fatima or Hagar, at once extinct and extant, served as signs. Aunt Khanzada's heroic sacrifice to save her brother in war would emerge in flashes. The way she turned her face away upon meeting Babur after ten years was for Gulbadan an enduring image. She raised her hand imperiously, expressing distaste for the man who had traded her for his kingly interests.[7] And yet she stood by him. Textured generosity, empathy, and grief reigned across epochs and geography.

To Gulbadan, the most significant embodiment of generosity was her own mother Dildar. She would once more ponder her mother's capaciousness. How stoically Dildar had shared the princess and her brother with Maham, the senior Mughal matriarch. For the itinerant princess, bold thinking was not novel. Meticulous reasoning had brought her this far into the majesty of the Arabian Desert. In this fabled land, she would augment her acts, find her truth, and claim the richness of feminine inheritance that she had garnered over time.

In Kuba and in Medina, Gulbadan's moment of truth came to be aligned with the neglected and disadvantaged. Fatima's unparalleled munificence, the healing waters, and the succulent dates upon majestic trees were all cues to give and share. Giving donations and alms and being charitable was a way to level the playing field with the less fortunate. In other words, when you aided the poor, *you* became the beneficiary, *you* were enriched. *Your* poverty was reduced. *You* expanded; *your* confines vanished. In a generous model like Fatima, the princess would locate a theologically grounded, empathic conception of Islam. In the near-symphonic invocations of Muhammad and his Qur'an by people of all kinds and everywhere—in her own caravan and all over the globe—she would find that boundaries and restrictions dissolved. Everyone could drink from any well and heal by eating the same dates. A thought formed; a new language emerged in Gulbadan's lush acts.

The air was soft and balmy at that time of the year, balmier if Gulbadan's convoy arrived in Medina in the evening. Bright foliage could be seen, the jingle of waterwheels heard. Luxuriant maize, wheat, barley, and patches of clover gleamed in the sun. Palms with stately columnar stems swayed majestically in the desert breeze. Well-known varieties such as *el-shelebi* or *ajwah*, loaded with ripening fruit, were found in this region. *El-hilwah*, a large date, was exceedingly sweet. Of *el-birni*, it was said that it could cure many sicknesses. *Sayhani* had a lovely legend. The Prophet, holding 'Ali's hand, happened to pass beneath this date tree. The tree cried: "This is Mohammed the Prince of Prophets, and this is Ali the Prince of the Pious."[8]

Ancient oases were spread out in these parts. Rings of topography enveloped Medina. High basaltic rocks first came into view for the traveler coming from the Syrian or northern road, the usual route of the Damascene caravan in which Evliya Celebi came. Then emerged Wadi al-Kura, a valley also called Old Medina, a former Jewish settlement that was three days' travel north of the city. It was also the area of the battle of Uhud, where Hamza, the Prophet's valiant uncle, had fought. Those coming from the west on the Yanbu road first came across barren clay fields, then the valleys, before entering Medina. For those arriving from the east on the Najd road, plains of clay were followed by a stretch of mausoleums.

Soon after crossing plains of clay and gravel, the Mughal cavalcade would see the orchards and gardens of Medina and the dome of the Mosque of the Prophet reaching to the sky. Their eyes dazzled by the luminous dome, the believers would cry out in awe. Men and women in the caravan would thank Allah that they had made it to his city. They would give blessings to Emperor Akbar for facilitating their visit. "The camels that were exhausted suddenly became strong again," wrote Celebi of his arrival. The horses whinnied and the donkeys cried out.[9]

The men, women, and children of Medina came out to greet the pilgrims. Boys holding little baskets they had bound themselves from palm branches raised them toward visitors atop camels and horses and on foot. Gulbadan would throw coins into their little baskets. The Mughal women followed suit. "Praise be to God. . . . May God accept your visit," the boys said. "Praise be to God," Gulbadan would reply. Singing eloquent odes, women and children walked alongside the caravan to Medina. In deep, melodious voices, women recited the *mawlid,* poems for Prophet Muhammad's birthday that made one's flesh tingle.[10]

The procession entered the walled city of Medina through the Egyptian gate, the one in closest proximity to the road from Kuba. A large tower bordered the gate on each side. Red, black, and white stones were pressed into the arches and on the walls. *Lord grant me a goodly entrance and a goodly exit, and sustain me with Your Power* was the subtle verse recited by all as they entered the gate.[11] Except for the Mosque of the Prophet, at the time there were no prayer houses or mosques inside the walled city of Medina. They were all outside. Local houses were mostly four or five stories tall, with lime-coated roofs. The houses had no orchards or gardens. Madrasas, water dispensaries, soup kitchens, Qur'an schools, and establishments for the poor and needy were to be found, as were many markets and public houses. A twelfth-century lunatic asylum was fully functional.

Evliya Celebi says that he pitched a tent outside the Egyptian gate. From his description, it appears that the governor of Damascus, in whose hajj caravan Celebi came, had a tent city set up at the northern entry point to Medina. From there, the governor could see Medina to the south and Mount Uhud to the north.[12]

Whether they stayed within the city limits or in royal tents pitched outside the walls, Gulbadan and her companions were surrounded by poor visitors, travelers, and wayfarers who elected to live in Medina. Poor visitors and dervishes crowded wells, mosques, gardens, and mausoleums, on streets or near the water fountains. Pilgrims, soldiers, and faqirs traveling in the Mughal caravan dwelt in these places, the Ottoman documents noted, making them "extremely crowded."[13] Ordinary people who traveled in the Mughal caravan camped all over Medina, noticeably around the sacred Mosque of the Prophet, which was, in the words of Sultan Murad's edict, "detrimental to the interests of the city of Medina as their crowding led to scarcity of provisions."[14]

The problem of living arrangements for the underprivileged haunted Sultan Murad at this time. Existing *ribats*, or hostels, were rundown. Several smaller sanctuaries supported by imperial foundations were in urgent need of repair. Murad's father had planned to construct a residential courtyard surrounded by cells on the famous Baki cemetery near the grave of the third caliph. What came of it, Ottoman sources don't mention. Murad's councilors pondered whether the courtyard of the storehouse where the city's grain was kept could be used. A large room with a stove and fireplace could easily be added to the premises.[15]

Sitting amid his ministers in the stately Istanbul chambers, Sultan Murad was preoccupied. He likely played with his long, full mustache, which tapered along his lower lip. As he pondered the state of damage in Medina, it would seem to him as if everything needed repair. Even the books in the library attached to the Mosque of the Prophet needed rebinding. In the entire city of Medina, there was not a single suitable bookbinder. "And if we find one, he will charge a lot of money," members of Murad's council noted.[16] The sultan's biggest problem was what to do with the poor in Arabia, who often slept on the streets and crowded sacred precincts.

Five years into his accession to the Ottoman throne, Murad had plenty on his mind. His claim to being the sultan of the Hijaz hinged upon providing safety and housing and daily amenities to pilgrims and residents. Obliged to make the Holy Land accessible and hospitable to everyone, he found the task challenging. Far from his Arabian domains, Murad had to work with an intricate web of bureaucracy and engage in complex and messy financial arrangements.

In Mecca, the sherif was the key authority in all matters. Although Sherif Abu Numay I recognized Turkish power soon after Murad's forefather conquered Egypt and the Holy Cities in 1516–17, successor sherifs remained predominant not only in the eyes of Meccans but also in the view of Islamic monarchs the world over, who regularly sent largesse, gifts, robes, and cash to him. According to one estimate, the sherif received one-quarter of the value of any ship that wrecked on the Mecca side of the Red Sea shore. From the donations for the upkeep of the people of Mecca that came from abroad, the sherif got one-fourth of the total. In addition, he received one-tenth of all imported goods, including one-tenth of all cargo on all Indian ships bound for Jeddah.[17] The same amount applied to *Salimi* and *Ilahi*, upon which Gulbadan and the haraman traveled. That sum was in addition to the cash and material donations that Emperor Akbar had sent to the sherif.

For much of the grain supply and general assistance for the yearly pilgrimage, Murad relied on the Egyptians. In 1577, the year Gulbadan and her group landed in Arabia, there was a massive shortage of grain. An additional administrative difficulty was that no Ottoman governor resided in the region. Only small detachments of soldiers or agents accountable to the governor of Egypt were stationed in Mecca and Medina. Permanent representatives of the governor of Egypt were based at Murad's court, serving as liaisons between their master and Istanbul. Such men were important agents in fostering Murad's power in Arabia.

Then there were the subjects of the shah of Persia, whom the Sunni Ottomans eyed with suspicion. They worried that Persian Shi'a pilgrims traveling to Arabia would contact supporters of the shah operating in Ottoman territory. Potential spy networks and rabble-rousing were worrisome affairs. For the Persians going on a pilgrimage, it was simplest to travel to Baghdad and from there to the port of Basra, which was in Ottoman hands. By 1565, it was no longer possible for them to take this route. The Ottomans required all Persian pilgrims to take the official caravan route by way of Damascus, Cairo, and Yemen. Basra was out of the question. The Portuguese had expansionist interests on the eastern coast of the Arabian Peninsula where Basra was located. In Basra and Bahrain, many notables supported the Portuguese and countered the Ottomans. Iran and Turkey were again at war. Inflation was raging. The prices of basic commodities had gone up.[18]

As if all this was not enough, Murad III received urgent word from the governor of Egypt that untoward happenings were taking place in Mecca and Medina. Presently in Medina, the harem matriarchs of Akbar the Great were the source of a special problem.

In and around Medina, customary sites would be on Gulbadan's itinerary. Local guides solemnly pointed out the important landmarks. North of Medina, on the road to Damascus, lay an orchard-lined mosque with two prayer niches. Fourteen years after Muhammad's migration from Mecca, it was here that Archangel Gabriel revealed a verse to him. After that revelation, the Prophet changed the *kibla*, the direction of prayer, from Jerusalem to Mecca. At this very mosque, he gave sermons to migrants. Prayer houses, gardens, prayer niches, flower and vegetable commons, and lemon and orange groves intoxicated visitors with sweet citrus smells. Sometimes the water in the wells was so close to the surface that there was no need to raise it with a rope—one could skim it by hand.[19]

Going by rocky roads full of date palms, acacia, and toothpick trees, the Mughal group would reach the Shrine of Hamza, an hour north of Medina. On the way, they performed two customary prostrations of prayer at the Stone Platform, where, dressed in Davidic coat-of-mail, his sword at his waist, Muhammad had called his community to prayer just before the battle in Uhud, where his "noble tooth was martyred."[20] At each of these memorials, Gulbadan came upon the consequence of generosity that was threaded through Islamic history. Camel sacrifices, great feasts, and losing one's life in battle exemplified magnanimity. The Qur'an emphasized caring for the weak and poor, and stressed that the wealth that came from God "is ultimately God's" and must be shared. *Karim*, the generous one, was one of the ninety-nine names of Allah.[21]

The Prophet's example was everywhere. And if you looked closely, stellar women embodied the spirit of sharing, giving, and nurturing—drawing from the life force embedded in the land itself. Natural sources for ailments, healing water, and powerful gardens were ubiquitous. At a popular stopover, pilgrims cooked sweet pudding and distributed it to the poor. The Prophet himself came once a year, it was said, and cooked *ashura*, a sweet pudding. Using the open-air fireplaces, Mughal assistants would follow tradition and distribute food to the poor.

Visiting the site of the battle of Uhud was a must. The ground of Uhud was red because of the blood from the Prophet's broken tooth. If they performed two prostrations, the women were told, they would be protected from natural disasters. Did the Mughal visitors touch the ground with their fingers and rub their teeth with it? It was a tested remedy.[22]

The party visited shrine after shrine, traversed dense wadis, and viewed bare mountains and rich corn fields. Bounties like dates and corn were available thanks to the warm springs in the valley floors. There was a constant call to prayer. The Prophet's imprints were all over, as if the earth was soaked with tradition and stories of his companions and women. There was no end to how much you could view and learn. Mujawiran lived in the desert their entire lives precisely so that time would not be a constraint.

Be it outside Medina or inside the city gates, vagabond lifeforce was essential to discovering, learning, and being mesmerized. Millions flocked each year to see and honor the Prophet's mosque and tomb, renowned as the Garden of Paradise. Friday prayers were performed only in this mosque, which was within the city limits. During the pilgrimage, it was hard to find a place to kneel. The head of the Prophet's mosque, or *shaikh al-haram*, was the main authority, assisted by a jurist, a castle warden of the city garrison, a chief gunner, and an artillery officer. No one was allowed into the Medina castle in the city—the fort or garrison of Medina, as it was variously called. The treasury of the city was located here.[23]

Girded in white loincloths, twelve black saintly eunuchs walked behind the shaikh al-haram to receive Gulbadan and the royal party. The shaikh, himself a eunuch, and his men had been in the Holy Sanctuary for much of their lives. By the late seventeenth century, there were seven hundred black eunuchs under the government of the shaikh al-haram. They controlled hundreds of gold and silver keys to the grave of the Prophet. Elegantly elongated, embedded with verses, sometimes recast or newly created, the keys were collected over centuries. The shaikh and his eunuchs ministered to exclusive guests during their visits.[24]

Bearing jeweled censers and rose water sprayers, they would take the Mughal group to the gate of the Prophet's grave. One reached here only by passing the grave of Fatima. Walking together at close quarters, Gulbadan, Salima, niece Salima, and others would bow to Fatima and ask for her intercession. The shaikh might have given them a broom. Brooms, having swept the sacred floors, brimmed with blessed energy. There were several highly regarded sweepers on the premises, their deputy the shaikh himself. They swept the outer parts of the mosque, entreated Fatima for her intercession, and recited a verse for her spirit. Praying and praising, the shaikh would welcome the visitors to the Prophet's mosque and the grave area.[25]

The interior decorations were in bad shape. The door curtains and coverings over the Prophet's tomb needed immediate repair. The shaikh had forwarded to Istanbul in 1577 a list of much-needed textiles. Ottoman documents show that fourteen years later, the covering for the Prophet's tomb was manufactured in Istanbul, and curtains and other items were ordered from Egypt.[26]

In this holiest of holy ground, the sanctified air and mythical tradition would take Gulbadan's breath away. But the declining condition of the Prophet's mosque and tomb would be jarring for the visitors. The building fabric of the dome of the small building in the mosque courtyard, used as a treasury, had dangerous fissures. Somehow this ancient section had escaped two major fires in 1256 and 1481. There was leakage in several roofs that covered the mosque compound. The books in the library had been partially eaten by insects. A new library room with bookcases was needed. The mosque wall as far as the Gate of Women needed a touch-up.[27]

The poor and indigent clustered around the monuments, shrines, and colleges. At each place, Gulbadan and the women came across people who needed food and a place to sleep—not only those with meager resources but also sojourners and religious men. Medina, the City of the Prophet, was also famous as the *dar al-hijrah,* the house of migration. Scholars, spiritualists, seekers, and refugees lived indefinitely in the area. At the time of Gulbadan's visit to Medina, by one Ottoman estimate, eight thousand people of meager means lived in pious retreats. An intimate connection with the Prophet's life gave the city a special status. Donations for the learned, devout, and poor of Medina were by the fifteenth century "a popular form of charity throughout the Islamic world."[28]

Courtesy demanded that no one hand out any contributions inside the Prophet's mosque. But there was no dearth of places for Mughal women to distribute food, water, alms, or gifts. The grave of Fatima, with its gilded sarcophagus, was crowded with many kinds of people. Near it dwelled poor residents and pilgrims, and visitors commonly gave them alms. When a girl was born in Medina, she was brought to Fatima's grave for an hour so that she could accrue blessings. Rich and poor frequently visited the grave and surrounding areas. Reciting *Peace Be upon you, O Fatima the Radiant*, Gulbadan and her companions would give out coins and food. Holy men sat around smaller mosques and broken hostels. They would donate coins to the "righteous men" sitting among the poor, who in turn performed for them "a complete recital of the Qur'an."[29]

So much is masked in *sadaqat*, a word of abundance repeatedly used in Ottoman documents for the alms the Mughal haraman gave. The words voluntary or beneficent donation cannot capture its depth. Ethical Judaic and Christian ideas that preceded Islam also amplify the word's meaning. *Sedaka* in Hebrew is a cognate of the Arabic *sadaqat*, and both share the root *sdk*—symbolizing a right, privilege, grant, or gift. In Hebrew, *sedaka* exemplified a moral sense, justice, or righteousness. The Hebrew word *hesed*, or graciousness, associated with hospitality and assistance for the needy, is also related to *sadaqat*. Early Christianity warned against attachment to money and material things; charity and asceticism were pivotal in the creation of monasteries. These "beneficent practices" are also similar to *sadaqat*.[30]

Along with *zakat*, compulsory giving, often in the form of tax, the legality of sadaqat was debated for centuries in theological literature. Theory and practice always blurred, and what mattered in the end was an individual's practice, the distinct choices and style she adopted in being benevolent. An astute donor understood that the right of the poor was essential to any giving.

In the open and in the privacy of the house of God, gifts and donations, including cash, coins, robes, sweet pudding, books, water, and clothes were welcome. Food was well known as "the most essential form of assistance." Words of solace and "small kindnesses" mattered.[31] "Guard yourself against Hellfire even by giving half a date, and if you have none to give, speak a kindly word," said Al-Bukhari, a ninth-century Persian scholar.[32]

Gulbadan and her co-hajjis rapidly became the talk of the town. The women resolutely went about dispersing sadaqat to the poor from India and those in Arabia—in Mecca, Kuba, and the sanctuary of Medina. Agents posted in Mecca and Medina looked on for nearly a year. Then they couldn't wait any longer and sent word to their lord and master, Masih, the governor of Egypt, who rushed a dispatch to Istanbul.[33] Sultan Murad was livid. Gulbadan and her harem co-dwellers' widespread benevolence would spawn political instability.

The Mughal women had stocks of Akbar the Great's gifts and donations—large amounts of cash, contributions in kind, and largesse such as the magnificent robes of honor for the shaikh al-haram, his eunuchs, and staff—and great offerings for the ordinary and poor. By the late seventeenth century, official offerings had to be made in secret. Any subscription given openly to the shaikh or eunuchs in Medina would result in their tearing it all to pieces. And tearing "you [the giver] to pieces as well."[34]

A great deal of cash was offered to the sherif of Mecca as well as to the shaikh al-haram in Medina. The amount that the Mughals gave the sherif of Mecca was large, and still the hajj commander complained to Emperor Akbar upon his return that he felt fleeced by how much extra cash he had to give.[35]

With the communication from the governor of Egypt, Sultan Murad had all the particulars in front of him. There was no doubt that the sultan had a delicate problem on his hands. He would have to deal firmly but subtly with the trouble brewed by the female relatives of the Mughal emperor. Civility was imperative. Already besieged by difficulties with Persia, Murad was at the time struggling to find ways to finance projects for the poor in Mecca and Medina.

As "Servitor of the Holy Cities," Murad had the responsibility of taking care of people in Arabia. His authority hinged on that very act. Murad was to be animated in the minds of people each time a house was built, a hostel erected, or food provided for the poor. It was all too clear to Murad that in her persistent almsgiving, the powerful patroness Gulbadan and her cohort had crossed a line. The princess, her almond-shaped eyes lined with kohl and strands of gray in her hair, stood resolutely and delivered donations in the Haram Sharif, the most sacrosanct Great Mosque in Mecca. She relieved and sustained the poor with her graceful bestowal of sadaqat.

As he considered the specifics, Murad became more and more irate. Self-assured Gulbadan and her companions handed out bounties to all and sundry. In Mecca and Medina, in the precincts of the great and smaller mosques, in front of mausoleums and sacred neighborhoods and hostels and fountains, the women flourished in the act of giving, visible to all in all sorts of places.

What was worse for Murad was that the harem denizens exuded by their very presence the might of Emperor Akbar. The Mughal's bid to project himself as a great, pious ruler was vividly apparent. Annual hajj caravans that matched the Egyptian and Damascene processions, lavish subventions, fountains, hostels, and significant sadaqat poured into Arabia. After Gulbadan's convoy of 1577, Akbar sent four more pilgrim caravans between 1577 and 1580 with large amounts of cash and robes of honor. The titles that Akbar took on in 1579, *Badshah-i Islam, Imam-i 'Adil*—King of Islam, Supreme Interpreter of Law—enhanced his claim to power in the Islamic world.

Although subservient to Shariah, Murad was the presumed supreme Muslim monarch. Not only was he the Servitor of the Holy Cities—the great protector of his subjects, visitors, and pilgrims—he was also the "Inheritor of the Great Khilafat."[36] *Khilafat* was a divinely ordained institution and the Qur'an attests to its origin. The *khalifa*, the holder of khilafat, was the head of the Muslim community and revered as the "Shadow of God on Earth." He was the symbol of the unity of the community (*ummah*) and the supremacy of law. By the fourteenth century, in the interpretation of an Egyptian qazi, the khilafat could be assumed by anyone who established his authority by might and military. In the fifteenth century, a distinguished jurist, Jalal al-Din Dawwani, outlined a theory that stressed the utmost importance of Shariah, the law, as the guiding light of the Muslim state. He argued that a monarch who governed with justice and who directed his state in accordance with Shariah "was entitled to hold the dignity of Khilafat." This doctrine became a standard exposition on khilafat among monarchs, including the Mughals, and the juridical ground upon which Akbar claimed his high titles.[37]

Enough, Murad would holler. The ensemble of Mughal harem women was now the target not only of the sultan's ire but also of his stringent orders.

In 1578, a *chawush*, or messenger, of Sultan Murad reached Arabia. He had with him two sovereign orders addressed to the authorities in the sacred cities. The first *farman* was jointly addressed to Qazi Husain, at the time civil governor, and to the shaikh al-haram of Mecca. The second was also jointly addressed, to the city judge of Medina and the shaikh al-haram. Mahmud, the agent of the governor-general Masih, would relay both the edicts to the addressees.

Written in Ottoman Turkish on paper scrolls, the royal decrees would be drafted by royal scribes in cursive script and adorned with beautiful imperial seals and the sultan's calligraphic signature. Housed presently in the Turkish State Archives in Istanbul are copies, not original farmans, which are lost. Murad's orders are preserved in Muhimme Defterleri, Registers of Important Affairs, the collection of the copies of the farmans of Ottoman sultans dispatched to provincial, religious, and military officers in all parts of the empire during the sixteenth and seventeenth centuries.

The 1578 orders that reached Mecca and Medina had four standard parts. The first section noted the name and designation of the addressee. Since these were jointly addressed, the name and rank of the senior person preceded those of the second. Then came a succinct summary of the incoming communication, followed by the sultan's reaction to the report. Usually stated in one or two sentences, the sultan used phrases such as "now," "this being so," and "I have commanded." The last part of the order was stern: "I command," "It is imperative that . . ." These were directives to the recipient to take immediate action. Sometimes the recipient was warned of the dire consequences of not carrying out sultanic orders.[38]

"Last year, a multitude of people [came] from India along with the Mughal caravan, but they did not return to their native country and dwelt in the Ka'ba Sharif as *mujawirs*," the sultan wrote to the qazi and shaikh al-haram of Mecca. Large numbers of people of India had been lodging around the Ka'ba, making it extremely crowded and "a source of distress and anxiety to the people of Mecca." "It is imperative," the order noted, that "no one should be permitted to stay outside the Haram Sharif," the Great Mosque. "It is necessary to eliminate the root of the problem," ordered the sultan. "I command," he said, that "as soon as this *farman* arrives . . . be it Mughal caravan or someone else, send them back."[39]

The second decree to the city judge and the shaikh al-haram of Medina featured similar wording. "Last year, a multitude of people had come from India along with the Mughal caravan, but they did not return to their native country and stayed in Medina . . . detrimental to the interests of the city. . . ."

They will become a source of distress and suffering to the people of Medina."
Murad underlined the scarcity of provisions and supplies in Medina. "A
noble decree for the expulsion of the aforementioned caravan has been issued," he noted firmly. "Pay utmost attention to this urgent matter. . . . Send
everyone back."[40]

Although outraged, Murad did not name the root of the problem in
the two eviction farmans that he sent out in 1578. But he firmly instructed
the recipients that be it Mughal caravan or someone else, they were to be
sent back. He maintained the customary graciousness in dealing with royal
Mughal women and Gulbadan, their leader. He did not name anyone specifically. He had hoped to solve the problem by sending everyone back to
their homes after the performance of pilgrimage. But that did not happen.

Gulbadan, the Mughal haraman, staff, and assistants stayed on beyond
1578. It was already a problem for Murad to deal with the sojourners who
had added immense burdens to the scant resources of Mecca and Medina.
And now to have the women of Akbar the Great, "may God eternalize him,"
still residing in Mecca? That was "contrary to Shariah," the sultan stressed.
Even though there was a robust tradition of sojourners in Arabia, enough
was enough.

Two years later, in 1580, Gulbadan and her companions were still on Arabian soil. Thrice more they had accomplished the pilgrimage rituals. Amid
scarcity, danger, and the perils of the raw elements, they lived insouciantly.
According to Akbar's court critic Badauni, they traveled to Karbala, Qom,
and Mashhad, key Shi'a cities.[41] Murad knew that the women had found their
truth and their freedom, which he characterized as indulging in "strange
activities." He sent out a third eviction order. "Stop the distribution of alms,"
ordered Murad. "Send them back," he ordered the sherif of Mecca.[42]

Murad was forced, at long last, to use that stringent and charged Ottoman Turkish word in his eviction order: na-meshru. Na-meshru meant
an inappropriate, erroneous act. It was a castigatory term for anyone who
crossed the limit, such as the Iranians who had been casually sauntering in
the Great Mosque, the Indians generating dirt and smells by crowding, the
stylish, ornamented, perfumed Meccan women at the sacred precincts of
the Great Mosque—and Gulbadan and her cohort. Mujawiran in Arabia,
they kept handing out alms, repeatedly stepping over Murad's sovereign
prerogative. Despite the expulsion orders, no one had been able to send them
back. Under the leadership of the princess, they firmly stood their ground.

Thirteen

Return

~

GULBADAN WOULD LOOK TOWARD THE ARABIAN COAST ONE last time as it faded into the distance. It was the third week of March 1580, when an unspecified number of vessels sailed out of the port of Jeddah. Gulbadan and her companions were upon the *Tezrav*, or Swift One, and Khwaja Yahya, the recent commander of pilgrimage, sailed on a second ship, the *S'ai*, or Effort.[1] Amid a convoy of unnamed boats with pilgrims and merchants, they were headed back to Hindustan. Gliding south from Jeddah, the same course that the harem inmates had taken four years earlier, they cruised upon the waters of the Red Sea. Seven days later, they passed the coral-laden, funnel-shaped channel of the Bab al-Mandab, from which they were expected to turn east into the Gulf of Aden.

Expert guides in trading and seafaring in the Indian Ocean had established that late August through early September, when the tail end of the southwesterly summer wind blew, was a good time to leave the Gulf of Aden for India.[2] Mughal ships typically sailed in consonance with established guidelines around monsoon wind and precipitation patterns. But this time, the *Tezrav* and the convoy of boats had sailed out hastily after Sultan Murad's fourth decree, dated March 16, 1580, in which he renewed the directive to evict the Mughal women. A fifth order of eviction reached Mecca in August 1580, but by that time the haraman had left.[3] They were reluctant to leave, Akbar's court historian noted, but in keeping with the emperor's earnest wish, Yahya persuaded them to return.[4]

Settling into their cabins, the women would express gratitude to God. They might quite possibly recall verses on the hajj from the Qur'an and remind themselves that "striving and fighting in defense of Truth . . . are necessary as tests of self-sacrifice."[5] In the final analysis, Allah knew.

> He knows what is before them
> And what is behind them
> And to God go back
> All questions (for decision).[6]

The gliding vessel gently swayed. A sense of loss would come over the vagabond princess. In the rarefied Arabian land, Gulbadan and the women of the imperial household had traveled to fabled places in the desert and seen the granular details of piety and the splendor of water. Their insights were sharpened and their political acumen was augmented. In their graceful engagements, spread over a long presence in the Holy Land, they reflected the power of the great Mughal emperor.

Gulbadan knew that the harem to which she was returning, a place bound by instruction and discipline, signaled more possibilities than she had thought. "Sometimes, *going back to* and *moving toward* coincide."[7] Since her adventures across the seas, she knew that the ground for freedom was generosity. That freedom was not absolute; it was "won and lost, again and again. It is a glimpse of possibility, an opening, a solicitation without any guarantee of duration."[8] Whether she contemplated such words we cannot say, but it is to be expected that she mused on what lay ahead.

Gulbadan would see her Arabian domicile as an allegory for opening outward—spreading knowledge, wisdom, and influence. A vagabond *within,* she was nourished by her own lush, benevolent actions. She would hold onto the freedom and the grace she had felt in giving sadaqat. She would preserve the abundance of experience that came in tackling kingly dreams, in pondering her generous actions, even though they were classified as na-meshru. *Send them back*—the women might have thought about this expression many times.

Sailors, merchants, and pilgrims on the ships awaited reunions with friends and relatives, perhaps looking at the sweet zamzam water they carried in a receptacle for an elder, rosary beads, or an incense burner for a neighbor. "May the hajj be abundantly rewarded [by God] . . . and sins forgiven."[9] When received with such ritual words, a returning pilgrim would extend blessings that she had accrued in accomplishing the pilgrimage rites, handing out the blessed water and gold-lined guidebooks purchased from the markets and in front of mosques in the Holy Cities.

Songs of praise, Qur'an recitations, auguries from Hafiz's poems, and recollections of the desert filled the royal cabins and the cuddies of ordinary men and women. Taking in the vastness of the sea, looking at the waters with awe, grateful and tired, and restless at the thought of a long sea voyage, royals and non-royals experienced their week upon the Red Sea. Then one day, as they were sailing south toward Aden at the tip of the Red Sea, ominous clouds came, so dark that "the sea became the sky and the sky the sea."[10]

Torrents of water rushed aboard the vessels. The boats began to oscillate. Would they crash on the fatal coral reefs? Sails tore; masts collapsed. How many passengers were pulled into the depths of the sea? The waves roared, and shouts and screams were heard. Khwaja Yahya was horrified, and the haraman panicked. Ancient Arabs and Jews had presciently likened the fragility of ships on the high seas to "a worm clinging on a log."[11] Since time immemorial, this is what sea-bound voyagers feared most of all.

Near Aden, most of the boats were wrecked. This is the only line describing the fate of the Mughal vessels in the imperial *Akbarnama*.[12] There are no other details. It would not have been difficult for experts in Aden to figure out the precise location of the wrecked ships. They frequently dealt with such disasters. Early in the twelfth century, commercial and administrative documents from the Red Sea region note that Aden had a good system of deciphering the location of missing ships. Maritime history records, including the medieval document repository known as the Cairo Geniza, which archaeologists and historians have mined, provide details of shipwrecks, rescue plans, and salvage operations. Specialists with intimate knowledge of weather, maritime topography, and the structure of a sunken ship were able to ascertain the chances of survival of those lost at sea.

The Mughal women, Khwaja Yahya, and other people were on board the ships. Whether their ships went down due to a storm or collision with the coral reefs, we do not know. There is no survivor list. But after disaster hit, Gulbadan, other haraman, and Khwaja Yahya were likely lowered from the ships in rescue boats.

Orchestrated from Aden, salvage was a routine operation, such as in the case of the ship that carried merchandise belonging to the twelfth-century Jewish Tunisian merchant Ben Yiju. His vessel was supposed to have docked in the vicinity of Berbera, an African port west of Aden but, driven against the rocky, constricted passage of the Bab al-Mandab, it went down. Divers went out to collect what they could and brought back half the supply of iron that was being transported on the ship. The operation lasted two days and there were no reported casualties, which meant that everyone got into lifeboats.[13]

That the Mughal boats wrecked "near Aden" suggests that the disaster may have taken place close to the Bab al-Mandab straits, a day and a night's sail away from Aden. How did the news reach Aden? From periodic coasting conducted from Aden? Flotsam? Debris? The fortuitous presence of a diver in the vicinity? How soon experts from the city responded and how quickly they recruited divers is hard to estimate, given the silence in the records. An expedition likely went out, as in other cases, on a "fast vessel, a galley with both sail and oar capability, to ensure speed and efficiency."[14] Gulbadan and others were brought to Aden, says Abul Fazl, and "were in trouble for seven months."[15]

The dazed Mughal party would land with their rescuers in the Sira Bay, with its widespread mud flats. As Aden's historic bay, Sira offered long-term anchorage. Oriented toward the sea, Aden was spread out like an amphitheater. The city was assembled on the narrow plain of an ancient crater. Behind the city, multiple hillocks rose. To anyone approaching from the sea, Aden presented itself as an urban theater. For those "gathered at an open elevated plaza," looking on from the edge, the maritime activities and vistas were gripping.[16]

Soon after the wreck of Gulbadan's ship, in the first week of April 1580, the royal group in Aden heard from Bayazid Bayat. The princess had first met him in Kabul. Since then, he had gained respect for his courage and efficiency, gone on several military operations, held posts in land assessment and revenue settlement, and become the darogha of the imperial treasury. Owing to an inquiry into his sources of wealth, he waited two years in Surat before Emperor Akbar gave him permission to go to Mecca with his wife and three sons.

Bayat sailed from Surat on Governor Qilich Khan Andijani's *Muhammadi*, filled with an assembly of poor pilgrims. As they came into the Daman estuary, they were stopped by the Portuguese, as Gulbadan had been on her out-bound journey in 1577. Demanding payment on behalf of poorer pilgrims, the tax officers boarded the *Muhammadi*, checked its hold, and held Bayat's son Iftikhar for the day. Bayazid paid the large sum, which he would later take from the travelers. After the evening prayer, Iftikhar returned to the ship, and on March 18, 1580, the *Muhammadi* set sail.

Within a fortnight, Bayat, his wife, three sons, and a host of fellow pilgrims were near the hills of Aden. One day, mid-morning, the captain, the pilot, and the people of the *Muhammadi* saw two small boats similar to skiffs coming out of Aden. When the boats drew near, Bayat later wrote, they found out that they had been sent by *Nawab* Gulbadan Begum, Salima Begum, niece Gul'izar Begum, and Khwaja Yahya to bring the news of who was on board the ship and from which port it had set out.

That's what Gulbadan was now called: *nawab*, or a person of high status, a holder of rank, or a powerful land holder—a ruler.[17] If from a royal family, a nawab was also someone upholding the sovereignty of the dynastic line, as Gulbadan had done in raising the flag of Mughal power in the faraway land of the Prophet.

Although the wind was favorable for cruising north on the Red Sea, Bayat asked the master of the ship and the pilot to lower the sails. He wrote out an account of all that had befallen his ship and the passengers and sent it to the royal ladies. Gulbadan praised Bayat's note and the information he provided.[18] Negotiating with the Portuguese and handing over Bulsar would flash through her mind. Along with the Khwaja, she wrote Bayat a reply that reached him after he arrived in Mecca. We do not know what was in the letter aside from words of praise.

It was a great loss that Bayat never got off the *Muhammadi* to pay his respects to the Mughal women. It is tantalizing to think what he might have added to his account had he seen Gulbadan on the final leg of her Arabian adventure.

If they had not in four years absorbed how profoundly an aquatic sensibility was ensconced in the reality of people's lives in the Hijaz, as in poetry and genealogy, the Mughal haraman would do so after their shipwreck.

The cosmology of the Holy Land was saturated with the immense power of seas, oases, ports, and many kinds of water. The sea held a core place in the Qur'an. The term *Arab* signified a space "soaked by the maritime element": Egypt to the north and Yemen to the south, extending into greater Syria and surrounded on all sides by "various seas."[19] Water was both nourishing and terrifying. It gave sustenance, and it killed.

Aden was immersed in creation myths and legends. The city came into being, it was said, with Alexander the Great's explorations. While not a demonic prison, says the sixteenth-century historian Abu Makhrama, Aden had dark origins. It was the site where Satan introduced the first wind instrument, seen in the Qur'an as a "symbol of moral degeneracy—the playing of which is regarded as, at best, inadvisable." Aden "sat near a gateway to hell."[20]

Another legend held that the monkey god Hanuman excavated a tunnel here connecting Arabia and India to save the heroine of the epic *Ramayana*. Enthralled by this version of the *Ramayana*, of which there are many forms and renditions, Ibn Mujawir noted the details in his thirteenth-century account. On top of the Sira Island in Aden's harbor was a well. In fact, it was an entrance to the tunnel Hanuman had dug, which had its other end in Malwa, central India. Sita was abducted by the demon Hadathar, who wanted to transform her into a jinni. After cutting the channel through the night, Hanuman reached Sita, who was asleep below a thorn tree on Sira. He threw her on his back and returned her safely to Rama, her husband, the hero of the *Ramayana*. The version that Mughals knew was the one in which Hanuman rescued Sita from the king of Lanka by building a bridge across the sea. If Gulbadan heard the Aden version, she would have marveled at the twist with jinnis and demons. Ideas and people from India thrived in Aden, as she saw in other parts of the Hijaz. Another story went that a deposed Yemeni prince roamed the coastal plains in southern Yemen disguised as a "one-eyed Indian."[21]

Gulbadan and her hajj cohort would hear many myths and accounts of the sea. Aden was home also to numerous mosques, Sufi hostels, and shrines. An important place of learning, the city attracted learned men, religious scholars, and pilgrims from Morocco to India. A local jurist by the name of Abdullah al-Hindi (from the land of Hind), the son of an enslaved porter, focused on studying the religious sciences. By the time Ibn Battuta came as a guest to his house, al-Hindi was one of the finest and best-known judges of Aden.[22]

Medieval geographers and travelers, among them thirteenth-century Yaqut al-Humani from Aden and fourteenth-century Ibn Battuta, note that Aden was very popular with Indian merchants. There were networks, passages, wind regimes, and the comings and goings of merchants, sailors, maritime patrols, and Muslims, Jews, Hindus, Portuguese, and Egyptians—the single largest "foreign community."[23] Surat would come alive for the Mughal women in Aden.

This place of lore and commerce had also accrued layers of hostile politics. In cataloguing legends, poems, and notes on prominent religious scholars, rulers, and merchants, Abu Makhrama recorded the emerging conflict between the Portuguese and Muslim powers of the western Indian Ocean in his *History of the Port of Aden*.[24] In March 1513, Afonso de Albuquerque, strategist of the Portuguese maritime empire in India, laid out a plan for the conquest of Asian ports that were at the confluence of major trading routes. Aden, Hormuz, Goa, and Malacca were to be sites for the intervention of the Portuguese crown in Asian affairs. The Portuguese succeeded with the other three ports, but failed in their attempt to conquer Aden. Through much of the sixteenth century, however, the Portuguese sailed along the Horn of Africa and the southern coast of Arabia, organizing raiding expeditions.

In 1517, the Egyptians attacked Aden. Then came the Ottomans. Even though they established suzerainty in parts of the Hijaz, they found it hard to maintain control over Yemen. There was discord among the imam in Sanaa, the tribal chiefs, and the Levantine and Circassian mercenaries. In 1538, an Ottoman fleet under the command of Pasha Hadim Suleiman arrived in Aden en route to India. Once in the city, the pasha invited the amir of Aden and his officers to a celebratory feast. After the party, the pasha had the amir executed. He forbade looting Aden and ordered nearly six hundred janissaries to secure the city for the Ottoman sultan. Aden would remain in Ottoman hands till 1635.[25]

To cut the story short, much of Yemen and the port city of Aden were still politically and economically fragile when the Mughal women landed there. Very much like the rest of Arabia that they had traversed, Aden was arid, dependent on food provision from trade and commercial networks. Buffeted by seasonal winds, the entire peninsula suffered from harsh heat. The climate was "stifling," wrote Ibn Mujawir in the thirteenth century. Five hundred years later, Arthur Rimbaud, writing in the 1880s, found Aden like a "horrible rock, without a single blade of grass or a drop of water." From June through September "the dog days [are] here!"[26]

Where did the women stay? Who made the day-to-day arrangements for them? "The governor there did not behave properly," wrote Abul Fazl, not naming the governor. Under Gulbadan's leadership, the Mughal haraman had posed a momentous challenge to the Ottoman sultan, also the overlord of the Yemen region. Her bold actions were by this time known to all key figures in Arabia, including Hasan Pasha, the governor of Yemen, and the unnamed local administrator of Aden. They would also know that Sultan Murad III had prohibited Mughal alms and evicted the harem women.[27]

That the matriarchs involved in the scandal landed in Aden certainly threw the local governor off guard. He was rude, inhospitable, and devoid of the required decorum. Clearly, he did not extend the obligatory courtesies to the royal women. That would mean enabling their stay, safe travel, and movement in the region if they wished—and their subsequent departure. Without the Ottoman laissez-passer, it would have been hard to get around. When Sultan Murad heard about the Aden governor's indecorous manner, Fazl adds, "he punished that ill-fated one."[28]

The women probably resided in the medieval city spread between the crater area and the harbor, amid stone houses, warehouses, palm thatch huts, and widespread sea vistas. Schools, mosques, irrigation channels, water cisterns, and bridges that the Tahirid dynasty built in the late fifteenth and early sixteenth centuries were still in use.

Although Aden was reliant on trade for food, the waters of the Gulf of Aden and the Arabian Sea provided much of the required fish. Dugong, a sea mammal from the tropical waters that was found in other seaports close to Aden, was part of the diet. Fish brought in funds because it was also used as fodder and fertilizer. Likewise, salt was used both for local consumption and preservation and for export.

Aden's advantageous location, close to Bab al-Mandab, meant that it controlled the commerce between India and the Red Sea, especially the supply of the highly popular frankincense, myrrh, and ambergris used in aromatics and perfumes. Southward facing, looking to the Gulf of Aden and the Arabian Sea, Hadramaut Valley was long renowned for its frankincense trees. Yemeni highlands in the north had a profusion of coffee plants. Coffee was new to the region, and only a few decades prior had become a favored drink.

After seven months in burning-hot Aden, the Mughal women left. Gulbadan's final exit from Aden is shrouded in silence.

The "noble caravan" landed in Surat, then went to Ajmer, where the handsome thirteen-year-old Prince Salim, "the pearl of the crown," received his great-aunt Gulbadan. Each day, court grandees came out to welcome the princess and her hajj companions. Salim escorted the women's group to the shrine of the beloved Sufi saint Muin al-Din Chishti, where they circumambulated the tomb and gave alms to the mendicants and poor. The royals then proceeded to Fatehpur-Sikri. The procession passed through Bagru, Kishangarh, Mehandipur, and other small places. Grandees kept coming to greet the returned Mughal hajj caravan.

On April 13, 1582, the convoy reached Khanwa, thirty-seven miles west of Fatehpur-Sikri. Recently back from a campaign against his half brother in Kabul, Emperor Akbar met the Mughal haraman here. In Gulbadan's "auspicious advent," he "received the light of bliss." Khwaja Yahya paid homage to the emperor and produced a petition from the dignitaries of the Hijaz along with a list of presents. Amid continued welcome and hospitality in the royal encampment in Khanwa, they stayed awake and spent the night "in pleasing discourses." With graciousness, Akbar inquired after the women's health. "The sorrowful ones of the arid desert were refreshed," wrote Abul Fazl. The next day, the "chaste, secluded ladies" went to Fatehpur-Sikri.[29]

Bega Begum had died while her haram friends were away in Arabia, but Hamida Banu Begum impatiently waited to salute her dear friend Gulbadan.

Father Rudolph Acquaviva and Father Monserrate—members of the first Jesuit mission to Akbar's court—were in Fatehpur-Sikri. Bible in hand, Acquaviva gave lessons in the Christian faith to Prince Murad.

Three years prior, to the bewilderment of the clergy and several court members, the emperor had promulgated the famous Infallibility Decree. Prepared by a leading jurist and signed by a premier judge, the document, *Mahzar*, gave Akbar the power to interpret the law of Islam. As supreme arbiter in civil and ecclesiastical matters in his land and a godlike king, Akbar would be the final authority in all legal matters concerning his state and people. Akbar styled himself as "Padshah of Islam," "Imam of Justice," and Caesar—all favored usages of the Ottomans. In bearing these titles, Akbar posed a challenge to the Ottoman dynasty's claim to be the protector of the Holy Muslim Cities. He went further and took the revered appellation "Amir-al-Muminin," Commander of the Faithful, which "even the Ottoman Sultans had not dared to assume publicly."[30]

Gulbadan would be ambivalent about her nephew's new legal claims. A year before her return, Akbar stopped the donations as well as the hajj caravan to the Holy Cities. Mughal amounts for disbursement—Yahya took 400,000 rupees, and the commander of the hajj, Hakimul Mulk Gilani, 500,000 rupees in 1580—were hugely welcome in Mecca and Medina. Akbar sent a polite letter to the sherif of Mecca expressing regrets that the subvention for 1581 could not be sent because of his engagements in suppressing a revolt in Kabul.[31] This was a subtle Mughal rejoinder to the Ottoman orders against the princess and the women of the royal household.

Akbar's authorized historian, Abul Fazl, would soon start work on the first official history of the Mughal Empire. Although there was no mention of Murad's edicts, Fazl devoted extensive paragraphs to Gulbadan's Arabian journey. In an illusive depiction, he labeled the vagabond princess a chaste and secluded lady.

Fourteen

The Books of Gulbadan

~

ON THE BANKS OF THE RIVER RAVI IN THE PROSPEROUS agrarian province of Punjab, Lahore was earning a reputation as a grand Mughal city. Three years after Gulbadan came back to Hindustan, in late 1585, Akbar moved his government there. For over a decade, the fort of Lahore had been getting a facelift, rebuilt handsomely in kiln-burnt brick and stone, its eleventh-century mud-brick foundations barely visible. In the interior of the solid Mughal fort was the stately harem where Gulbadan had relocated with the Mughal and Rajput Hindu women. A shortage of water, which was in any case of poor quality in Fatehpur-Sikri, was a catalyst for the royals to move. Lahore also was a strategic location for Akbar to keep track of his territories to the northwest; if required, he could take swift military action. Splendid guesthouses, awe-inspiring pilgrimage centers, bustling bazaars, delightful gardens, and a potpourri of languages and cultures added to Lahore's appeal.[1]

Gulbadan was not in pursuit of legendary gardens, shrines, or mosques. Curiosity, she knew, began *within*—a wandering instinct created a mujawir— a thought likely to have become entrenched during her Arabian sojourn. Five years after her return, she began another astonishing journey, this time from behind the parapets of the harem in Lahore. A new vision within the ramparts, her venture was linked once more with her nephew's ambitions.

Around 1587, Akbar made an announcement that would transform the idea of record keeping in Mughal history. Like his idea of the stone-walled Sikri harem, his latest declaration was in line with his determination to be remembered as an unprecedented monarch. The emperor could not read or write; he was an *ummi*, an inspired mystic, or someone whose knowledge came directly from divinity, not schooling. Each evening, select reciters read books aloud to Akbar. Badauni wrote that he had been chosen as one of Akbar's readers because of his sweet voice. Over twenty-four thousand book and manuscript collections were in the imperial library and the harem precincts. Books even accompanied battles in the armed cortege.[2]

The *kitabdar*, or head librarian, his assistants, and staff catalogued, numbered, and classified works, entering their details into separate registers for each subject, including astronomy, music, astrology, mythology, books of advice, and commentaries on the Qur'an. Scribes, calligraphers, and bookbinders busily worked in the library and ateliers, encasing manuscripts in silk, binding them with lacquer or leather, and engraving and inscribing them.[3]

This book-loving, greatly ambitious Emperor Akbar arrived at a historic decision. It was time to compile a monumental history of his empire so that posterity would never forget his grandeur or his dynasty. *Akbarnama*, or the History of Akbar, was to be *the* official history of the Mughal Empire, unrivaled in scope. Abul Fazl, the emperor's chosen chronicler and devotee, felt that such a history had to start at the very beginning. Even though it was to be all about the emperor and the splendid empire he created, ancestors were imperative to the story, as grand roots gave legitimacy to power.

And so in 1587, Akbar sent out orders to several "servants of the state" and "older members of the Mughal family" to write their impressions of earlier times, which would be used for Abul Fazl's official history.[4] Among the officers and servants, the emperor selected Bayazid Bayat, who had sent a letter to Gulbadan from aboard his ship in the Aden peninsula. Presently, he oversaw the imperial kitchen. Jawhar, the former water carrier of Humayun, was among the invitees.

Akbar also approached one venerable woman: his accomplished Aunt Gulbadan, now sixty-three, the astute witness of events of the Mughal dynasty who had recently returned from her own glorious adventures. The emperor considered her the best person he could turn to for accurate and detailed information about his dynasty.

"An order is handed out," Gulbadan wrote in the first line of her book. *Hukm*, imperial command, the Persian word she used, was suggestive of the urgency and importance of the royal project. She spelled out the directive: "Write down whatever you know of the doings of *Firdaus-makani* and *Jannat-ashyani*," and featured the posthumous descriptions of Babur and Humayun: *dwelling in paradise, nestling in paradise.*[5]

Akbar's selection of his aunt for his new project to record the history of the empire speaks of his admiration for her as a dynastic memory keeper— his salute to her unique experiences. He could have asked Hamida, his proficient mother, an ardent book collector and patron of some of the finest visual works of the Mughal atelier. She was more involved in the day-to-day events of his rule. In any case, he knew that his mother and aunt were intimate. Without doubt, the two would work together in reconstructing the Mughal past. During royal hunting expeditions, the tents of these two women were always next to Akbar's, signifying their elevated status. In a delightful painting of Hamida's wedding celebrations that she herself commissioned—the picture likely grounded in Gulbadan's text's vivid scene of the marriage negotiations—the princess sits across from Hamida and Humayun.[6] Joined at the hip through time and space, the two worked in concert in the new imperial endeavor, carefully documenting the polychromatic women's world in movement.

The men invited to contribute to the new imperial history busied themselves with famed books and tracts by men, met with religious and court authorities to compile the feats of kings, and wrote their own odes to Mughal wars and victories. Meanwhile, Gulbadan began to gather information in storytelling sessions. *Stories:* that is how royal women—heirs to Scheherazade— spoke and shared the stuff of human history, stories within stories that may have been told over a thousand and one nights or more. The harem in Lahore bustled with women recalling and sharing tales. The princess's vision, which had unfolded in the peripatetic life that she and her circle embodied, would now be recorded in the pages of her book.

Nearly sixty, dressed in a classic long *kurta* and *salwar* narrowing at her ankles, her head concealed in a *dupatta* dotted with sparkling silver sequins, Hamida enlivened the female deliberations. Gulbadan adds the phrase "Hamida Banu says" to her sentences. Queen Salima, companion in adventures across the seas, was part of the assembly. Perhaps she jogged

Gulbadan's memory or fine-tuned her recollections. Queen Harkha, mother of Prince Salim, may also have joined them. Fairly stooped by this time but still sprightly, Bibi Fatima was there. It is certain that the women held many assemblies. Attendants brought food and wine. Together, they looked at prized books and paintings housed in the harem, and shared their stories. Gulbadan's nieces, daughters of Kamran and also pilgrimage companions, would add their points of view. The elderly Gulnar would simply be amazed at how far the Mughal household had come since the days of their arrival in Agra.

Women attendants, companions, and caretakers gathered below a red awning in front of Gulbadan's quarters. Hamida sat beside Gulbadan, the princess relaxed as she looked at the women. Gulbadan typically dressed in a long top, as in Mughal miniatures, as well as embroidered trousers and a dupatta thrown over her shoulders. Her luminous eyes, a striking feature, were agile and attentive to detail.[7]

Her book originated from shared stories, which she wrote in conversational Persian laced with words in Turki, her mother tongue, and Hindavi. This was an accessible book from a master storyteller who weaved stories within stories and created dramatic pauses in her prose by shifting the narrative from one time to another, a sign of vital connections. Events do not always appear chronologically in Gulbadan's book, for she would reflect on older times as she wrote about new ones.

Gulbadan offered a unique chronicle suffused with feeling. We saw in the pages of this book that although she did not describe her husband, son, or a presumed daughter, she keenly documented childbirth, children killed in war, unfulfilled desires, anticipation in love and marriage, and the simultaneity of war and peace. Individualism does not inform her narration, although she brings individuality to each person. Her recollections of joy, sorrow, matrimony, motherhood, and sovereignty illustrate a collective, universal experience.

Thanks to her recognition of the fragility of human beings, we meet in her book human kings, uncertain leaders, and emotional, demanding women who raise with Babur and Humayun the thorny subject of the lack of time spent together. Heart-wrenching discussions; the pain of infertility; the bold questions that Hamida posed to Humayun before she agreed to marry him; royal women's abductions; special pleading by matriarchs on behalf of their sons; women dressed as men; anguish, laughter, and tears are all part of her narrative. Odd places, ordinary people, kind and evil servants, gentle eunuchs, resourceful women, and playful children—and the lives of people who do not normally appear in the annals of the Mughal Empire—all take center stage in Gulbadan's history.

Her writing was distinct from anything that official chroniclers or servants produced.[8] Invited male contributors favored *tarikh*, a historical, chronological narrative; *tazkireh*, a linear biographical or autobiographical mode; *qanun*, a normative account or legal text; *vaqi'at*, the narration of happenings, events, and occurrences; or *nama*, a genre that includes histories, epistles, or accounts of exemplary deeds.[9] All of these were firm assertions of male thinking.

The power of Gulbadan's book is that it is a constellation, not a categorizing of episodes. Patterns of peripatetic Mughal times emerge in her assembling, but not through an instructive mode. She called her book *Ahval-i Humayun Badshah*, or Conditions in the Age of Humayun Badshah. Conditions, states, and circumstances—an open-endedness animates the word *ahval*, perfectly befitting the Mughal era in which men and women were frequently on the move while celebrating births, mourning setbacks and losses, and learning new philosophies of artful living.

In the first portion of her two-part book, Gulbadan explores her father's daily life. We see the dynamic facets of his wanderings in Afghanistan and Hindustan, his desperation and longing during wars and victories, and the messy early years of Mughal rule in Hindustan. We also find rare, nuanced, and complex accounts of Mughal home life—especially in comparison to how those issues are discussed in other chronicles.[10] We meet the young Gulbadan in Kabul, amazed at the curiosities of Hind, traversing the Khyber Pass to begin a new life in Agra in the aftermath of her father's Hind victories. This is the only fully autobiographical part of her writing.

In the second part, she devotes substantial space to her favored half brother Humayun's exile and kingship. We glean fabulous details of his desert wedding to Hamida, and her legendary prenuptial negotiation. We learn about Mughal women lost in wars, the debacle in Chausa, Akbar's birth in the harsh circumstances of his parents' itinerant life, and senior women's feasts at Humayun's accession and Hindal's wedding. The lost world of the court in camp is animated in a way that no other chronicler of the time even approaches.

What books did Gulbadan own? Did she draw inspiration from any of them? We know that she read the masters of poetry Jami and Mir ʿAli Sher Navaʾi, whom her father adored. She grew up on the fabulous allegorical tales of Saʿdi's *Rose Garden* and his *Bustan* (The Orchard), with chapters on justice, mercy, love, humility, contentment, and education. She memorized the Qurʾan. She took auguries from Hafiz. She likely saw the colorful visual folios of the *Tuti-Nama* (Tales of the Parrot), India's *Thousand and One Nights*, produced in Akbar's atelier.

She is bound to have seen, after she came back from Kabul in the late 1550s, the masterly paintings of the *Hamzanama*, the Epic of Hamza, being created in Akbar's atelier, which displayed the valor of the uncle of Prophet Muhammad. Hamza's adventures were "represented in twelve volumes, and clever painters made the most astonishing illustrations for no less than one thousand and four hundred passages of the story."[11]

She read memoirs, including her father's *Baburnama*. Bayazid Bayat sent her a copy of his *Tazkireh-i Humayun va Akbar*, a history of the reigns of Humayun and Akbar from 1542 to 1591, which she kept in her library. She likely read Jawhar's portrayal of Humayun, composed in a "shaky and rustic" Persian, in the words of Hermann Ethé, who catalogued it for the British Library.[12] Gulbadan would have loved Jawhar's intimate book, but at what stage she read it or Bayat's book, both concurrent with her own, is hard to say. She inscribed her name on her copy of courtier Khwandamir's book about Humayun's ordinances and buildings.[13]

She would have known the didactic texts and famous books of advice such as the *Akhlaq-i Nasiri* and the *Qabusnama*, both ubiquitous in Islamic courts. Rumi's *Masnavi*, an epic poem, was a cherished work. *Shahnama*, Firdawsi's Book of Kings, a monument of poetry and history, and thousands of other books were in the harem and the imperial library, and were regularly read aloud to Akbar.[14]

None of these works served as a literary model for Gulbadan's writing, which differed radically from most court chronicles of her time. For one thing, her work has no didactic charge; it falls outside the prevalent "mirror for princes" genre, which emphasized pragmatic guidance and the role of rulers as moral exemplars.

Instead, the wide world and its people were her books. Her knowledge germinated from gardens, tents, pavilions, caravans, ships, rivers, oceans, deserts, camels, mosques, water fountains, hills, mansions, and the red sandstone harem. Babur, Dildar, Maham, Khanzada, her Rose sisters, little 'Aqiqa, Bega Begum, the Afghan Lady, Humayun, Hamida, Khizr, Kamran, Atun Mama, Lady Gulnar, gentle 'Asas, and Mama were her books. The Portuguese, the Surat governor, her nephew Akbar, the Ottoman emperor Murad, the sherif of Mecca, the sherif of Medina, and the local officer in Aden were her books. Women in history—Scheherazade, Zubaida, Fatima, her brave grandmother Isan Daulat—were her books.

Experience was her book. Crossing the Khyber Pass in a caravan at the age of six, being a young woman in exodus to Kabul, and her time as a sagacious woman lodged in the harem: all informed her writing. Indoors and outdoors, upon the seas or on land, her own body was her experience. Experience is in the body. Memory is *embodied*. She commenced writing from embodied memory and from events as she experienced and thought of them. She created tapestries of court life, domestic life, political intrigues, and ceremonies as she interpreted them.

The result was not what Akbar or his dear Abul Fazl had imagined. They were not looking for the quotidian occurrences of Mughal households that she included along with each extraordinary event. Rather, they wanted a document of the undertakings of Mughal ancestors in full splendor, as an established imperium. The kingdoms of her father and brother that the princess sketched were far from "historic" in that way. She shows the Mughal Empire and its history *being formed*, evoking a powerful impression of a dynasty not already known or made, a political formation taking unsteady steps from its early stages to maturity. She gives snapshots of the less tangible aspects of history, unfamiliar and unexpected evidence of the rough and tumble of Mughal domestic dramas, everyday struggles, and hidden fears and pleasures.

Like most books of the era, the *Ahval* is written in *nasta'liq,* or cursive script. Is this Gulbadan's writing? Whether it is or not, the princess's work is both audacious and unclassifiable. It would not fit the stately magnificence centered on kings that Abul Fazl sought to establish. He wanted accuracy and objectivity for his official history of emperors, their lieutenants, official policies, and actions—something resembling a modern state's gazetteers and archive.

When Annette Beveridge began work on the first English translation of Gulbadan's book in the 1890s, she had only one copy of her manuscript, the one from the Hamilton collection that I later consulted. As she briskly translated the princess's memoir, her husband Henry Beveridge, another distinguished colonial-era scholar, translated the *Akbarnama.* In 1899, Henry went back to India for further research and spent seven months looking for other extant copies of Gulbadan's book, to no avail.[15] Only one copy of her work survives, even though it was a standard practice in the court to make multiple copies of any work.

Muslim, Kayastha, Khatri, and Brahmin scribes routinely prepared copies of royal and non-royal works. A *khatib,* or scribe, waited upon the old Bayazid Bayat, who had suffered a stroke but was still supervising the imperial kitchen. Bayat spoke and the khatib wrote. Of the nine copies of his work, notes Bayat, he sent two to Abul Fazl, one to the imperial library, where an earlier copy had been mislaid, and one to Gulbadan. Even those authors not attached to the court but with resources would get dozens of copies transcribed and would gift them to patrons and friends. "It was very rare that fewer copies were made," notes an eminent Mughal historian.[16]

It is also mysterious that Gulbadan's manuscript breaks off mid-sentence, as she describes the 1553 blinding of her half brother. Is this Gulbadan's *ellipsis,* an abridgment of a scene well known, or someone else's redaction? Jawhar, who was with Kamran, wrote a moving passage about the blind prince's condition. Did Gulbadan write more? What was in those pages, and what happened to them? In 1899, Beveridge noted that the manuscript was "rebound (not recently, I believe), plainly, in red leather. . . . The folio that stands last is out of place, an error apparently made in the rebinding."[17]

It would not be surprising if Gulbadan had added rich pictures of her beloved brother Humayun's short reign in Delhi, and of Akbar's coronation and his noteworthy ascent. Akbar had commissioned Gulbadan to write, and while he expected her to include memories of olden times, she would elevate him, as she had her father and brother. Progressive thinker, writer, and educationist Maulana Shibli Nomani was certain that Gulbadan's book covered Akbar's reign. Delighted at the publication of Annette Beveridge's English translation of 1902, Shibli Nomani wrote a review explaining the distinctive features of Gulbadan's work, noting that it likely "contained an account of Akbar's reign up to his 22nd regnal year which is clear from Shahjahan's note on the manuscript."[18] Shibli was referring to an autograph of Akbar's grandson Shah Jahan on the princess's book. "This history, which contains an abridgement of the affairs of His Majesty . . . [Timur] and of his glorious descendants and of the events of the days of 'Arsh—Ashiyani [Akbar]—May God make clear his proof!—down to the twenty-second year of his reign, was written in the time of Shah Baba [Akbar]."[19]

Chances are that the princess would solemnize Akbar's permission for her hajj, which was as important to him as it was to her. All this Akbar and Fazl would love. But in so doing, she would describe things as she saw them and as her co-haraman heard them, in tune with the rest of the work. The virtues of movement were celebrated. Arabian peregrinations were recalled. Women standing in front of the Great Mosque in Mecca, distributing sadaqat, were highlighted. Abul Fazl likely "read it and despised it," wrote Annette Beveridge.[20] As expected, he complained to the emperor. Upon hearing of the princess's behavior on the hajj, Akbar might be disturbed.

In 1580, when the Ottoman emperor insisted on the expulsion of Mughal women from the Hijaz, Akbar ignored Murad's complaints, which likely reached him from his own officials. His ambition to dominate the Islamic world and be the next millennial sovereign was so great that the mention of "un-Islamic" acts committed by Mughal women, let alone any record of them, would be shameful. Gulbadan had gone beyond imperial expectations. While in Arabia, the Mughal women had transgressed the boundaries of life designed for them in the sacred harem that Akbar had fashioned. To be visible, to be the focus of the public gaze, was not why Akbar had sent them on the hajj. Even though the emperor gained prominence through his aunt's protracted distribution of the sadaqat, for many male authorities, her bold presence thousands of miles away from Fatehpur-Sikri amounted to *fitna*—disorder or chaos.

Would Akbar find the recording of such damning acts unacceptable? In the *Akbarnama*, Abul Fazl rendered Gulbadan's Arabian voyage as a holy act, the hajj—something that the usually secluded elderly women performed in the interest of their dynasty, not as the bold adventure or royal peregrination that Gulbadan executed. There was no scandal in the *Akbarnama*, no sign of dynastic storms; the astute court historian kept all this under wraps. Even if these stories appeared only in *Ahval*, and even if only a small group of courtiers or harem women read Gulbadan's writing, it would still be a problem. Thinking differently, especially for women, was dangerous.

It was not difficult to expunge some pages of a woman's "little" book from the record.[21] For the Great Mughal, it was no different from excluding the name of Harkha, the mother of his coveted son Salim, from the main record of the empire, the new imperial history. Akbar's earlier children had died one after another. Then, with the blessings of a mystic, the much-coveted Prince Salim was born, and lived. The single reference in the *Akbarnama* to the unnamed mother is a metaphor: the prince was the "shell of her womb." The person celebrated in this moment of joy was the emperor, "the just and perfect Muhammad Akbar." The infant Salim was "a pearl of Shahinshah's mansion," "a pearl of Akbar Shahi's casket." In the performance of that single act of consequence, Harkha's name went missing."[22]

A critic of Akbar's policies, Badauni was so fearful of the emperor's wrath and control that he hid to write his own account of the times. Badauni's three-volume history of Akbar's reign, a counterpoint to the official *Akbarnama*, was revealed only after the emperor's death. So intolerant was Akbar to any opposing view that he banished to Mecca two jurists who disagreed with his policies.

The princess wrote in consultation with Hamida, Akbar's powerful mother, whom he worshipped. Did the emperor decide nevertheless to purge certain pages of his aunt's book, and have no more copies transcribed? We do not know. What we have is a record of Akbar's censorial policies, and the noteworthy fact that no other copies of the *Ahval* exist. According to one renowned Mughal historian, "while transferring information, Abul Fazl sometimes censored . . . primary texts."[23] While the official historian used Gulbadan's work for some parts of his *Akbarnama*, he did not mention her book.

The layers of actions that surround the lost pages of the princess's book paint raw pictures of the sixteenth-century world and of acts seldom connected with imperial power. They suggest a world of ambition, intrigue, resilience, women's masterly thinking, and the making of history. Yet, despite the machinations, Gulbadan's *Ahval* never completely disappeared.

It emerged again and again: in a box smuggled from Delhi to London, in a colonial-era translation, and in a postcolonial woman's history—as did Gulbadan in a Mughal miniature painting, holding a book in her hand.

In a dynamic scene painted in 1602–3, now part of the British Library's *Akbarnama*, Humayun and Hamida sit upon an elevated, opulently carpeted floor in front of a garden pavilion. Mughal artist Madhu drew the backdrop and scenes of this painting.[24] Three kings arriving in adoration of Christ adorn the chrome-yellow wall of the pavilion. In a theatrical scene, they gallop to the site, then dismount and kneel before Christ, the child held in the arms of his mother. Below the fresco is another painting fringed by cypress trees and flowering creepers. Hamida wears lilac-colored clothing from head to toe; a soft white muslin stole covers her shoulders and wraps around her conical hat. Robed in an olive-green *jama*, a salmon-pink flowing jacket upon it, Humayun gestures to Akbar, who is sitting on his mother's lap. The prince wears an embroidered yellow shirt, red trousers, and a little red headdress. The royals mark Akbar's circumcision ceremony, a scene described in Gulbadan's book.[25]

Scores of women participate in the festivities. Clad in clothes like Hamida's, three of them sit under a red awning. A woman in yellow robes, a red stole, and a red and yellow conical hat stands out. Was Nar Singh, who drew the portraits, signifying that she was Khanzada? A woman stands behind Humayun, fanning him. To her left, dressed in a long, soft green garb and a diaphanous muslin stole, is an elegant woman holding a wine-red book.[26]

Gathered below the Mughal family, women attendants prepare wine jars, cups, and refreshments. Other women dance under the observant eyes of the chief eunuch, who stands to the left of the woman with the book. In a somber gray and white costume, a mature chaperone appears on the left side of the painting. She is in the exposed outside area, separated from the younger women sheltered under a canopy. Generations of women and their different stations, each indicating different points of authority, are featured.[27]

"One of the ladies is almost certainly Gulbadan," notes a British Library blog about the *Akbarnama* image, though it does not say which one. Art

Celebrations in the women's quarters at the time of Akbar's circumcision
(from the *Akbarnama*). The British Library blog notes,
"One of the ladies is almost certainly Gulbadan."

historians observe that pictures of people with books or bound manuscripts appeared frequently in the Mughal world. A bound manuscript, like a religious text or a portrait of a leading ruler or saint, was a precious object, both materially and as a repository of memory or spiritual meaning.[28] People carrying such valuable manuscripts in paintings were mostly holy persons or master artists. Only master artists were drawn carrying bound folios of paintings as signs of their stature. Sometimes ascetics and saints were pictured offering prized books to rulers. The legendary Mughal painter Kesu Das, a contemporary of Gulbadan, made a self-portrait with a bound volume tucked under his right arm. He also painted a Jain ascetic carrying a work in the same way.

Which venerable woman would Nar Singh draw with a book other than Gulbadan? In the line of eminent persons carrying books, she was the only woman of the era who could rightfully hold her own. By the 1590s, Nar Singh had worked on folios of some of the finest poetry collections. He "shows himself a skillful technician and master in creating a quiet, restrained mood," notes an art historian, adding that only major historical personages appear as distinct figures in his works.[29] The princess in the British Library *Akbarnama* painting is quietly observant and composed. Her body is intimately connected with the book she holds, a bound manuscript. Its color suggests that it was made of either leather or lacquer, materials reserved for precious manuscripts. And she enjoys a special status, standing on the edge of the central frame. The placement immediately draws our attention to her.[30]

Nar Singh thus delicately posits a relationship between her body and her book as an extension of it. The princess is among the few women and men shown in full profile; most others are in three-quarter profile. This is a sign of the dignity Nar Singh wishes to bestow upon her. Her book enhances her distinction, an artist's reflection on her eminence and her standing as a chronicler of her times.

When the princess passed away in February 1603 at the age of eighty, Akbar helped to carry her bier for some distance. This was a great honor—an imperial nod to Gulbadan's preeminence.

Note on Sources

Oblivion and erasure are themes that have been at the core of my work since I began my career as a historian. I explore not only what happened in the past, and why certain figures do not take center stage in Mughal history, but also how women, girls, ordinary people, ambiguous figures (eunuchs, concubines, wet nurses), spaces (harems, gardens, tents), and multiple forms of desire are *made* deviant, redundant, or obscure in history. The fact is that scholars are largely complicit in how history is designed, presented, made available, and preserved.

In my first book, *Domesticity and Power in the Early Mughal World*, I opened up the *process* and *becoming* of the Mughal Empire by giving historical depth to the institution of the royal harem. Romanticized and stereotyped in both colonial and postcolonial writings, the harem warranted further study. I sought to lay out its basics, explain its complex creation, and elaborate on the richly layered lives, tastes, and passions of its denizens. That book was inspired by Gulbadan's *Ahval-i Humayun Badshah*. However, as I began my doctoral research at Oxford, which led to the writing of *Domesticity and Power*, a senior male colleague asked me, "How are you going to write this history? There are no sources for it." This echoed a question that generations of feminist historians have heard.

Domesticity and Power garnered praise for interrupting the so-called "lack of sources." Nevertheless, the "lack" reappeared when I wrote my second book, which historicized the girl-child in nineteenth-century India. It emerged yet again when I turned to the history of as public a figure as Nur Jahan, the only woman co-sovereign of Mughal India and the subject of my third book, *Empress: The Astonishing Reign of Nur Jahan*. There is an abundance of sources on her life and reign. So the question was asked with a bit more nuance by another distinguished Mughal scholar, again male: "But doesn't Nur Jahan appear only in representation?" He was puzzled that she didn't order or write a chronicle herself. "And who doesn't? What is *not* representation?" I responded.

Over the years, I have thought about the historiographical challenges to my thinking and writing: *There are no sources* and *Isn't this representation?*, both of them underpinned by a fundamental male disbelief in the veracity of feminine experiences and the possibility of women's thinking. These objections symbolize the obstacles that all critical oppositional histories—feminist, left-wing, indigenous, and minority—face in confounding and expanding upon received histories: that is, histories with a capital H, supposedly grounded in the only authentic archive—state and official records.

Who decides what history is? Who decides what counts as a source? Who decides what is memorable and deserving of the name *archive*? How does a source become "official" or "marginal"? How have the most important Mughal sources been preserved and become available to us? Who writes them, for what purpose, and what happens to their narrative and information in the process of collating, editing, and translating? Surely these procedures are critical to the way in which a source is archived (made into a source) and read.[1] Such questions are not frequently asked in Mughal history because both the history and the archive are considered established for all eternity.

I will add that the availability of sources does not automatically ensure their use in writing histories. I showed in *Domesticity and Power* the subtle ways in which historians were complicit in marginalizing and silencing the groundbreaking, well-known, and abundant work of Gulbadan. This generated a specific silence—an absence or lacuna. Similarly, it does not matter that manuscripts, paintings, or fabulous architectural data exist, as in the case of Nur Jahan. The problem of fundamental male disbelief remains.

This inadequacy or "lack" requires further thinking. Are sources so scarce as not to provide even the possibility of raising new questions and hypotheses? Are there other forms of inadequacy that we need to address? How do we work with fragments, a concept that several thinkers have fruitfully deployed?

With that, I turn to the present book. You have met Gulbadan in full splendor: a royal girl, she arrives in India, settles in a new home, and forms new relationships. As a young person, she becomes involved in the machinations of Mughal politics surrounding her brother and half brothers. As a married woman, she is forced back to Kabul. As an itinerant matriarch, she finds herself back in India, and then in a harem previously unknown to her, from which she leads Mughal women across the seas to western Arabia. Her bold and generous actions lead to an unspoken but massive tiff between the Ottomans and the Mughals. How did I assemble these pictures of her complex life for which there are no obvious sources?

I have not been content with the well-known fact that there is only one available manuscript of her work. As the reader knows, Gulbadan's manuscript breaks off at folio 83. I am absorbed in considering how this fact was created, how a void is generated. What layers of action surround it?

Gulbadan's *Ahval* is at the center of my thinking, and it is around this book that I visualize my encounters with other texts and paintings. Because of her *Ahval*, I began to read the official Mughal court chronicles very differently, for these, too, are richer in meaning and content than historians have suggested to date. Among these court histories are those of Abul Fazl, Badauni, and Nizam al-Din Ahmad, familiar to the reader from the pages of this book, imperial letters and orders, and the accounts of officers and servants such as Bayazid Bayat and Jawhar.

Other sources required equally careful, sustained reading over a long period, as well as the command of distinct visual and literary languages. It took patience to learn and engage with the technicality of each genre. To grapple with the place of Gulbadan's *Ahval* and the intriguing presentation of people with books in Mughal miniatures narrated in the last chapter, I leaned on the expertise of art historians to understand the iconography embedded in such paintings. A subject carrying a book or a bound manuscript was meant to be a singular and distinguished person. Again, I found myself glued to the British Library image, very likely of Gulbadan, in which the artist imbued her with immense dignity by showing her entire profile, whereas most others are in three-quarter profile. Her book enhanced her distinction.

Note on Sources

I faced dead silence in the Mughal records about the conditions and character of Gulbadan's years in Arabia. I had to explore sources that could lead me to the sixteenth-century worlds of Arabia—and to the nature of pilgrimage back then. The popular pictures of Arabia and the hajj practices and rites come from late nineteenth-century accounts, such as the fabulous writings of Sir Richard Burton and Arthur Rimbaud, among others.

So I delved into sixteenth-century histories such as Ibn Faraj's magnificent *Bride of the Sea* on Jeddah. I read extensively about Islamic urbanism, the Red Sea's imperial politics, the role of the sherif of Mecca, the intricacies of architecture, especially in relation to the water problem in desert lands, and the lives of royals and non-royals who stayed in western Arabia. Many of the mujawirs, or spiritual and nonspiritual sojourners, as they were called, left behind copious documentation. Their wide-ranging travelogues, observations, and accounts are key to picturing Gulbadan's visit to Arabia, for which there are no extant Mughal sources. But the writings of Ibn Jubayr, Ibn Faraj, Ibn Battuta, and Evliya Celebi—and those of medieval geographers and observers such as Abu Makhrama for Aden—come with their own visual and linguistic tradition, for which I leaned on scholarly and public intellectual debates on the Ottoman age.

In order to enliven the places where Gulbadan and her companions lived—the Afghan mountains, the riverine tracts of northern India, the western Indian port city of Surat, the vast waters of the Indian Ocean and the Red Sea, and the legendary Arabian cities Jeddah, Mecca, Medina, and Aden, I studied maritime geographies and economies, states and styles of ships and shipbuilding, sea monsters, sea and land routes, legends of saints and tombs, and histories and topographies of medieval Islamic cities. Shipwrecks, salvage operations, the very geography of wreckage in the sixteenth-century Indian Ocean and the Red Sea worlds fascinated me.

You will recall that Ottoman sultan Murad III's orders are immensely rich, their language and words soaked with meaning. Why had we not paid attention to the words in these imperial orders? As I read the orders in Ottoman Turkish with the help of Ottoman scholars, I kept thinking, why did Murad repeatedly mention the words *mujawir* and *sadaqat*? Why did he refrain from using the charged and punitive word *na-meshru* until his final order?

Words carry histories and working through them is a vital analytical move for me. Here is another example: Father Monserrate noted in his *Commentary* that Gulbadan gave a town named Butzaris to the Portuguese. It was then that the royal party was able to set sail from Surat to Arabia. No other records tell us about Gulbadan's time in the city of Surat or her departure. We saw that according to the *Akbarnama*, everything was ready when the women left Fatehpur-Sikri, including the cartaz that the Portuguese issued to royal and ordinary pilgrims and merchants. When Gulbadan and her royal retinue reached Surat, however, there was no pass.

Where is Butzaris? Searching, I found two leads: a letter from Akbar to his aunt suggesting that she defer her trip to the Holy Land, and the mention of Bulsar in one of the records as Gulbadan's jagir. Several Mughal women had jagirs, estates with fiscal rights. Bulsar, or Butzaris as Monserrate called it, was a new allotment for Gulbadan. Sixty miles south of Surat, this piece of land, a Portuguese holding, was at the northern tip of coastal Daman. The vast Arabian Sea was to the west of Bulsar. It was a rich agricultural area.

Why did Emperor Akbar ask his aunt to defer her plans? Why did he allocate a piece of land on the border of the Portuguese properties to her when there was some tussle with them? Monserrate's one line was tantalizing. Why did Gulbadan give Bulsar to the Portuguese? Learning about Portuguese stakes in the Indian Ocean world created a robust image of Gulbadan's diplomatic negotiation before she embarked on her journey. Her negotiation with a foreign power, often a male prerogative in the princess's times, shaped my understanding of her authority.

I stumbled upon tantalizing words: a turn of phrase here, an image there, an event, a paragraph about a child falling in the sea. Thus, gradually, each chapter of this book found its rhythm, and the bigger picture of Gulbadan's daring life emerged.

In writing this book, my goal has been to stand beside Gulbadan, lingering over her broken manuscript, her long years in a distant land, and her holding of a book in visual renderings. I pause at the offhand remarks and the breaks in narration, and work through both the pictorial iconography and the language of manuscripts. Per Adrienne Rich's advice, I search "for symbolic arrangements, decoding difficult and complex messages left to us by women of the past."[2] Butzaris, the recurring mention of cisterns in medieval Arabia, the shipwreck in Aden, a Mughal officer's one-line report that the princess did not want to return home, and Murad's eviction of Akbar's aunt—all this shapes the great adventures of Gulbadan.

Finally, a word regarding the title of this book. I pondered at length on the word *mujawir*, used in Murad's eviction orders as well, delving into its history. It emerges from the Arabic verb *jawara*, which means literally to be a neighbor or to stay in the vicinity of someone or something. Frequently used as an adjective in Persian and Arabic, it means "adjacent" or "neighboring." Used as a noun since the early Islamic era, it means someone who seeks residence in or near a Holy Place, like a shrine, a saint's tomb, Mecca, and so on. Both extended residence and clear intention are essential to being a mujawir. The term signifies more than a regular pilgrim visiting a Holy Place; the residence of a mujawir is much longer than needed for the usual purpose of benefiting from the blessings of nearness to Holy Places and spaces, and spending time in prayer and seclusion for worship.[3] *Sojourner* or *spiritual sojourner* are closer English translations.

Mujawir carries richly layered meanings, encompassing curiosity, travel, movement, and intention—compelling descriptors of Gulbadan's itinerant lifestyle in Arabia. What English word could capture her life of continual movement, not only in Arabia but also in Afghanistan and in Hindustan, where she spent long stretches of time?

I wanted a word that could capture the vigor of life-in-movement, even as Gulbadan lived in mansions, tents, and the harems for long periods. I wanted a word that could convey the flavor of a philosophy of movement. I wanted a word that was rigorous enough to encompass the central motif of Gulbadan's spiritual, political, and bodily movement. So, I found myself leaning toward the word *vagabond,* a taut English word conveying numerous connotations: sauntering, moving, wayfaring, wayward, itinerant, explorer, wanderer, pilgrim, trailblazer. *Vagabond Princess,* I hope, will capture the textures, complexity, and paradoxes of the worlds of Gulbadan, and of her diverse roles as a seeker, adventurer, sojourner, writer, and princess.

Notes

There is voluminous fine writing on Mughal history and the wider Islamic world of the sixteenth century. I have opted not to provide an exhaustive bibliography, only details of archival sources, published books and essays, and visual and architectural materials that are central to the history of Gulbadan. The notes that follow are based upon my consultation of Persian and other documents that animate the sociocultural context in which Gulbadan was born, grew up, and traveled.

Translation of Persian manuscripts and books, unless noted otherwise, is mine. There is no standard system for transliterating Persian into English. I have used the modified version of the *IJMES* (*International Journal of Middle East Studies*) system developed by Layla S. Diba and Maryam Ekhtiar for their edited volume *Royal Persian Paintings: The Qajar Epoch, 1785–1925* (London: I. B. Tauris, 1998). However, I have retained the common English form of all well-known names of persons, places, and Persian texts. Thus: *Baburnama* and *Akbarnama* rather than *Baburnameh* and *Akbarnameh*; Agra rather than Agreh; and Begum/Beg rather than Bigum/Biyg.

INTRODUCTION

1. Annette Beveridge, Private Papers, 1902, MSS. EUR C.176/195–196, British Library, London.

2. *Humayun at the Celebrations Held at the Time of Akbar's Circumcision, Akbarnama,* Or.12988, fol. 114r, British Library.

3. The Delhi Collection, British Library, https://www.bl.uk/collection-guides/the-delhi-collection.

4. For a detailed discussion of the history of the production of Gulbadan's book and Annette Beveridge's translation, see Ruby Lal, *Domesticity and Power in the Early Mughal World* (Cambridge: Cambridge University Press, 2005), especially chapter 3.

5. Gulbadan Banu Begum, *Ahval-i Humayun Badshah,* Ms.Or.166, fols. 82a–82b, British Library.

6. Henry Beveridge, trans., *The Akbar Nama of Abu-l-Fazl,* vol. 3 (1902–39; repr., Delhi: Low Price Publications, 1993), 205.

7. George S. A. Ranking, W. H. Lowe, and Sir Wolseley Haig, trans. and eds., *Muntakhabu-t-tawarikh* (1884–1925; repr., Delhi: Renaissance, 1986), 2:253.

8. A. Azfar Moin, *The Millennial Sovereign: Sacred Kingship and Sainthood in Islam* (New York: Columbia University Press, 2012), 9.

9. Wheeler M. Thackston, trans. and ed., *Three Memoirs of Homayun,* vol. 1 (Costa Mesa, Calif.: Mazda, 2009), xii.

10. Lal, *Domesticity and Power.*

11. N. R. Farooqi brought these orders to the attention of scholars and used them as part of his broader investigations into Ottoman-Mughal relations: "Six Ottoman Documents on

Mughal-Ottoman Relations during the Reign of Akbar," in *Akbar and His Age,* ed. Iqtidar Alam Khan (New Delhi: Northern Book Center, 1999), 209–22; "An Overview of Ottoman Archival Documents and Their Relevance for Medieval Indian History," *Medieval History Journal* 20, no. 1 (2017): 192–229. I consulted the copies of the orders preserved in the National Archives in Istanbul with the help of Alexis Wick, historian of the Red Sea, who also helped with close translations of these edicts. The registers (fully digitalized) are housed at the State Archives of the Presidency of the Turkish Republic (formerly and still often known as the Ottoman Archives of the Office of the Prime Minister, the Babakanlık Osmanlı Arşivi, BOA). Muhimme Defterleri, vol. 35, fol. 292, farman 740; A_{DVNSMHM_00035_00149; Muhimme Defterleri, vol. 35, fol. 292, farman 741; A_{DVNSMHM_00035_00149; Muhimme Defterleri, vol. 39, fol. 160, farman 349; A_{DVNSMHM_00039_00082; Muhimme Defterleri, vol. 39, fol. 238, farman 471; A_{DVNSMHM_00039_00121; Muhimme Defterleri, vol. 43, fol. 54, farman 107; A_{DVNSMHM_00043_00030; Muhimme Defterleri, vol. 62, fol. 205, farman 457; A_{DVNSMHM_00062_00119. A fuller discussion of these orders appears in later chapters of this book.

12. There is another scandal, I might note: the scandal of historians who easily condemn exceptional, not easily unclassifiable works—especially by women—to the margins of history. Nearly a hundred years after the first English translation of Gulbadan's work, in 1902 by Annette Beveridge, a well-known scholar writing about the historians of Akbar's age added this in a footnote: "I have not included a study of the *Humayun Nama* of Gulbadan Begam in this chapter though it falls in the same class of [minor historical] works. . . . The reason is that I feel I have practically nothing to add to what its translator, Mrs. Beveridge, has said in her introduction to the translation." He distinguished between major works (political-administrative and emperor-centered) and minor ones (of royal women, servants, and so forth), privileging the "hard politics" of the former against the "soft society" of the latter. Harbans Mukhia, *Historians and Historiography during the Reign of Akbar* (New Delhi: Vikas, 1976), 154n1; Annette S. Beveridge, trans., *The History of Humayun: Humayun Nama,* 2nd ed. (1902; repr., Delhi: Low Price Publications, 1994). Another scholar put his views more forthrightly: "The foundations of any historical study of Akbar must rest solidly upon Abu-l-Fadl's *Akbarnamah.* It is full, detailed and mainly authentic, because it was written by a man who was fully familiar with the official policies and actions of the government and enjoyed not only confidence but actually the friendship of the emperor." Ishtiaq Husain Qureshi, *Akbar: The Architect of the Mughul Empire* (1978; repr., Delhi: Idarah-i Adabiyat-i Delli, 1987), 2, 6.

13. Adrienne Rich, *On Lies, Secrets, and Silence: Selected Prose, 1966–1978* (New York: Norton, 1979), 13–14.

ONE. The Rose Princess and Her Circle

1. Only the upper section of the citadel was in existence then. Although it is now in complete ruins, mid-nineteenth-century observations and present-day research suggest that royal residential quarters may have been located on the north side of the upper fort. On the ground, adjacent with but separated from the city, was the royal palace built in the nineteenth century. It had a fabulous garden that Babur likely initiated and a mosque as well. On the history of Bala Hisar fort, see C. W. Woodburn, "The Bala Hissar of Kabul: Revealing a Fortress Palace in Afghanistan," *The Institution of Royal Engineers Professional*

Paper, no. 1 (2009): 1–50; Howard Crane, "The Patronage of Zahir al-Din Babur and the Origins of Mughal Architecture," *Bulletin of the Asia Institute,* n.s. 1 (1987): 95–110; Bill Woodburn and Ian Templeton, "From Bala Hissar to Arg: How Royal Fortress Palaces Shaped Kabul, 1830–1939," *Court Historian* 17, no. 2 (2012): 171–88. For an understanding of the wider geography, see also Sir E. Denison Ross, trans., and N. Elias, ed., *The Tarikh-i Rashidi of Muhammad Haidar Dughlat: A History of the Moguls of Central Asia* (London: S. Low, Marston, 1895).

2. Babur mentions several of his marriages and wives in the *Baburnama;* Gulbadan provides a more complete list of the women and their children. In 1488–89, when Babur was five, he was betrothed to ʿAyesha Sultan Begum, daughter of Sultan Ahmad Mirza Miranshahi (Babur's paternal uncle). She gave birth to Fakhr-un-Nisa, who died about a month later. ʿAyesha Sultan Begum left Babur before 1503. Babur and Zainab Sultan Begum, daughter of Sultan Mahmud Mirza (Babur's paternal uncle) were married in 1504 or 1505. Zainab Sultan Begum died childless two or three years after this. Babur was also married to Maʿsuma Begum, another daughter of Sultan Ahmad Mirza Miranshahi, in 1507. She gave birth to Maʿsuma (same name as the mother) and died in childbirth. In Niyaz Muhammad Khukandi's *Tarikh-i Shahrukhi* and Nalivkine's *Khanate of Khokand,* it is mentioned that when Babur left Samarkand in 1512 after his defeat by the Uzbeks, one of his wives, Sayyida Afaq, accompanied him in his flight and gave birth to a son in the desert between Khujand and Kand-i badam. For details of Babur's wives and concubines, see Ruby Lal, *Domesticity and Power in the Early Mughal World* (Cambridge: Cambridge University Press, 2005), 111–20. He had four wives at the time of Gulbadan's birth, including her mother, Dildar.

3. Mughal paintings are the best sources for understanding royal births. They show the birth chamber as well as indicate the ranks of women according to where they stand in the miniatures. I am grateful to Cathy Benkaim for bringing to my attention a wide range of miniatures with birth scenes, among them Birth of Jahangir, 14.657, c. 1618, Museum of Fine Art, Boston; Birth of Timur, c. 1590–95, *V&A Akbar Nama;* M.A. 5674, Guimet Museum, Paris; Birth of Ghazan Khan, from a *Jami al-Tawarikh* manuscript, 1596, 1935.12, Worcester City Art Gallery and Museum, Worcester, U.K. For details of birth in Akbar's times, see Lal, *Domesticity and Power,* 183–88.

4. Ruby Lal, *Empress: The Astonishing Reign of Nur Jahan* (New York: Norton, 2018), 24–25.

5. I discuss painterly traditions of allocation of spaces to female figures in "From the Inside Out: Spaces of Pleasure and Authority," in *Art and Stories from Mughal India,* ed. Sonya Rhea Quintanilla (Cleveland: Cleveland Museum of Art, 2016), especially 296–97.

6. Babur's first child was born during his campaign in Samarkand. ʿAyesha Sultan Begum gave birth to Fakhr-un-Nisa, who died a month later. Gulbadan notes examples of several other children who died during campaigns. On the question of children's death, see Ruby Lal, "Recording Death: Invocations from the Early Mughal World," in *Death at Court,* ed. Karl-Heinz Spiess (Leiden: Brill, 2013), 301–19.

7. Henri Masse, *Persian Beliefs and Customs* (New Haven, Conn.: Human Relations Area Files, 1954), 7, 12; details of the rituals of birth on 13–14.

8. Gulbadan uses this phrase several times in her *Ahval.*

9. Wheeler M. Thackston, trans. and ed., *Zahiruddin Muhammad Babur Mirza: Babur-nama*, parts 1–3, Turkish transcription, Persian edition, and English translation (Cambridge, Mass.: Near Eastern Languages and Civilization, Harvard University, 1993), 481; Annette Susannah Beveridge, trans., *Babur-nama (Memoirs of Babur) of Zahiru'd-din Muhammad Babur Padshah Ghazi* (1921; repr., Delhi: Low Price Publications, 1997), 385.

10. Abul Fazl emphasizes the union of "celestial fathers" and "terrestrial mothers" that results "every spring [in] a fresh flower [that] blooms in the garden of fortune." It must be acknowledged that there is at least some indirect reference to the mother, the "terrestrial mother," the necessary instrument in this royal birth. In June 1570, once again, a noble son on "whose forehead the lights of high fortune were visible, appeared in the fortunate quarters of Shaykh Selim in Fathpur." Henry Beveridge, trans., *The Akbar Nama of Abu-l-Fazl*, 3 vols. (1902–39; repr., Delhi: Low Price Publications, 1993), 2:514–15. Badauni records the *qit'ah* of Mawlana Qasim Arsalan, composed especially for the occasion of Murad's birth. The first hemistich refers to the birth of Salim and the second to that of Murad; George S. A. Ranking, W. H. Lowe, and Sir Wolseley Haig, trans. and eds., *Muntakhabu-t-tawarikh* (1884–1925; repr., Delhi: Renaissance, 1986), 2:136.

11. On Khanzada's presentation of Khalil Sultan, see Priscilla P. Soucek, "Timurid Women: A Cultural Perspective," in *Women in the Medieval Islamic World: Power, Patronage, and Piety*, ed. Gavin R. G. Hambly (New York: St. Martin's, 1998), 211. On Gulbadan's and Hindal's adoption, see Lal, *Domesticity and Power*, 120–28.

12. Among the examples that haunt the chronicles of the time are Barbul, Mihr-jan, Ishan Dawlat, and Faruq, all of whom died in infancy (children of Maham Begum and Babur). Ma'suma (same name as her mother) died at the time of her birth (daughter of Ma'suma Begum and Babur). Dildar Begum (wife of Babur) lost Alwar, the last of her five children, who died in childhood. Bibi Mubarika Yusufzai and Zainab Sultan Begum (wives of Babur) died childless. Gulbadan reports that 'Aqiqa Begum (daughter of Humayun and Bega Begum) died during the war of Chausa between Humayun and Sher Shah. More on this in chapter 6.

13. Annette S. Beveridge, trans., *The History of Humayun: Humayun Nama*, 2nd ed. (1902; repr., Delhi: Low Price Publications, 1994), 116; Gulbadan Banu Begum, *Ahval-i Humayun Badshah*, Ms.Or.166, fol. 23b, British Library, London.

TWO. The Rose Garden

1. Shaykh Mushrifuddin Sa'di of Shiraz, in Wheeler M. Thackston, trans., *The Gulistan (Rose Garden of Sa'di): Bilingual English and Persian Edition with Vocabulary* (Bethesda, Md.: Ibex, 2008).

2. C. W. Woodburn, "The Bala Hissar of Kabul: Revealing a Fortress Palace in Afghanistan," *The Institution of Royal Engineers Professional Paper*, no. 1 (2009): 1–50; Howard Crane, "The Patronage of Zahir al-Din Babur and the Origins of Mughal Architecture," *Bulletin of the Asia Institute*, n.s. 1 (1987): 95–110; Bill Woodburn and Ian Templeton, "From Bala Hissar to Arg: How Royal Fortress Palaces Shaped Kabul, 1830–1939," *Court Historian* 17, no. 2 (2012): 171–88.

3. For an example of the arrangements of the khasa-tabin, see the description of the battle of Panipat in 1526, Wheeler M. Thackston, trans. and ed., *Zahiruddin Muhammad Babur*

Mirza: Baburnama, parts 1–3, Turkish transcription, Persian edition, and English translation (Cambridge, Mass.: Near Eastern Languages and Civilization, Harvard University, 1993), 568–72. See also the example of Babur's victory over Qandahar in 1508, Annette Susannah Beveridge, trans., *Babur-nama (Memoirs of Babur) of Zahiru'd-din Muhammad Babur Padshah Ghazi* (1921; repr., Delhi: Low Price Publications, 1997), 333–37. Babur includes in his "household," among others, Mir Shah Qawchin, Sayyid Qasim Eshik-aqa Jalayir (also "Lord of the Gate"), Qasim Ajab, 'Ali Dust Taghayi's son Muhammad Dust, Muhammad 'Ali Mubashshir (messenger of good tidings), Khudaberdi Tughchi Mughul, Yarak Taghayi, Baba 'Ali's son Baba Quli, Pir Ways, Shaykh Ways, Yar 'Ali Balal (great-grandfather of 'Abdur Rahim *Khan-i Khanan*, the Persian translator of the *Baburnama* at the court of Akbar), Qasim Mirakhvur (chief equerry), and Haidar *Rikabadar* (stirrup holder).

4. Pulad (literally, steel) was a son of Kuchum, the Khaqan of the Uzbeks, and Mihr-ban, who Annette Beveridge thinks was a half sister of Babur. She was captured on one of the occasions when Babur lost to the Uzbeks. The *diwan* that he sent to Pulad contained a verse on its back that looks to be addressed to his sister through her son; Beveridge, *Babarnama*, 402nn2, 3, and 632n3.

5. For a chart that shows the imperial camp and its layout, see Henry Blochmann, ed., and H. S. Jarrett, trans., *The A'in-i Akbari*, 3 vols. (1873, 1894; repr., Calcutta: Royal Asiatic Society, 1993), the plate facing 1:48. And for a discussion of Mughal tent cities, see Stephen P. Blake, *Shahjahanabad: The Sovereign City in Mughal India* (Cambridge: Cambridge University Press, 1993), especially 83–99. For architecture and meanings attached to tents in Central Asia, Afghanistan, and Iran, past and present, see Peter Alford Andrews, *Nomad Tent Types in the Middle East* (Wiesbaden: L. Reichert, 1997), 13.

6. Gulbadan Banu Begum, *Ahval-i Humayun Badshah*, Ms.Or.166, fol. 11b, British Library, London.

7. Gulbadan, *Ahval*, fol. 2a.

8. Most of the details of Babur's favorite residential places are drawn from Crane, "The Patronage of Zahir al-Din Babur," especially 98–101.

9. Babur employs the word *Mongol* in his *Baburnama* for the Turkicized descendants of Chingiz Khan. His usage *Mughulistan* covers the same region as Mongolia of today, but the Chaghatayid Turks and Mongols of today's Mongolia are different.

10. Annette S. Beveridge, trans., *The History of Humayun: Humayun Nama*, 2nd ed. (1902; repr., Delhi: Low Price Publications, 1994), 244; Stanley Lane-Poole, *Babar* (1890; repr., Delhi: Low Price Publications, 1997), 23.

11. This poem was first mentioned in *Tazkira Sobh Golshan*, written by Sayyed Mohammad Ali Hassan Khan Bhupali and published in 1878 in Bhopal. Mohammad Ali Hassan Khan Salim Bhupali, *Tazkira Sobh Golshan* (Bhopal, 1878), 348.

12. I discuss the books that Gulbadan owned and read in chapter 14. Maria Szuppe, "The Jewels of Wonder: Learned Ladies and Princess Politicians in the Provinces of Early Safavid Iran," in *Women in the Medieval Islamic World: Power, Patronage, and Piety*, ed. Gavin R. G. Hambly (New York: St. Martin's, 1998), 342n45.

13. Quite popular in those times was the pseudonym *Makhfi*, or the Hidden One, which holds a clue to the modest and secreted side of women's creative ventures. Royal women's

poems remained tucked in the margins of manuscripts, noted outside buildings, or conjured anew in the agile public imagination with attributions to past female poets. Later male collectors and restorers of poetry believed that a successful female poet was one who wrote like a man. This was certainly the view of Valeh Dhagestani, an Iranian, who in the mid-eighteenth century assembled the works of Muslim elite and royal women in twenty-five hundred entries. There was also Azar Begeli's *Atashkhand*, completed in 1760–61, and a Mughal officer in Bengal, Shir Khan Lodi, whose short *tezkerah*, or a memorial of poets compiled in the form of a biographical anthology, lists, among others, the seventeenth-century Empress Nur Jahan, who used the popular pseudonym Makhfi. For a history of these compilations, see Sunil Sharma, "From A'esha to Nur Jahan: The Shaping of a Classical Persian Poetic Canon of Women," *Journal of Persianate Studies* 2 (2009): 148–64.

14. G. M. Wickens, trans. and ed., *The Nasirean Ethics* (London: George Allen and Unwin, 1964), 169–70.

15. Wickens, *Nasirean Ethics*, 173.

16. Wickens, *Nasirean Ethics*, 167–68.

17. The literature on women's literacy in Islamic societies is extensive. The following books are good examples: Hambly, *Women in the Medieval Islamic World*; D. Fairchild Ruggels, ed., *Women, Patronage, and Self-Representation in Islamic Societies* (Albany: State University of New York Press, 2000); and, more recently, collected essays on women's education in the Muslim world, especially Nadia Maria el-Cheikh, "Observations on Women's Education in Medieval Islamic Societies," in *Enfance et jeunesse dans le monde musulman: Childhood and Youth in the Muslim World*, ed. François Georgeon and Klaus Kreiser (Paris: Maisonneuve and Larose, 2007), 57–72.

18. Szuppe, "The Jewels of Wonder," 329.

19. K. M. Asharf, *Life and Conditions of the People of Hindustan*, 3rd ed. (New Delhi: Munshiram Manoharlal, 1988), 269.

THREE. Curiosities of Hind

1. Gulbadan Banu Begum, *Ahval-i Humayun Badshah*, Ms.Or.166, fols. 9b–10b, British Library, London. Gulbadan's description of the gift-giving ceremony is on 10a–11a. Her expression "Curiosities of Hind" is on 9b.

2. Gulbadan does not name the garden, but the Kabul Chahar Bagh outside the city walls, built sometime after 1504, appears to have served along with Bala Hisar as one of Babur's primary places of residence. Gulbadan mentions the garden's excellent audience hall (*divankhana*), and Babur refers to the garden on several occasions. For an architectural discussion, see Howard Crane, "The Patronage of Zahir al-Din Babur and the Origins of Mughal Architecture," *Bulletin of the Asia Institute*, n.s. 1 (1987): 95–98.

3. Crane, "The Patronage of Zahir al-Din Babur," 98; Annette Susannah Beveridge, trans., *Babur-nama (Memoirs of Babur) of Zahiru'd-din Muhammad Babur Padshah Ghazi* (1921; repr., Delhi: Low Price Publications, 1997), 417.

4. Gulbadan, *Ahval*, fols. 9a–9b.

5. The evocative translation is from Wheeler M. Thackston, trans. and ed., *The Babur-nama: Memoirs of Babur, Prince and Emperor* (New York, Modern Library, 1996), 353–55. Babur's speech is on 354.

6. Gulbadan, *Ahval*, fol. 9b.

7. Thackston, *Memoirs of Babur,* 353.

8. Gulbadan, *Ahval*, fol. 11a.

9. The description of the dress of the dancers is derived from a painting made in the court of Gulbadan's nephew Akbar: *The Celebrated Dancers from Mandu Perform before Akbar, Akbarnama,* Ms. fol. I. S.2/ 1896, Acc. No. 16/17. For a detailed discussion of this painting and the event, see Ruby Lal, *Domesticity and Power in the Early Mughal World* (Cambridge: Cambridge University Press, 2005), 200–202.

10. Gulbadan, *Ahval,* fol. 9b.

11. A. Yusuf Ali, *The Holy Qur'an: Text, Translation and Commentary* (n.p.: Amana, 1983), 14–15.

12. Gulbadan, *Ahval,* fols. 10a–11a.

13. Wheeler M. Thackston, trans. and ed., *Zahiruddin Muhammad Babur Mirza: Baburnama,* parts 1–3, Turkish transcription, Persian edition, and English translation (Cambridge, Mass.: Near Eastern Languages and Civilization, Harvard University, 1993), 367–68.

14. Thackston, *Baburnama,* 335.

FOUR. The First *Kafila*

1. Gulbadan Banu Begum, *Ahval-i Humayun Badshah,* Ms.Or.166, fol. 14a, British Library, London. Fakhr-un-Nisa is several times mentioned. She was the mother-in-law of the celebrated Maham Anaga, the foster mother of Akbar, the third Mughal emperor. Annette S. Beveridge, trans., *The History of Humayun: Humayun Nama,* 2nd ed. (1902; repr., Delhi: Low Price Publications, 1994), 101n9.

2. Wheeler M. Thackston, trans. and ed., *The Baburnama: Memoirs of Babur, Prince and Emperor* (New York: Modern Library, 1996), 424.

3. Cited in Subhash Parihar, *Land Transport in Mughal India: Agra-Lahore Mughal Highway and Its Architectural Remains* (New Delhi: Aryan Books, 2008), 84.

4. For a detailed history of the Kabul-Agra route, see Parihar, *Land Transport in Mughal India,* 49–58.

5. Father Antonio Monserrate, *The Commentary of Father Monserrate, S.J., on His Journey to the Court of Akbar,* trans. J. S. Hoyland, and ed. S. N. Banerjee (1922; repr., New Delhi: Asian Educational Services, 1992). Among European travelers who traversed this route in the late sixteenth and seventeenth centuries are John Mildenhall, William Finch, and Edward Terry.

6. Monserrate, *Journey to the Court of Akbar,* 149.

7. Arif Qandhari, *Tarikh-i Akbari,* trans. Tasneem Ahmad (Delhi: South Asia Books, 1993), 64, 131.

8. Nicolao Manucci, *Storia Do Mogor or Mogul India, 1653–1708 by Niccolao Manucci Venetian,* trans. William Irvine (London: John Murray, 1907), 2:101.

9. Monserrate, *Journey to the Court of Akbar,* 143.

10. Sir Alexander Burnes, *Cabool: Being a Personal Narrative of a Journey to, and Residence in That City* (London: John Murray, 1842), 127.

11. Burnes, *Cabool*, 128.

12. This account is drawn from two manuscripts in the British Library, I.O. 581 in Pashtu and I.O. 582 in Persian, and from Annette Susannah Beveridge, trans., *Babur-nama (Memoirs of Babur) of Zahiru'd-din Muhammad Babur Padshah Ghazi* (1921; repr., Delhi: Low Price Publications, 1997), xxxvi–xli, citation on xli. For Gulbadan's rendering, see Gulbadan, *Ahval*, fol. 7b.

13. Burnes, *Cabool*, 120–21.

14. Monserrate, *Journey to the Court of Akbar*, 122.

15. Muzaffar Alam, *The Languages of Political Islam in India, c. 1200–1800* (New Delhi: Permanent Black, 2004), 121, 123, 135.

16. Gulbadan, *Ahval*, fol. 14a.

17. Gulbadan, *Ahval*, fol. 14a.

18. Gulbadan, *Ahval*, fol. 14a.

19. Babur repeatedly stressed the weight of protocol, most notably in 1506 on his way to Herat on a strategic mission in which he was to ally with a cousin against their ardent enemy the Uzbeks. En route, hearing that his cousin had passed away, he changed direction and went toward Badakhshan to pay condolences to his nephews, the sons of his deceased cousin, and other relatives who were based there. When they heard that Babur was approaching their city, his relatives came out to meet him, except his nephew Badi-uz-zaman Mirza, whose officers explained that since he was fifteen years older than Babur, custom required that he enter the Mirza's premises, kneel, and offer condolences. Babur did so. Although it was not a social gathering, fruit, syrups, and sherbet were brought out in gold and silver vessels. When Babur returned a second time, the Mirza did not show him the courtesy of honored reception or adequate hospitality. Babur spoke to his officers and made clear that although he was younger in age, his place was high. He sat twice on the throne of Samarkand, the seat of the great Timur. Valor and triumph signified Babur's rank. The noblemen conveyed Babur's displeasure and reminded the Mirza of the protocol. He admitted to his mistake at once and showed Babur the respect he claimed.

20. Gulbadan, *Ahval*, fol. 14b.

21. Gulbadan, *Ahval*, fol. 15a.

22. Gulbadan, *Ahval*, fol. 15a.

23. Gulbadan, *Ahval*, fol. 15a.

FIVE. My Royal Father

1. For early town planning of Agra, see Javed Hasan, "Mapping the Mughal City of Agra," *Proceedings of the Indian History Congress* 51 (1990): 241–45; William G. Klingelhofer, "The Jahangiri Mahal of Agra Fort: Expression and Experience in Early Mughal Architecture," *Muqarnas* 5 (1988): 153–69.

2. I visited Ram Bagh in January 2016 with the support of the Archaeological Survey of India team led by Mr. R. K. Singh.

3. Gulbadan Banu Begum, *Ahval-i Humayun Badshah*, Ms.Or.166, fol. 15a, British Library, London. This was the Garden of Victory, or Bagh-i Fath, that Babur launched after his triumph over Rana Sanga.

4. Gulbadan, *Ahval*, fol. 15b.

5. Gulbadan, *Ahval*, fol. 15b.

6. Gulbadan, *Ahval*, fol. 11a.

7. Henry Blochmann, ed., and H. S. Jarrett, trans., *The A'in-i Akbari*, 3 vols. (1873, 1894; repr., Calcutta: Royal Asiatic Society, 1993), 1:277.

8. Gulbadan, *Ahval*, fol. 21a.

9. Gulbadan, *Ahval*, fol. 11b.

10. Gulbadan, *Ahval*, fol. 15b.

11. Gulbadan, *Ahval*, fol. 15b.

12. Gulbadan, *Ahval*, fol. 15b.

13. Stephen F. Dale, *Babur: The Timurid Prince and Mughal Emperor, 1483–1530* (New Delhi: Cambridge University Press, 2018), 163–64. The work that Babur copied was *Risala-i Validiya*.

14. Ruby Lal, "From the Inside Out: Spaces of Pleasure and Authority," in *Art and Stories from Mughal India*, ed. Sonya Rhea Quintanilla (Cleveland: Cleveland Museum of Art, 2016), 293–94. The painting *Lady Smoking a Hookah by a Pool* (Mughal 1680–1700), held in the Cleveland Museum of Art's collection, is discussed in this essay.

15. Gulbadan, *Ahval*, fol. 16b.

16. Gulbadan, *Ahval*, fol. 16b.

17. Gulbadan, *Ahval*, fol. 17a.

18. *A'in-i Akbari*, 1:275.

19. *A'in-i Akbari*, 1:276.

20. Gulbadan, *Ahval*, fol. 17a.

21. The image of Babur performing the sacrificial rite is from the British Museum version of Maulavi Khuda Bakhsh Khan Bahandur, *Tarikh-i Khandan-i Timuriyya*. The original manuscript is at the Khuda Bakhsh Oriental Public Library, Patna, India.

22. Gulbadan, *Ahval*, fol. 17a.

23. Gulbadan, *Ahval*, fol. 17a.

24. For details of the wedding discussion, see Gulbadan, *Ahval*, fol. 18b. Gulrang was born between 1511 and 1515. She was given in marriage to Isan Timur Sultan. Gulchihra, born between 1515 and 1517, married Sultan Tukhta-bugha. For a biographical sketch of the two princesses, see Annette S. Beveridge, trans., *The History of Humayun: Humayun Nama*, 2nd ed. (1902; repr., Delhi: Low Price Publications, 1994), 231–33.

25. Wheeler M. Thackston, trans. and ed., *Zahiruddin Muhammad Babur Mirza: Baburnama*, parts 1–3, Turkish transcription, Persian edition, and English translation (Cambridge, Mass.: Near Eastern Languages and Civilization, Harvard University, 1993), 741. This text is in Chaghatay Turki only. Not available in Persian in Thackston's edition.

26. Annette Beveridge's discussion of this tussle for succession is in her notes in the *Baburnama*: Annette Susannah Beveridge, trans., *Babur-nama (Memoirs of Babur) of*

Zahiru'd-din Muhammad Babur Padshah Ghazi (1921; repr., Delhi: Low Price Publications, 1997), 702–11.

27. Among them, Nizam al-Din Ahmad and Abul Fazl.

28. *A'in-i Akbari*, 1:277; B. De and Baini Prasad, trans., *The Tabaqat-i Akbari of Khwajah Nizammudin Ahmad*, 3 vols. (1936; repr., Delhi, 1992), 2:28.

29. Gulbadan, *Ahval*, fol. 19b.

30. Gulbadan, *Ahval*, fol. 20a.

31. Gulbadan, *Ahval*, fols. 20b–21a. Each Mughal emperor customarily had an official posthumous name/title that was used by all court historians.

SIX. Female Guardians of the Empire

In addition to the references that follow for this chapter, the key concepts and ideas on the making and conditions of court society in Humayun's reign are based upon my investigations in *Domesticity and Power in the Early Mughal World* (Cambridge: Cambridge University Press, 2005), especially chapters 4 and 5.

1. Gulbadan Banu Begum, *Ahval-i Humayun Badshah*, Ms.Or.166, fol. 29a, British Library, London.

2. For an extended discussion, see Lal, *Domesticity and Power,* chapters 4 and 5.

3. Gulbadan, *Ahval*, fol. 21b.

4. On Miva-jan's hysterical pregnancy, Ruby Lal, "Historicizing the *Harem:* The Challenge of a Princess's Memoir," *Feminist Studies* 30, no. 3 (Fall/Winter 2004): 590–616.

5. My discussion of the feasts is drawn from Gulbadan, *Ahval,* fol. 24a–28b. For gift-giving and its significance, see Lal, *Domesticity and Power,* 126–28.

6. Gulbadan, *Ahval*, fol. 27b.

7. Gulbadan, *Ahval*, fol. 28a.

8. Gulbadan, *Ahval*, fol. 28b.

9. Gulbadan, *Ahval*, fol. 29a.

10. Except for the discussion of the building of Dinpanah in Delhi in Khwandamir's *Qanun-i Humayuni,* and a brief mention of the beginnings of the construction of buildings in Agra and Gwalior by Gulbadan, there is no reference to the buildings constructed by Humayun. Jawhar, Bayazid Bayat, Abul Fazl, Nizam al-Din Ahmad, and Badauni are silent on this matter. M. Hidayat Hosain, ed., *The Qanun-i Humayuni of Khwandamir,* Bibliotheca Indica Series 260, no. 1488 (Calcutta: Royal Asiatic Society of Bengal, 1940), Persian edition; *Tadhkira-i Humayun wa Akbar of Bayazid Biyat,* Bibliotheca Indica Series 264, no. 1546 (Calcutta: Royal Asiatic Society of Bengal, 1941), Persian edition. See also B. Prasad, "A Note on the Buildings of Humayun," *Journal of the Royal Asiatic Society of Bengal: Letters* 5 (1939).

11. Hosain, *Qanun-i Humayuni,* 34–35. The *Akbarnama* translates *Ahl-i Sa'adat* as "learned or literary men," Henry Beveridge, trans., *The Akbar Nama of Abu-l-Fazl,* 3 vols. (1902–39; repr., Delhi: Low Price Publications, 1993), 1:610, and on p. 643, the translation of the three words is given as follows: *murad* (joy), *dawlat* (dominion), and *sa'adat* (auspiciousness). For Gulbadan's discussion of the *ahl-i Dawlat,* the *ahl-i Sa'adat,* and the *ahl-i Murad* at the time of the feast organized by Khanzada Begum, see Gulbadan, *Ahval,* fols. 26b–28a.

12. Gulbadan, *Ahval*, fols. 30a–30b.

13. Michael Fisher, *A Short History of the Mughal Empire* (London: I. B. Tauris, 2016), 61–62.

14. Gulbadan, *Ahval*, fol. 32a.

15. Gulbadan, *Ahval*, fols. 33b–34a; Beveridge, *The Akbar Nama of Abu-l-Fazl*, 1:338. When Humayun found out about Hindal's attempt to usurp the Mughal throne, he dispatched a close political adviser to Agra. Among the growing number of Indian Muslims at the court, Shaikh Bahlul was resented by the older nobles with origins in other lands. When this trusted messenger offered words of advice, Hindal murdered him.

16. Beveridge, *The Akbar Nama of Abu-l-Fazl*, 1:339, and n1.

17. Gulbadan, *Ahval*, fol. 33a.

18. K. R. Qanungo, *Sher Shah and His Times* (New Delhi: Orient Longman, 1965), 205.

19. Gulbadan, *Ahval*, fol. 33b.

20. Gulbadan, *Ahval*, fol. 34b.

21. Gulbadan, *Ahval*, fol. 35a.

22. Annette S. Beveridge, trans., *The History of Humayun: Humayun Nama*, 2nd ed. (1902; repr., Delhi: Low Price Publications, 1994), appendix, p. 219.

23. Gulbadan, *Ahval*, fol. 35a.

24. I use the simultaneous Persian/English edition of Jawhar Aftabchi, *Tadhkirat-ul-Vaqi'at*, trans. and ed. Wheeler M. Thackston: *Three Memoirs of Humayun* (Costa Mesa, Calif.: Mazda, 2009), 1:90.

25. Gulbadan, *Ahval*, fols. 35a–35b.

26. In a meeting he convened soon after Hindal's return, the issue utmost in the emperor's mind was Shaikh Bahlul's murder. Hindal explained that the shaikh had sent arms and military appurtenances to Sher Shah, a clarification Gulbadan agreed with and recorded in her book. Humayun, Kamran, and other members of the court concluded that the prince was carried away under the influence of a dissatisfied court faction threatened by the rising influence of Muslims from Hindustan. For further details, see Munis D. Faruqui, *The Princes of the Mughal Empire, 1504–1719* (Cambridge: Cambridge University Press, 2012), 57.

27. Gulbadan, *Ahval*, fol. 36a.

28. Gulbadan, *Ahval*, fol. 36a.

29. Gulbadan, *Ahval*, fol. 37b.

30. Gulbadan, *Ahval*, fol. 37b.

31. Gulbadan, *Ahval*, fol. 39a.

SEVEN. Great Expectations

1. Gulbadan Banu Begum, *Ahval-i Humayun Badshah*, Ms.Or.166, fols. 54a–54b, British Library, London.

2. Jawhar Aftabchi, *Tadhkirat-ul-Vaqi'at*, trans. and ed. Wheeler M. Thackston: *Three Memoirs of Humayun* (Costa Mesa, Calif.: Mazda, 2009), 1:116.

3. Jawhar, *Tadhkirat-ul-Vaqi'at*, 1:116–17.

4. Jawhar, *Tadhkirat-ul-Vaqi'at*, 1:116–17.

5. More on Gulbadan's style and writing in chapter 14.

6. Gulbadan, *Ahval*, fols. 68a–68b.

7. Gulbadan, *Ahval*, fol. 48b.

8. Henry Beveridge, trans., *The Akbar Nama of Abu-l-Fazl*, 3 vols. (1902–39; repr., Delhi: Low Price Publications, 1993), 1:455.

9. Gulbadan, *Ahval*, fol. 62b.

10. Gulbadan, *Ahval*, fol. 65a.

11. Gulbadan, *Ahval*, fols. 63a–63b.

12. Gulbadan, *Ahval*, fol. 63a.

13. For a brief biography of Mah Chuchak, see Annette S. Beveridge, trans., *The History of Humayun: Humayun Nama*, 2nd ed. (1902, repr., Delhi: Low Price Publications, 1994), 260.

14. See, for example, Gulbadan, *Ahval*, fol. 52b.

15. Privy to fine-grained, intimate detail, Gulbadan later penned the entire account, as though she was present in Sind. Even Jawhar, the water bearer with an eye for daily happenings who was present at Hamida's wedding, couldn't possibly know what Gulbadan gathered from her sister-in-law. For a discussion of the different presentations of Gulbadan and Jawhar, see Ruby Lal, *Domesticity and Power in the Early Mughal World* (Cambridge: Cambridge University Press, 2005), 99–102.

16. Annette Susannah Beveridge, trans., *Babur-nama (Memoirs of Babur) of Zahiru'd-din Muhammad Babur Padshah Ghazi* (1921; repr., Delhi: Low Price Publications, 1997), 551, and index 1, p. 749n1.

17. Gulbadan says Dildar Begum gave a party, *majlis-i dadand*; Gulbadan, *Ahval*, fols. 42a–42b.

18. Gulbadan, *Ahval*, fol. 42b.

19. S. Haim, *Shorter English Persian Dictionary*, 3rd ed., 691; F. Steingass, *A Comprehensive Persian-English Dictionary*, 2nd ed., 1265.

20. Gulbadan, *Ahval*, fols. 43a–43b.

21. Gulbadan, *Ahval*, fols. 43a–43b. In her words: lawful, or *jayiz ast*; a second time it is forbidden, or *na-mahram ast.*

22. Gulbadan, *Ahval*, fols. 43a–43b.

23. Gulbadan, *Ahval*, fol. 65b.

24. Gulbadan, *Ahval*, fols. 66a–66b. On the exact date of Akbar's circumcision, see Beveridge, *History of Humayun*, 179n2.

25. B. N. Goswamy, "Humayun and His Painters," *Tribune*, April 14, 2013, https://www.tribuneindia.com/2013/20130414/spectrum/main2.htm#top.

26. Gulbadan, *Ahval*, fol. 78b.

27. Gulbadan, *Ahval*, fols. 67a–67b.

28. Gulbadan, *Ahval*, fols. 68a–68b.

29. Gulbadan, *Ahval*, fols. 68a–68b.

30. Gulbadan, *Ahval*, fol. 69a.

31. Gulbadan, *Ahval*, fols. 69a–70b.

32. Gulbadan, *Ahval*, fol. 73b. The reader thus meets Saru-qad, or Straight Cypress, another Persian woman who likely came back with Humayun and Hamida. She will be a future companion of the princess in her long travels.

33. Gulbadan, *Ahval*, fol. 83a.

34. Gulbadan, *Ahval*, fol. 80a.

35. Gulbadan, *Ahval*, fols. 82a–82b. Gulbadan's manuscript breaks off here. The tussles and machinations in Mughal history after Kamran's blinding did not stop. Many men wrote about the times ahead. There was Jawhar, the ewer-bearer. There was Bayazid Bayat, the officer. There were rich monumental court histories of Akbar that recounted dynastic events.

EIGHT. Butzaris

1. Two dates are mentioned in the *Akbarnama* for Gulbadan's departure from Fatehpur-Sikri: October 8 or 9, 1575 (Henry Beveridge, trans., *The Akbar Nama of Abu-l-Fazl*, 3 vols. [1902–39; repr., Delhi: Low Price Publications, 1993], 3:206), and October 1576 (3:570n1). The date of her return is given as April 13, 1582, in the *Akbarnama* (3:206n3), which is clearly not compatible with the fact that the pilgrimage lasted three and a half years. Judging by Sultan Khwaja's return, as I suggest above, we can establish that Gulbadan left Surat in the spring of 1577. It was spring 1580 when she started her homeward journey. Bayazid Bayat had an exchange of letters with the royal party when he reached Aden in early April 1580. Taking into account the time she spent in Surat, the shipwreck in Aden, and on to Ajmer, where she performed a supplementary pilgrimage, it would be another year before she finally returned to Fatehpur-Sikri (3:570n1).

2. The women in the hajj caravan included:

—Sultanam Begum, the wife of Mirza 'Askari (Akbar's step-aunt, who looked after him when Humayun was in exile).

—Umm-Kulsum Khanum, the granddaughter of Gulbadan Begum (perhaps the daughter of Gulbadan Begum's son Sa'adat-yar, though this is not entirely clear).

—Gulnar Aghacha, a wife of Babur *padshah*, one of the two Circassians sent as a present to him by Shah Tahmasb in 1526 (Akbar's step-grandmother).

—Bibi Safiyeh, Shaham Agha, and Sarv-i Sahi, the servants of Humayun. Bibi Saru-qad, also called Sarv-i Sahi (Straight Cypress) later married Munim Khan-i Khanan. A widow by the time of this journey, she had been, according to Annette Beveridge, a singer, a "reciter," and a "reliable woman." Bibi Safiyeh and Bibi Saru-qad "sang in the moonlight on the road to Laghman in 1549."

—The last-named member of the group was Salima Khanum, daughter of Khizr Khwaja Khan, Gulbadan Begum's husband. Whether Gulbadan was the mother is not known.

For this list, see Annette S. Beveridge, trans., *The History of Humayun: Humayun Nama*, 2nd ed. (1902, repr., Delhi: Low Price Publications, 1994), 70; Beveridge, *The Akbar Nama of Abu-l-Fazl*, 3:206; Ruby Lal, *Domesticity and Power in the Early Mughal World* (Cambridge: Cambridge University Press, 2005), 208–13.

3. Beveridge, *The Akbar Nama of Abu-l-Fazl*, 3:275.

4. Beveridge, *Humayun*, 71; Beveridge, *The Akbar Nama of Abu-l-Fazl*, 3:206n2.

5. Ruby Lal, *Empress: The Astonishing Reign of Nur Jahan* (New York: Norton, 2018), 38.

6. I am grateful to Rana Safvi and the Archaeological Survey of India for the tour of Arab Ki Sarai. For Arab masons and the work in the area, see Rana Safvi, trans. and ed., *Sayyid Ahmad Khan, Asar-us-Sanadid* (New Delhi: Tulika Books, 2018), 49. Art historians continue to debate who designed Humayan's tomb.

7. Beveridge, *The Akbar Nama of Abu-l-Fazl,* 2:503, 530.

8. *hazrat-i-sarapardeh-i-saltanat* (Majestic, Highnesses, Veiled Ones of the Kingdom); see references to senior women in B. De and Baini Prasad, trans., *The Tabaqat-i Akbari of Khwajah Nizammudin Ahmad,* 3 vols. (1936; repr., Delhi, 1992), 2:78, 96, 110, 559.

9. Work on Akbar's religious and ethical life is extensive. See, as examples, S. A. A. Rizvi, "Dimensions of Sulh-i Kul (Universal Peace) in Akbar's Reign and the Sufi Theory of Perfect Man," in *Akbar and His Age,* ed. Iqtidar Alam Khan (New Delhi: Northern Book Center, 1999), 17; Irfan Habib, "Commemorating Akbar," in Khan, *Akbar and His Age,* xii, xiii, xiv; S. A. A. Rizvi, *Religious and Intellectual History of the Muslims in Akbar's Reign* (New Delhi: Munshiram Manoharlal, 1975); Muzaffar Alam et al., eds., *The Making of Indo-Persian Culture: Indian and French Studies* (New Delhi, Manohar, 2000); and, more recently, Ali Anooshahr, "Shirazi Scholars and the Political Culture of the Sixteenth-Century Indo-Persian World," *Indian Economic and Social History Review* 51, no. 3 (2014): 342–43.

10. For the history of the making of Mughal harem, see Lal, *Domesticity and Power,* chapter 7; Lal, *Empress,* chapter 4.

11. Henry Blochmann, ed., and H. S. Jarrett, trans., *The A'in-i Akbari,* 3 vols. (1873, 1894; repr., Calcutta: Royal Asiatic Society, 1993), 1:45–46.

12. For Akbar's marriages and sources for Mughal marital alliances, see Lal, *Domesticity and Power,* 166–75.

13. Lal, *Domesticity and Power,* 237–42.

14. M. N. Pearson, *Merchants and Rulers in Gujarat: The Response to the Portuguese in the Sixteenth Century* (Berkeley: University of California Press, 1976), 36.

15. Pearson, *Merchants and Rulers,* 40–41.

16. Naim R. Farooqi, "Moguls, Ottomans, and Pilgrims: Protecting the Routes to Mecca in the Sixteenth and Seventeenth Centuries," *International History Review* 10, no. 2 (May 1988): 200.

17. *Akbarnama,* Add.27, 247, fol. 285b, British Library. For a discussion of this passage, see Shireen Moosvi, "Shipping and Navigation under Akbar," *Proceedings of the Indian History Congress* 60 (1999): especially 252–53.

18. George S. A. Ranking, W. H. Lowe, and Sir Wolseley Haig, trans. and eds., *Muntakhabu-t-tawarikh* (1884–1925; repr., Delhi: Renaissance, 1986), 1:480.

19. Beveridge, *The Akbar Nama of Abu-l-Fazl,* 3:206. For Gulbadan's hajj, see Lal, *Domesticity and Power,* 208–13; Beveridge, *The Akbar Nama of Abu-l-Fazl,* 3:205; Ranking, Lowe, and Haig, *Muntakhabu-t-tawarikh,* 2:216, 320.

20. Mahmood Kooria, "'Killed the Pilgrims and Persecuted Them': Portuguese *Estado da India*'s Encounters with the Hajj in the Sixteenth Century," in *The Hajj and Europe in the Age of Empire,* Leiden Studies in Islam and Society, vol. 5 (Leiden: Brill, 2017), 24.

21. Pearson, *Merchants and Rulers,* 41, 43.

22. Beveridge, *The Akbar Nama of Abu-l-Fazl*, 3:205.

23. Sayed Moinuddin Nadwi, Saiyeed Azhar Ali, and Imtiaz Ali Arshi, eds., *Arif Qanda-hari, Tarikh-i Akbari* (Rampur: Rampur Raza Library, 1962), 232–33.

24. Simon Digby, "Bayazid Beg Turkman's Pilgrimage to Makka and Return to Gujarat: A Sixteenth Century Narrative," *Iran* 42, no. 1 (2004): 160.

25. The sultans of Gujarat had successfully secured the land routes from the coast to the inner agricultural hinterlands, but in 1535, the Portuguese seized the island of Diu in the southwest and imposed the decree about acquiring cartaz in order to navigate the sea waters. Surat resisted the Portuguese under the governorship of a man named Khwaja Safar Safar. The well-known conquistador João de Castro, after a bloody war with Safar's forces in 1546, sent messages to nearby towns asking local merchants to return to trade and settle in Diu. Safar was killed in this second siege of Diu: Pearson, *Merchants and Rulers*, 33.

26. Mentioned in Akbar's farman to Qilich Khan, E. Blocket Supplement Pers. 482, document no. 15, fols. 30b–31a, Bibliothèque Nationale, Paris; cf. Moosvi, "Shipping and Navigation under Akbar," 260–61.

27. The men in the pilgrim party, Gulbadan's uncle 'Abdur Rahman Beg, the emperor's foster brother Baqi Khan, and accompanying officers were still en route to Surat. The *mir-i hajj* consulted Gulbadan and hurriedly dispatched a messenger named 'Ali Murad Uzbeg to the emperor to send orders. Ranking, Lowe, and Haig, *Muntakhabu-t-tawarikh*, 2:243.

28. Beveridge, *The Akbar Nama of Abu-l-Fazl*, 3:276.

29. Beveridge, *The Akbar Nama of Abu-l-Fazl*, 3:205.

30. Akbar first met a group of Portuguese in 1573 during the siege of Surat. A year later he received Peter Tavares, a Portuguese commandant at his court, and inquired a great deal about Christianity. At Tavares's recommendation, Akbar sent for Father Gil Eanes Pereira, vicar general of Bengal, who arrived in Fatehpur-Sikri in 1578. Unable to satisfy Akbar's curiosity about Christianity, Pereira put to the emperor the idea of inviting a Jesuit mission to the court. A group of three Jesuit missionaries arrived in February 1580. This mission, headed by Rudolph Acquaviva, stayed in Fatehpur-Sikri for three years. A second mission went to Lahore, the new capital, in 1591, and stayed a year. Father Jerome Xavier led the third mission to Akbar's court in 1594. Arnulf Camps, *An Unpublished Letter of Father Christoval Ce Vega, S. J. Its Importance for the History of the Second Mission to the Mughal Court and for the Knowledge of the Religion of Emperor Akbar* (Cairo, 1956), 7.

31. Pearson, *Merchants and Rulers*, 32. On Surat's history and rise, see Ashin Das Gupta, *Indian Merchants and the Decline of Surat, c. 1700–1750* (Wiesbaden: Franz Steiner, 1979); Sanjay Subrahmanyam, "A Note on the Rise of Surat in the Sixteenth Century," *Journal of the Economic and Social History of the Orient* 43, no. 1 (2000): 32.

32. Gupta, *Indian Merchants*, 20.

33. Gupta, *Indian Merchants*, 21, citation on 35.

34. Ira Mukhoty, *Akbar, the Great Mughal* (New Delhi: Aleph, 2020), 141.

35. Gupta, *Indian Merchants*, 22. The description of the wharf area is from this text. Gupta discusses the seventeenth-century landscape. On ships and their technology, see A. Jan Qaisar, "Shipbuilding in the Mughal Empire during the Seventeenth Century," in *Medieval India, a Miscellany*, vol. 2 (London: Asia Publishing House, 1972), 149–70.

36. Beveridge, *The Akbar Nama of Abu-l-Fazl*, 3:205; Ranking, Lowe, and Haig, *Muntakhabu-t-tawarikh*, 2:216, 320.

37. *Akbarnama*, Add.27, 247, fol. 285b, British Library.

38. A number of Mughal miniature paintings depict ships. See, for example, *Alexander Is Lowered into the Sea*, folio from a *Khamsa* (Quintet) of Amir Khusrau Dihlavi, drawn for Akbar by painter Mukunda, dated 1597–98, accession no. 13.228.27, the Metropolitan Museum of Art, New York. There is also the painting in the Victoria and Albert Museum, London, Museum No. IS.2:4–1896, that is from the official history of Akbar's reign that depicts his mother Mariam Makani traveling to Agra by river.

39. Moosvi, "Shipping and Navigation under Akbar," 256–57.

40. *Nishan* of Jahanara to Sharfuddin Husain and the officers of the Sahebi, dated 1642. E. Blochet, Supplement Pers. 482, document no. 15, fol. 36a, Bibliothèque Nationale, Paris. For a discussion of this Nishan, see Shireen Moosvi, "A State Sector in Overseas Trade: The Imperial Mughal Shipping Establishment at Surat," *Studies in People's History* 2, no. 1 (2015): 71–75.

41. Moosvi, "A State Sector," 74.

42. Henry Blochmann, ed., and H. S. Jarrett, trans., *The A'in-i Akbari*, 3 vols. (1873, 1894; repr., Calcutta: Royal Asiatic Society, 1993), 1:222, 229.

43. I use the simultaneous Persian/English edition of Bayazid Bayat's *Tarikh-i Humayun*, trans. and ed. Wheeler M. Thackston: *Three Memoirs of Homayun* (Costa Mesa, Calif.: Mazda, 2009), 2:166–67, citation on p. 167; fol. 150b.

44. Moosvi, "Shipping and Navigation under Akbar," 254.

45. Moosvi, "Shipping and Navigation under Akbar," 261.

46. As the imperial historian described her. Beveridge, *The Akbar Nama of Abu-l-Fazl*, 3:206.

47. Father Antonio Monserrate, *The Commentary of Father Monserrate, S.J., on His Journey to the Court of Akbar*, trans. J. S. Hoyland and ed. S. N. Banerjee (1922; repr., New Delhi: Asian Educational Services, 1992), 166n255.

NINE. The Promised Land

1. Alexis Wick, *The Red Sea: In Search of Lost Space* (Berkeley: University of California Press, 2016), 18, 26.

2. G. Rex Smith and Ahmad 'Umar al-Zayla'I, eds., *Bride of the Sea, a 10th/16th Century Account of Jeddah: al-Silah wa-'l-'uddah fi tarikh bander Juddah*, Occasional Papers Series (Durham: University of Durham, 1984), 3–14.

3. On features and amenities on ships, see Ahsan Jan Qaisar, "Merchant Shipping in India during the Seventeenth Century," in Aligarh Muslim University Department of History, Centre of Advanced Study, *Medieval India, a Miscellany*, vol. 2 (London: Asia Publishing House, 1972), 195–220.

4. A. Jan Qaisar, "Shipbuilding in the Mughal Empire during the Seventeenth Century," in *Medieval India, a Miscellany*, vol. 2, 158.

5. Qaisar, "Merchant Shipping in India," 197.

6. Venetia Porter, ed., *Hajj: Journey to the Heart of Islam* (Cambridge: Harvard University Press, 2012), 127.

7. Doris Behrens-Abouseif, "The *Mahmal* Legend and the Pilgrimage of the Ladies of the Mamluk Court," 93, https://doi.org/10.6082/M1C24TJJ.

8. Hatoon Ajwad Al-Fassi, "A Note on Meccan Women in the Fifteenth Century," *Journal of Women of the Middle East and the Islamic World*, no. 14 (2016): 248; Behrens-Abouseif, "The *Mahmal* Legend," 91.

9. El-Qutlugh Khatun was the daughter of Abagha Ilkhan (r. 1265–82). On her life, see Jonathan Brack, "A Mongol Princess Making Hajj: The Biography of El Qutlugh, Daughter of Abagha Ilkhan (r. 1265–82)," *Journal of the Royal Asiatic Society*, 3rd ser., 21, no. 3 (July 2011): 331–59.

10. Brack, "A Mongol Princess Making Hajj," 333. See also Suraiya Faruqhi, "Slave Agencies Compared: The Ottoman and Mughal Empires," in *Slaves and Slave Agency in the Ottoman Empire*, ed. Stephen Conermann and Gul Sen (Gottingen: V&R Unipress, 2020), 55–85.

11. Claudine Dauphin, Mohamed Ben Jeddou, and Jean-Marie Castex, "To Mecca on Pilgrimage on Foot and Camel-back: The Jordanian Darbal-Hajj," *Bulletin for the Council for British Research in the Levant* 10, no. 1 (2015): 23–36, doi: 10.1179/1752726015Z.00000000029; Andrew Peterson, "The Archaeology of the Syrian and Iraqi Hajj Routes," *World Archaeology* 26, no. 1 (June 1994): 47–56.

12. For discussion of the *Chingiznama* folios, see Marie Swietochowski and Richard Ettinghausen, "Islamic Painting," *Metropolitan Museum of Art Bulletin* 36, no. 2 (Autumn 1978): 42–43; Michael Brand, "Art from the Mughal City of Victory," in *Akbar's India* (New York: Asia Society, 1985), 74–75, 145; Maryam Ekhtiar, Sheila R. Canby, Navina Haidar, and Priscilla P. Soucek, eds. *Masterpieces from the Department of Islamic Art in the Metropolitan Museum of Art* (New York: Metropolitan Museum of Art, 2011), 351–52.

13. Rana Safvi, trans. and ed., *Sayyid Ahmad Khan, Asar-us-Sanadid* (New Delhi: Tulika Books, 2018), 49.

14. For detailed references to artistic productions of the Wak-Wak tree, see Marcus Fraser, *Deccan and Mughal Paintings: The Collection of Catherine Glynn Benkaim and Ralph Benkaim*, 2 vols., Private Research Document (London: Pureprint, n.d.). These volumes were a private gift to me.

15. Fragment of a Pile Carpet, Wool on Cotton Ground, Mughal India, 1600, the David Collection, Inv. No. Tex 32, Copenhagen, Denmark, https://www.artoftheancestors.com/blog/islamic-art-david-collection-part-1.

16. *Akbarnama*, Add.27, 247, fols. 297a–297b, British Library. The Khwaja wrote this letter from Gujarat after returning from Arabia. Before he reached Fatehpur-Sikri, he sent this communication.

17. *Akbarnama*, Add.27, 247, fols. 297a–297b, British Library. The Khwaja does not specify how long the operation took nor the identity of the child, his name or that of his parents, or the state of his health after he was brought on board. He does not say how far along they were in the voyage when this episode took place.

18. Wick, *The Red Sea*, 26.

19. Wick, *The Red Sea*, 20.

20. For the legend and a discussion of the architecture of Al-Balad, the historic core of Jeddah, see M. Bagader, "The Old City of Jeddah: From a Walled City to a Heritage Site,"

WIT Transactions on Built Environment 143 (2014): 365–74. See also Stefan Maneval, *New Islamic Urbanism: The Architecture of Public and Private Space in Jeddah, Saudi Arabia* (London: University College London Press, 2019), 22–29.

21. Smith and Ahmad ʿUmar al-ZaylaʿI, *Bride of the Sea*, 1. Ibn Faraj noted that it took seven days to travel from the Bab al-Mandab to Jeddah (11).

22. Porter, *Hajj*, 126.

23. Wheeler M. Thackston, Jr., trans. and ed., *Naser-e Khosraw's Book of Travels, Safarnama* (Albany: Bibliotheca Persica, 1986), 67.

24. Smith and Ahmad ʿUmar al-ZaylaʿI, *Bride of the Sea*, 5.

25. H. A. R. Gibb et al., trans. and eds., *The Travels of Ibn Battuta, A.D. 1325–1354* (New Delhi: Munshiram Manoharlal, 1962), 360.

26. George Percy Badger, *The Travels of Ludovico Di Varthema in Egypt, Syria, Arabia Deserta and Arabia Felix, in Persia, India, and Ethiopia, A.D. 1503 to 1508* (London: Hakluyt Society, 1863).

27. Smith and Ahmad ʿUmar al-ZaylaʿI, *Bride of the Sea*, 15.

28. Smith and Ahmad ʿUmar al-ZaylaʿI, *Bride of the Sea*, 15.

29. Smith and Ahmad ʿUmar al-ZaylaʿI, *Bride of the Sea*, 14–15.

30. On why pilgrims undertake the pilgrimage to the Hijaz, see Porter, *Hajj*, 19–23.

31. Gavin R. G. Hambly, ed., *Women in the Medieval Islamic World: Power, Patronage, and Piety* (New York: St. Martin's, 1998); D. Fairchild Ruggels, ed., *Women, Patronage, and Self-Representation in Islamic Societies* (Albany: State University of New York Press, 2000); Nadia Maria el-Cheikh, "Observations on Women's Education in Medieval Islamic Societies," in *Enfance et jeunesse dans le monde musulman: Childhood and Youth in the Muslim World*, ed. François Georgeon and Klaus Kreiser (Paris: Maisonneuve and Larose, 2007), 57–72.

32. The *Taʾrikh-i Alfi*, or History of 1,000 Years, was commissioned by Akbar to commemorate the millennium of Islam, corresponding to 1591–92 CE. The manuscript was written for Akbar between 1582 and 1588 and revised in 1594, after which it was illustrated. It is a book of history containing a historical narrative of the world (*ʿalam*) as it was known to the Mughals. It opens with the death of the Prophet Muhammad in 632 CE and continues till the reign of Akbar.

33. Porter, *Hajj*, 95, 102; italicized lines from 103, below figure 64.

34. Smith and Ahmad ʿUmar al-ZaylaʿI, *Bride of the Sea*, 5.

35. I take inspiration for the idea of physical removal from the fabulous novel by Nicole Krauss, *Forest Dark* (London: Bloomsbury, 2018), 264–65.

36. Thackston, *Naser-e Khosraw's Book of Travels*, 67.

TEN. The Road to Mecca

1. For an excellent discussion of the desert landscape, camels, and visual history of Arabia, I use Venetia Porter, ed., *Hajj: Journey to the Heart of Islam* (Cambridge: Harvard University Press, 2012), in addition to the other references below.

2. Porter, *Hajj*, 144.

3. Suraiya Faroqhi, *Pilgrims and Sultans: The Hajj under the Ottomans* (London: I. B. Tauris, 2014), 128.

4. B. De and Baini Prasad, trans., *The Tabaqat-i Akbari of Khwajah Nizammudin Ahmad*, 3 vols. (1936; repr., Delhi, 1992), 2:472.

5. On the hajj routes, see Porter, *Hajj*, 146–52.

6. A few months into Gulbadan's arrival in Mecca, Sultan Murad III issued an imperial decree directed at the Mughal party, instructing the local authorities to ask the pilgrims to return. In both the farmans dated October 21, 1578, and the one following them, undated, the phrase "multitude of people," appears. N. R. Farooqi, "Six Ottoman Documents on Mughal-Ottoman Relations during the Reign of Akbar," in *Akbar and His Age*, ed. Iqtidar Alam Khan (New Delhi: Northern Book Center, 1999), 212–13. More on the documents in the chapters that follow.

7. Wheeler M. Thackston, Jr., trans. and ed., *Naser-e Khosraw's Book of Travels, Safarnama* (Albany, N.Y.: Bibliotheca Persica, 1986), 67. By the time Carsen Niebuhr traveled there in the eighteenth century, he noted the trip could be accomplished in one full day. Robert Heron, trans., *M. Niebuhr, Travels through Arabia and Other Countries in the East*, vol. 2 (Dublin: Printer for Gilbert, Moore, Archer, and Jones, 1792), 32.

8. On the Egyptian and Damascus caravans, see Faroqhi, *Pilgrims and Sultans*, 33–37. For the conditions of the performance of the pilgrimage, see Porter, *Hajj*, 32.

9. Henry Beveridge, trans., *The Akbar Nama of Abu-l-Fazl*, 3 vols. (1902–39; repr., Delhi: Low Price Publications, 1993), 3:206.

10. Beveridge, *The Akbar Nama of Abu-l-Fazl*, 3:145.

11. George Percy Badger, *The Travels of Ludovico Di Varthema in Egypt, Syria, Arabia Deserta and Arabia Felix, in Persia, India, and Ethiopia, A.D. 1503 to 1508* (London: Hakluyt Society, 1863), 38.

12. Maria Sardi, "Weaving for the Hajj under the Mamluks," in *The Hajj: Collected Essays*, ed. Venetia Porter and Liana Said (London: British Museum Press, 2013), 172.

13. Doris Behrens-Abouseif, "The *Mahmal* Legend and the Pilgrimage of the Ladies of the Mamluk Court," 91, https://doi.org/10.6082/M1C24TJJ; Porter and Said, *The Hajj*, 196. Many mahmal legends relate to Shajarat al-Durr, the first queen and the first of the Mamluk family to rule in thirteenth-century Egypt. A Turkic slave of the last caliph of Baghdad, she had a brief but stellar reign of eighty days. She never went to Mecca but is counted among the early Egyptian rulers to send the *Kiswa*, or the gold thread–brocaded black silk cover for the Ka'ba, the holiest shrine in Islam, in the heart of the Great Mosque in Mecca where Gulbadan was headed. At some point in telling the tales of Shajarat, narrators entangled the kiswa and the mahmal, adding to her allure. Legends accumulated that she had sent the gorgeous litter to Mecca, "giving her a kind of a patron role." Doris Behrens-Abouseif, "The *Mahmal* Legend," 90–91. For a scholarly discussion of the origins of the mahmal, see also M. Gaudefroy-Demombynes, *Le pelerinage a la Mekke* (1923; repr., Paris: P. Geuthner, 1977), 160–61; A. E. Robinson, "The Mahmal of the Moslem Pilgrimage," *Journal of the Royal Asiatic Society of Great Britain and Ireland*, no. 1 (1931): 120–22.

14. This information comes from Venetia Porter, "The *Mahmal* Revisited," in Porter and Saif, *The Hajj*, 196–97, quote on 198. Porter leans on the research of Doris Behrens-Abouseif.

15. Mahmals went to Mecca throughout the thirteenth and fourteenth centuries. After the 1543 Ottoman conquest of Yemen, the Yemeni litter continued to grace caravans for another hundred years. Porter, "The *Mahmal* Revisited," 199.

16. H. A. R. Gibb et al., trans. and eds., *The Travels of Ibn Battuta, A.D. 1325–1354* (New Delhi: Munshiram Manoharlal, 1962), 59.

17. Porter, *Hajj,* 139, 140. The ceremonial canopy refers to later Mamluk times. See Porter, *Hajj,* 139, 140; Behrens-Abouseif, "The *Mahmal* Legend," 89.

18. Porter and Said, *The Hajj,* 195.

19. Behrens-Abouseif, "The *Mahmal* Legend," 94.

20. In the early sixteenth century, a Persian man named Muhyi al-Din Lari composed and illustrated a guide in verse for pilgrims called *Revelations of the Two Sanctuaries.* He dedicated it to Mahmud Shah, the sultan of Gujarat. Several copies of the work survive, speaking to its popularity. Porter, *Hajj,* 46. Or see Safi ibn Vali's late seventeenth-century *Anis al-Hujjaj,* The Pilgrim's Companion. Zeb-un-nisa, the daughter of the last great Mughal, Aurangzeb, sponsored his journey to Mecca. The work is housed in Nasser D. Khalili Collection of Islamic Art, The Khalili Family Trust.

21. M. Sari, "Stability Analysis of Cut Slopes Using Empirical, Kinematical, Numerical and Limit Equilibrium Methods: Case of Old Jeddah—Mecca Road (Saudi Arabia)," *Environmental Earth Sciences* 78, no. 621 (2019); Arthur E. Robinson, "The Mahmal of the Moslem Pilgrimage," *Journal of the Royal Asiatic Society of Great Britain and Ireland,* no. 1 (1931): 117–27, http://www.jstor.org/stable/25194179.

22. Rasul Ja'fariyan, ed., *Safarnama-i Manzum-i hajj,* in *Miras-i Islami Iran* (1994–95), 9:337–91. For a discussion of this work, see Muzaffar Alam and Sanjay Subrahmanyam, *Indo-Persian Travels in the Age of Discoveries, 1400–1800* (Cambridge: Cambridge University Press, 2007), 27, 38.

23. Gibb et al., *The Travels of Ibn Battuta,* 1:187.

24. Faroqhi, *Pilgrims and Sultans,* 6–7, 9, 85.

25. Faroqhi, *Pilgrims and Sultans,* 76–78, 80, 84.

26. Faroqhi, *Pilgrims and Sultans,* 74–75.

27. All modern Ottoman history books provide discussions of the titles that Ottoman sultans of Turkey took.

28. Faroqhi, *Pilgrims and Sultans,* 17–18.

29. Ayad Akhtar, "The Breath of Miraj," in *Shahzia Sikander: Apparatus of Power* (Hong Kong: Asia Society, Hong Kong Center, 2016), 239.

30. Robert Dankoff and Sooyong Kim, trans. and eds., *An Ottoman Traveller: Selections from the Book of Travels of Evliya Celebi* (London: Eland, 2011), 348.

31. For an excellent discussion of the layout near the Great Mosque, see Faroqhi, *Pilgrims and Sultans,* 100, 107–8; Atef Alshehri, "Ottoman Spatial Organization of the Pre-modern City of Medina," *ABE Journal,* October 15, 2018, 23, http://journals.openedition.org/abe/4341.

ELEVEN. Everyone's Mecca

Much of the widely known information on the Muslim pilgrimage rites comes from the later nineteenth century on. To decipher the early modern setting of the pilgrimage and its rituals, I have used a number of early modern accounts, such as those of Naser-e Khosraw, Ibn Jubayr, Ibn Battuta, Evliya Celebi, and others cited here and in the previous chapters. Suraiya Faroqhi's *Pilgrims and Sultans* and N. R. Farooqi's writings on Mughal-Ottoman relations have been very helpful in understanding the late sixteenth-century Ottoman Hijaz, the politics of pilgrimage, bureaucratic arrangements, and the architectural refashioning of the Holy Cities at the time of Sultan Murad's rule.

1. Suraiya Faroqhi, *Pilgrims and Sultans: The Hajj under the Ottomans* (London: I. B. Tauris, 2014), 100, 107–8.

2. Robert Dankoff and Sooyong Kim, trans. and eds., *An Ottoman Traveller: Selections from the Book of Travels of Evliya Celebi* (London: Eland, 2011), 359, dress discussion on 360.

3. H. A. R. Gibb et al., trans. and eds., *The Travels of Ibn Battuta, A.D. 1325–1354* (New Delhi: Munshiram Manoharlal, 1962), 1:215–16.

4. Gibb et al., *The Travels of Ibn Battuta*, 1:216.

5. For a discussion of this ban, see Marion Holmes Katz, *Women in the Mosque: A History of Legal Thought and Social Practice* (New York: Columbia University Press, 2014), especially chapter 3.

6. Ziaduddin Sardar, *Mecca: The Sacred City* (London: Bloomsbury, 2014), 150.

7. Faroqhi, *Pilgrims and Sultans*, 111, 132.

8. Faroqhi, *Pilgrims and Sultans*, 111.

9. Faroqhi, *Pilgrims and Sultans*, 107–8, 131, citation from 132.

10. At the time of Battuta's travels there were five minarets on the sacred mosque. Gibb et al., *The Travels of Ibn Battuta*, 1:203; On minarets and their changing numbers, Faroqhi, *Pilgrims and Sultans*, 101; on gates, Wheeler M. Thackston, Jr., trans. and ed., *Naser-e Khosraw's Book of Travels, Safarnama* (Albany, N.Y.: Bibliotheca Persica, 1986), 72–73 and footnotes on these pages; Gibb et al., *The Travels of Ibn Battuta*, 1:201–4.

11. Faroqhi, *Pilgrims and Sultans*, 46.

12. Faroqhi, *Pilgrims and Sultans*, 101–2.

13. Gibb et al., *The Travels of Ibn Battuta*, 1:188.

14. Venetia Porter, ed., *Hajj: Journey to the Heart of Islam* (Cambridge: Harvard University Press, 2012), 36 and sidebar with figure 12; on Muhyi al-Din Lari, 46.

15. The work was made for Jalal-al Din Iskander ibn Umar Shaikh (d. 1415), a grandson of Timur, same family line as Gulbadan's father Babur. Porter, *Hajj*, 24.

16. Rachel Milstein, "Futuh-i Haramayn: Sixteenth-Century Illustrations of the Hajj Route," in *Mamluks and Ottomans: Studies in Honor of Michael Winter*, ed. David J. Wasserstein and Ami Ayalon (London: Routledge, 2006), 167.

17. Porter, *Hajj*, 30–31. The tradition is well known and well documented in all books concerning the hajj.

18. Muzaffar Alam and Sanjay Subrahmanyam, *Indo-Persian Travels in the Age of Discoveries, 1400–1800* (Cambridge: Cambridge University Press, 2007), 38.

19. Faroqhi, *Pilgrims and Sultans*, 107–8.

20. Gibb et al., *The Travels of Ibn Battuta*, 1:194–95; Faroqhi, *Pilgrims and Sultans*, 118. The figures of the measurement of the Ka'ba can be acquired from any of the works cited here as well as encyclopedias and online sources.

21. F. E. Peters, *The Hajj: The Muslim Pilgrimage to Mecca and the Holy Places* (Princeton: Princeton University Press, 1994), 238–40.

22. The note about pigeons comes from Battuta; Gibb et al., *The Travels of Ibn Battuta,* 1:196.

23. Porter, *Hajj,* 41.

24. M. J. Kister, "Maḳam Ibrahim," in *The Encyclopedia of Islam,* vol. 6, 2nd ed., ed. C. E. Bosworth et al. (Leiden: Brill, 1991), 105; Peters, *The Hajj,* 16–17.

25. Thackston, *Naser-e Khosraw's Book of Travels,* 78; Gibb et al., *The Travels of Ibn Battuta,* 1:198.

26. Porter, *Hajj,* 30; Peters, *The Hajj,* 17–18; Gibb et al., *The Travels of Ibn Battuta,* 1:200.

27. Gibb et al., *The Travels of Ibn Battuta,* 1:206.

28. Faroqhi, *Pilgrims and Sultans,* 112.

29. Thackston, *Naser-e Khosraw's Book of Travels,* 74.

30. The approximate distance between Marwa and Safa is a quarter of a mile.

31. Faroqhi, *Pilgrims and Sultans,* 46.

32. Faroqhi, *Pilgrims and Sultans,* 21–23.

33. Faroqhi, *Pilgrims and Sultans,* 23; Porter, *Hajj,* 49–51, citation on 51.

34. Faroqhi, *Pilgrims and Sultans,* 169.

35. On gifts from the Hijaz, Porter, *Hajj,* 52, 72.

36. Amy Singer, *Charity in Islamic Societies* (Cambridge: Cambridge University Press, 2008), 148.

37. Henry Beveridge, trans., *The Akbar Nama of Abu-l-Fazl,* 3 vols. (1902–39; repr., Delhi: Low Price Publications, 1993), 3:306; Shah Nawaz Khan and Abdul Hayy, *The Maathir-Ul-Umara,* 3 vols. (Patna: Janaki Prakashan, 1979), 1:143; M. N. Pearson, *Pious Passengers: The Hajj in Earlier Times* (London: Hurst, 1994), 125 and footnotes.

38. Pearson, *Pious Passengers,* 114.

39. Faroqhi, *Pilgrims and Sultans,* 86.

40. Singer, *Charity,* 170.

TWELVE. Send Them Back

1. Key documents used in this chapter are the imperial orders of Sultan Murad III, issued between 1578 and 1581, located in the State Archives of the Presidency of the Turkish Republic. One of the premier repositories, the Bashvekalet Arshivi, the collection of Ottoman state documents, also holds the Register of Important Affairs, the Muhimme Defterleri in which copies of the dispatches of Ottoman sultans to different parts of the empire are preserved. For the phrase "a multitude of people," see Muhimme Defterleri, vol. 35, fol. 292, farman 740, issued on October 21, 1578; Muhimme Defterleri, vol. 35, fol. 292, farman 740, n.d. These two farmans are identical except that the latter is issued to the qazi and shaikh-al haram of Medina. It is likely that the second order was issued at the same time as the first.

2. Suraiya Faroqhi, *Pilgrims and Sultans: The Hajj under the Ottomans* (London: I. B. Tauris, 2014), 124.

3. For entry into Kuba and the description of geography, see Robert Dankoff, trans., and Nurettin Gemici, ed., *Evliya Celebi in Medina: The Relevant Sections of the Seyahatname*

(Leiden: Brill, 2012), 147, citation on 149; Richard Burton, *A Personal Narrative of a Pilgrimage to Al-Madinah and Meccah* (London: Tylston and Edwards, 1855), 2:197.

4. Faroqhi, *Pilgrims and Sultans*, 75.

5. Dankoff and Gemici, *Evliya Celebi in Medina*, 151, 153.

6. Firoozeh Kashani-Sabet, "Who Is Fatima? Gender, Culture, and Representation in Islam," *Journal of Middle East Women's Studies* 1, no. 2 (Spring 2005): 4, 6.

7. A symbolic representation of Khanzada's power and the respect that she commanded as a senior woman may be seen in an illustration from the British Library *Baburnama, Babur Reunited with His Sister After a Ten-Year Separation (1493)* (plate 1), Ms. Or.3714. fol. 13b, British Library, London. Though drawn much later, in the atelier of Akbar in 1590, the folio is significant for its depiction of Khanzada Begum. This miniature portrays a time when Khanzada Begum returned to Qunduz and joined Babur after a ten-year separation. Here, Khanzada Begum is in a clear mode of authority. The gesture of her hand is royal and imperious. Far from any stigma or question mark attaching to the status of this returned relative, she is the main focus of the cast and is represented in a commanding position. For a description of this meeting, see also Annette Susannah Beveridge, trans., *Babur-nama (Memoirs of Babur) of Zahiru'd-din Muhammad Babur Padshah Ghazi* (1921; :pr., Delhi: Low Price Publications, 1997), 352.

8. On date palms, see Burton's excellent description in chapter 19, for general information in this paragraph, Burton, *Al-Madinah and Meccah*, 1:199, 200.

9. Dankoff and Gemici, *Evliya Celebi in Medina*, 19.

10. Dankoff and Gemici, *Evliya Celebi in Medina*, quote on 21, see also 23.

11. Robert Dankoff and Sooyong Kim, trans. and eds., *An Ottoman Traveller: Selections from the Book of Travels of Evliya Celebi* (London: Eland, 2011), 349; for the description of the gate, Dankoff and Gemici, *Evliya Celebi in Medina*, 37.

12. Dankoff and Gemici, *Evliya Celebi in Medina*, 349.

13. *Extremely crowded*, a description used in the first two farmans: Muhimme Defterleri, vol. 35, fol. 292, farman 740, issued on October 21, 1578; Muhimme Defterleri, vol. 35, fol. 292, farman 740, n.d.

14. Muhimme Defterleri, vol. 35, fol. 292, farman 740, n.d.

15. Faroqhi, *Pilgrims and Sultans*, 122–23.

16. Faroqhi, *Pilgrims and Sultans*, 96.

17. Gerald de Gaury, *Rulers of Mecca* (London; George G. Harrap, 1951), 107.

18. Faroqhi, *Pilgrims and Sultans*, 135–36.

19. Dankoff and Gemici, *Evliya Celebi in Medina*, 25, 27, 29.

20. Dankoff and Gemici, *Evliya Celebi in Medina*, 157, 159.

21. For an excellent discussion of charity and the wide-ranging meanings of zakat and sadaqat in Islamic history, see Amy Singer, *Charity in Islamic Societies* (Cambridge: Cambridge University Press, 2008), 21.

22. Dankoff and Gemici, *Evliya Celebi in Medina*, 157, 159.

23. Dankoff and Kim, *An Ottoman Traveller*, 352.

24. Dankoff and Gemici, *Evliya Celebi in Medina*, 99.

25. Dankoff and Kim, *An Ottoman Traveller*, 357.

26. Faroqhi, *Pilgrims and Sultans*, 121.

27. Faroqhi, *Pilgrims and Sultans*, 120–21.

28. Faroqhi, *Pilgrims and Sultans*, 75, 85.

29. Dankoff and Gemici, *Evliya Celebi in Medina*, 95, 99.

30. Singer, *Charity*, 4–5.

31. Singer, *Charity*, 18.

32. Cited in Singer, *Charity*, 67.

33. The two Ottoman orders referenced above give this information.

34. Dankoff and Gemici, *Evliya Celebi in Medina*, 99.

35. Henry Blochmann, ed., and H. S. Jarrett, trans., *The A'in Ain-i Akbari*, 3 vols. (1873, 1894; repr., Calcutta: Royal Asiatic Society, 1993), 1:467; Henry Beveridge, trans., *The Akbar Nama of Abu-l-Fazl*, 3 vols. (1902–39; repr., Delhi: Low Price Publications, 1993), 3:271–72.

36. For a detailed discussion on Akbar's hajj policies, see N. R. Farooqi, "An Overview of Ottoman Archival Documents and Their Relevance for Medieval Indian History," *Medieval History Journal* 20, no. 1 (2017): 205–9. For the importance of debates on khilafat and Muslim monarchs' declaration of being the khalifa within their own territories, as well as Mughal and Ottoman attitudes to khilafat, see Farooqi, *Mughal-Ottoman Relations: A Study of Political and Diplomatic Relations between Mughal India and the Ottoman Empire* (Delhi: Idarah-I Adabiyat-I Delli, 2009), chapter 5.

37. Farooqi, *Mughal-Ottoman Relations*, 179; for an extended discussion, see chapter 5, "Mughal Attitude towards the Ottoman Khilafat." On the Ottomans and Akbar, and for other titles above, see Giancarlo Casale, *The Ottoman Age of Exploration* (New York: Oxford University Press, 2010), 153–54, 159, 184.

38. N. R. Farooqi, "Six Ottoman Documents on Mughal-Ottoman Relations during the Reign of Akbar," in *Akbar and His Age*, ed. Iqtidar Alam Khan (New Delhi: Northern Book Center, 1999), 208–11. For details of the farman structure, see 210.

39. Muhimme Defterleri, vol. 35, fol. 292, farman 740, issued October 21, 1578.

40. Muhimme Defterleri, vol. 35, fol. 292, farman 741, n.d.

41. George S. A. Ranking, W. H. Lowe, and Sir Wolseley Haig, trans. and eds., *Muntakhabu-t-tawarikh* (1884–1925; repr., Delhi: Renaissance, 1986), 2:216–17. Qom in northwest Iran is also a center of ancient Zoroastrianism; Karbala, sixty-two miles southwest of Baghdad, is the home of Husain's tomb, the Prophet's martyred grandson. A major oasis along the silk road, Mashhad lay to the northeast in Persia. According to Farooqi, a report said that Akbar desired to have the khutba read in his name in the sacred city of Mashhad. Farooqi, *Mughal-Ottoman Relations*, 190.

42. Muhimme Defterleri, vol. 39, fol. 160, farman 349, issued February 13, 1580.

THIRTEEN. Return

1. The name of the second ship is spelled differently in the various *Akbarnama* manuscripts: *jihaz-i S'ai*, or the Ship of Effort, or the *jihaz-i Safi*, which means the Swift Ship. Henry Beveridge, trans., *The Akbar Nama of Abu-l-Fazl*, 3 vols. (1902–39; repr., Delhi: Low Price Publications, 1993), 3:570n2.

2. Among the earliest of these guides is the anonymous *Periplus of the Erythrean Sea*, from the first century CE. Roxani Margariti, *Aden and the Indian Ocean: 150 Years in the Life of a Medieval Arabian Port* (Chapel Hill: University of North Carolina Press, 2007), 40.

3. Muhimme Defterleri, vol. 39, fol. 238, farman 471, issued on March 16, 1580; and Muhimme Defterleri, vol. 43, fol. 54, farman 107, issued on August 25, 1580, State Archives of the Presidency of the Turkish Republic. For a discussion of Gulbadan's departure dates, see also Simon Digby, "Bayazid Beg Turkman's Pilgrimage to Makka and Return to Gujarrt: A Sixteenth Century Narrative," *Iran* 42, no. 1 (2004): 162.

4. Beveridge, *The Akbar Nama of Abu-l-Fazl*, 3:568–69.

5. A. Yusuf Ali, *The Holy Qur'an: Text, Translation and Commentary* (Brentwood, Md.: Amana, 1983), 849.

6. Ali, *The Holy Qur'an*, 871–72.

7. Saidiya Hartman, *Lose Your Mother: A Journey into the Atlantic Slave Route* (New York: Farrar, Straus and Giroux, 2007), 96.

8. Hartman, *Lose Your Mother*, 170.

9. Venetia Porter, *The Art of Hajj* (London: British Museum Press, 2012), 88.

10. This description is based upon the records of the shipwreck of Shaikh 'Abd-ul Haqq (d. 1642), South Asian Sufi and hadith scholar, as well as those of the twelfth-century ship carrying Ben Yiju's merchandize mentioned later. Scott Kugle, *Hajj to the Heart: Sufi Journeys across the Indian Ocean* (Chapel Hill: University of North Carolina Press, 2021), quote on 1.

11. Margariti, *Aden and the Indian Ocean*, 39.

12. Beveridge, *The Akbar Nama of Abu-l-Fazl*, 3:570.

13. Margariti, *Aden and the Indian Ocean*, 173–74. For the Cairo Geniza, Ben Yiju, and the wider universe of his time, see the eloquent work of Amitav Ghosh, *In an Antique Land: History in the Guise of a Traveler's Tale* (New York: Vintage, 1994).

14. Margariti, *Aden and the Indian Ocean*, 174.

15. Beveridge, *The Akbar Nama of Abu-l-Fazl*, 3:570.

16. Margariti, *Aden and the Indian Ocean*, 71.

17. Bayat was not the only court writer giving precedence to Gulbadan as the leader of the hajj. As the previous chapters show, the *Akbarnama*, *Muntakhab-ut-Tawarikh*, *Tabaqat-i Akbari*, and all other sources note Gulbadan's leadership.

18. I use the following Persian edition for Bayazid Bayat, *Tarikh-i Humayun*, trans. and ed. Wheeler M. Thackston: *Three Memoirs of Homayun* (Costa Mesa, Calif.: Mazda, 2009), especially 2:166–68.

19. Alexis Wick, *The Red Sea: In Search of Lost Space* (Berkeley: University of California Press, 2016), 91.

20. Quotation from Scott S. Reese, *Imperial Muslims: Islam, Community and Authority in the Indian Ocean, 1839–1937* (Edinburgh: Edinburgh University Press, 2018), 25.

21. For a detailed discussion of this legend, see Reese, *Imperial Muslims*, chapter 1, quote on 17. Paula Richman has studied the many renditions, forms, and diverse tellings of the *Ramayana*. Paula Richman, *Many Ramayanas: The Diversity of a Narrative Tradition in South Asia* (Berkeley: University of California Press, 1991).

22. Reese, *Imperial Muslims*, 20.

23. Reese, *Imperial Muslims*, 19.

24. Along with a number of other contemporary authors of works such as the *Tarikh Ba Fakih al-Shiri* and the *Tarikh Shanbal*—R. B. Serjeant's famed "Hadrami Chronicles"—Makhrama was one of a number of local writers who commented on the emerging political tensions.

25. The Ottomans had participated in 1538 in the siege of the Portuguese fortress of Diu in Gujarat. The expedition, led by Hadim Suleiman Pasha, ended in complete victory for the Portuguese. The Turkish admiral was able to secure Ottoman hegemony in the Red Sea and surrounding areas, most notably the port of Aden. The literature on Portuguese commercial ambitions and movement in the Indian and Arabian Ocean is rich and vast. I have consulted these works to understand the context of Gulbadan's time in Aden. For a general survey of Portuguese contacts with Asia, see Sanjay Subrahmanyam, *The Portuguese Empire in Asia, 1500–1700* (London: Longman, 1993). For Portuguese contacts with the Red Sea area, see R. B. Serjeant, *The Portuguese off the South Arabian Coast* (Beirut: Librairie du Liban, 1974); Andreu Martínez d'Alòs-Moner, "Conquistadores, Mercenaries, and Missionaries: The Failed Portuguese Dominion of the Red Sea," *Northeast African Studies* 12, no. 1 (2012): 1–28. For the Ottoman side, see Salih Ozbaran, *Ottoman Expansion towards the Indian Ocean in the 16th Century* (Istanbul: Istanbul Bilgi University Press, 2009); and, for a recent analysis of Ottoman contacts with the Indian Ocean, Giancarlo Casale, *The Ottoman Age of Exploration* (New York: Oxford University Press, 2010). Although not directly related to the sixteenth-century issues surrounding Gulbadan's time in Arabia and the wider political and economic context, I have found Nile Green's work especially helpful in understanding the making of "global" Muslim communities—in the Atlantic, Pacific and Indian Ocean worlds.

26. Margariti, *Aden and the Indian Ocean*, 34.

27. From 1580 to 1604, Hasan Pasha was the governor of Yemen. The reference to the unnamed Aden governor in the sources indicates the local governor of Aden.

28. Beveridge, *The Akbar Nama of Abu-l-Fazl*, 3:570. For Gulbadan's return, see also B. De and Baini Prasad, trans., *The Tabaqat-i Akbari of Khwajah Nizammudin Ahmad*, 3 vols. (1936; repr., Delhi, 1992), 2:557.

29. Beveridge, *The Akbar Nama of Abu-l-Fazl*, 3:569.

30. N. R. Farooqi, *Mughal-Ottoman Relations: A Study of Political and Diplomatic Relations between Mughal India and the Ottoman Empire* (Delhi: Idarah-I Adabiyat-I Delli, 2009), 192. On the Ottomans and Akbar, and for other titles above, see Giancarlo Casale, *The Ottoman Age of Exploration* (New York: Oxford University Press, 2010), 153–54, 159, 184. On khilafat and titles, see earlier notes and Farooqi, *Mughal-Ottoman Relations*, chapter 5, "Mughal Attitude towards the Ottoman Khilafat."

31. For a discussion of Akbar's annulment of alms and its reinstatement by later emperors, see Farooqi, *Mughal-Ottoman Relations*, 115–31.

FOURTEEN. The Books of Gulbadan

The title of this chapter is inspired by Olga Tokarczuk, *The Books of Jacob*, trans. Jennifer Croft (New York: Riverhead Books, 2022).

1. For historical details of Lahore, see M. Baqir, *Lahore: Past and Present* (Delhi: Low Price Publications, 1996), 309, 363, 364.

2. J. S. Hoyland, trans., *The Empire of the Great Mogol. A Translation of De Laet's Description of India: Fragment of Indian History* (Delhi: Idarah-i Adabiyat, 1975), 108–9. Vincent Smith, *Akbar the Great Mogul* (Oxford: Clarendon, 1917), 424, notes that these numbers were copied independently from Mughal registers by Sebastian Manrique, who visited the court during Shah Jahan's reign.

3. For a study on cataloguing, evaluation, and details of Mughal manuscripts, see John Seyller, "The Inspection and Valuation of Manuscripts in the Imperial Mughal Library," *Artibus Asiae* 57, nos. 3/4 (1997): 243–349.

4. Henry Beveridge, trans., *The Akbar Nama of Abu-l-Fazl*, 3 vols. (1902–39; repr., Delhi: Low Price Publications, 1993), 1:29.

5. Gulbadan Banu Begum, *Ahval-i Humayun Badshah*, Ms.Or.166, fol. 2b, British Library, London.

6. *Feasting and Music Following the Marriage of Humayun and Hamida*, which is in the private collection of Cynthia Hazen Polsky in New York.

7. I draw this scene from a highly unusual painting of harem life, *Feasting and Music Following the Marriage of Humayun and Hamida*, which is in the collection of Cynthia Hazen Polsky in New York. It comes from an *Akbarnama* termed the "third" one, circa 1595–1600. Linda Leach suggests that Hamida Banu commissioned it. Only a small number of folios from this manuscript are known, all dispersed around various collections. For a discussion, see Linda York Leach, "Pages from an Akbarnama," in *Arts of Mughal India, Studies in Honour of Robert Skelton*, ed. Rosemary Crill, Susan Stronge, and Andrew Topsfield (London: Victoria & Albert Museum and Mapin, 2004), 42–55. The picture was also published in an exhibition catalogue of the Polsky collection in 2004: Andrew Topsfield, ed., *In the Realms of Gods and Kings* (New York: Philip Wilson, 2004), no. 165, 372–73.

8. The list of the sources for the compilation of the *Akbarnama* shows this. Beveridge, *The Akbar Nama of Abu-l-Fazl*, vol. 1: see introduction, especially 29–33, including footnotes.

9. For the meanings of the words, see S. Haim, ed., *Dictionary English-Persian, Persian-English*, rev. ed.; F. Steingass, *A Comprehensive Persian-English Dictionary*, 2nd ed.; and S. Haim, *Shorter English Persian Dictionary*, 3rd ed., s.v. "tarikh," "tazkireh," "nameh," "qanun," "vaqiʿat."

10. Take the example of the inventory of gifts and instructions for their distribution after Babur's victory of Panipat discussed in the chapter "Curiosities of Hind." In his brief discussion of the same event, Babur makes only a casual, and far less interesting, mention of the presents. Wheeler M. Thackston, trans. and ed., *Zahiruddin Muhammad Babur Mirza: Baburnama*, parts 1–3, Turkish transcription, Persian edition, and English translation (Cambridge, Mass.: Near Eastern Languages and Civilization, Harvard University, 1993), 634–35; and Annette Susannah Beveridge, trans., *Babur-nama (Memoirs of Babur) of Zahiru'd-din Muhammad Babur Padshah Ghazi* (1921; repr., Delhi: Low Price Publications, 1997), 525–26.

11. Henry Blochmann, ed., and H. S. Jarrett, trans., *The Aʾin-i Akbari*, 3 vols. (1873, 1894; repr., Calcutta: Royal Asiatic Society, 1993), 1:115.

12. Hermann Ethé, *Catalogue of Persian Manuscripts in the Library of the India Office*, vol. 1 (Oxford: H. Hart, 1903), 222.

13. For Persian and English editions of Bayazid Bayat, Jawhar, and Gulbadan, see Wheeler M. Thackston, trans. and ed., *Three Memoirs of Homayun* (Costa Mesa, Calif.: Mazda, 2009). Khwandamir wrote his *Qanun-i Humayuni* (also called *Humayun-nama*), in 1534 under Humayun's patronage. The author spent time at the court of 'Abdul Ghazi Sultan Husiyn bin Mansur bin Bayqura, the ruler of Herat (1468–1505), and in Khurasan and Persia before joining Babur in 1528. He spent his last days in the court of Humayun. Khwandamir's memoir is, by his own claim, an eyewitness's account of the rules and ordinances of Humayun's reign, accompanied by descriptions of court festivities and of buildings erected by the *padshah* (king). See Beveridge's note on Gulbadan's ownership of this work: Annette S. Beveridge, trans., *The History of Humayun: Humayun Nama*, 2nd ed. (1902, repr., Delhi: Low Price Publications, 1994), 76, 78.

14. *A'in-i Akbari*, 1:110.

15. MSS Eur C176/ 221, 1–2, British Library, London; M. A. Scherer, "Woman to Woman: Annette, the Princess, and the Bibi," *Journal of Royal Asiatic Society*, ser. 3, 6, no. 2 (1996): 208–9.

16. Irfan Habib, "Persian Book Writing and Book Use in the Pre-printing Age," *Proceedings of the Indian History Congress* 66 (2005–6): 522.

17. Beveridge, *Humayun Nama*, 79.

18. Tuhina Islam, "Literary Contribution of Mughal Court Lady Gulbadan," *Journal of History and Social Sciences* 4, no. 1 (January–June 2013): 9.

19. Shah Jahan's autograph can be seen opposite p. xiv of Annette Beveridge's English translation. Translation mine.

20. Annette S. Beveridge, "Life and Writings of Gulbadan Begum (Lady Rosebody)," *Calcutta Review* no. 213 (April 1898): 345.

21. Quote from Beveridge's publisher, Annette Beveridge, Private Papers, 1902, MSS. EUR C.176/195–196., British Library. See my "Introduction: Complex Messages" above.

22. Beveridge, *The Akbar Nama of Abu-l-Fazl*, 2:503, 507; Maulawi 'Abd-ur-Rahim, ed., *Akbarnamah by Abul-Fazl I Mubarak I 'Allami*, 3 vols. (Calcutta, 1873–86), 2:347. For a fuller discussion, see Ruby Lal, *Domesticity and Power in the Early Mughal World* (Cambridge: Cambridge University Press, 2005), chapter 7.

23. Habib, "Persian Book Writing," p. 515.

24. Madhu was a leading painter in the royal atelier of Akbar and contributed to the Jaipur *Razmnama*, the Keir Collection *Khamsa*, the British Library (Dyson Perrins) *Khamsa*, the Bodleian Library Baharistan, the *Baburnama*, the Victoria and Albert Museum *Akbarnama*, the Chester Beatty Library/British Museum version of the same text, and the British Library *Nafahat al-Uns*. Verma notes that he was recorded as being in the employ of 'Abd al-Rahim Khan-e Khanan in 1614 and suggests that he moved from the imperial atelier to that of the Khan-e Khanan sometime after 1605; Som Prakash Verma, *Mughal Painters and Their Work: A Biographical Survey and Comprehensive Catalogue* (Delhi: Oxford University Press, 1994), 234–38. Three other artists who used the name Madhu (Madhu Kalan, Madhu Khurd, and Madhu Gujarati) are considered by Verma to be separate artists (234–40).

25. In an email exchange dated September 27, 2022, Ursula Sims-Williams, curator of Persian collections at the British Library, clarified that the subject of this painting

is celebrations for Akbar's circumcision, rather than his presentation to his parents, as was previously thought. The British Library caption comes from an Asian and African studies blog dated January 13, 2013: https://blogs.bl.uk/asian-and-african/2013/01/a-mughal-princesss-auto biography.html.

For details of *The Young Akbar Recognizes His Mother,* see Milo Cleveland Beach, *The Imperial Image: Paintings for the Mughal Court* (Washington, D.C.: Freer Gallery of Art, 1981), 103. For a discussion of fol. 114r of the British Library *Akbarnama,* Or.12988, see J. P. Losty and Malini Roy, *Mughal India: Art, Culture and Empire: Manuscripts and Paintings in the British Library* (London: British Library, 2012), 66–68.

26. *Humayun at the Celebrations Held at the Time of Akbar's Circumcision, Akbarnama,* Or.12988, fol. 114r, British Library. Illustrations of the *Akbarnama* are held at Victoria and Albert Museum, London (116 folios with the text), the British Library (thirty-nine illustrations), and the Chester Beatty Library, Dublin (sixty-six scenes). For details of these three *Akbarnamas,* see Leach, "Pages from an Akbarnama," 43–44.

27. For an expanded discussion of these themes, see Ruby Lal, "From the Inside Out: Spaces of Pleasure and Authority," in *Art and Stories from Mughal India,* ed. Sonya Rhea Quintanilla (Cleveland: Cleveland Museum of Art, 2016), especially 296–97.

28. This tradition is different from the Indian and Persian literary and painterly tradition of depicting women and men holding portraits. A wife gazes at a portrait of her husband; a princess observes a portrait of herself or of someone else; a lone heroine draws a portrait of her lover or an absent husband. Women seeing portraits are found, for example, in the following museums: Freer Gallery of Art and Arthur M. Sackler Gallery (Washington, D.C.), F.1984. 43 2 and 1985. 1. 354; Bonhams (London), 3.19. 2012 lot. 1167; and *Jahangir Viewing a Portrait of Akbar,* Louvre (Paris), OA 3676 b (1). For further examples and details, see Klaus Ebeling, *Ragamala Painting* (New Delhi: Ravi Kumar, 1973), 76, C26. In Nizami of Ganja's twelfth-century collection there is a story, "Khusrau va Shirin," that is a parable of love, unity, and divinity in which the painter Shapur, highly skilled at lifelike presentations, tells the hero, Khusrau, about the beautiful Shirin (literally, "sweet"). Khusrau's grandfather once told him that he would meet a beloved of great sweetness. And so Khusrau asks Shapur to find Shirin. He can only do so through Khusrau's portrait. Shapur, disguised as a monk, goes to Armenia to find Shirin. He finds out from a priest where she and her attendants spend time. Early one morning, he goes to that meadow, paints a portrait of Khusrau, and suspends it from a branch of a tree. Shirin and her companions arrive. Her eyes fall upon the portrait. The women bring the portrait to her, and looking at it she becomes absorbed "in rapt contemplation." She embraces it as if it were alive. Fearful, thinking that the portrait is the work of demonic creatures, the women take it away from her. The next day Shapur makes a second painting, exactly like the first. When Shirin sees it, she is overwhelmed, unable to speak. Her companions destroy the painting again, burn rue to dispel the evil spirits, and move to a new meadow. And yet, Shapur embarks on a third, exactly like the first two. Shirin finds and holds up the portrait. The portrait that Shirin held, says Nizami, "contained her own reflection." "In the mirror (ayina) she saw her own reflection (nishan) [and] when she seized it, she fainted." Priscilla Soucek, "Nizami on Painters and Painting," in *Islamic Art*

in the Metropolitan Museum of Art, ed. Richard Ettinghausen (New York: Metropolitan Museum of Art, 1972), 17, 18.

29. Beach, *The Imperial Image,* 95.

30. I am grateful to Mughal art and architecture historians Molly Aitken and Monica Juneja for an extended conversation about this image. The iconography of the painting that I describe above—Gulbadan in profile, placement of her book—follows from these discussions. I also consulted, as mentioned above, Ursula Sims-Williams of the British Library. In an untitled picture from circa 1600, held at the Chester Beatty Library in Dublin, Gulbadan sits wearing a long veil that flows down her caftan in the Mongol and Chagatai style of her predecessors. She is in private quarters on a verandah, with a bolster behind her. An authoritative figure, she holds an open book in her raised right hand, as if explaining something to the two women who sit across from her. The smaller sizes of the latter figures denote their youth in stylized paintings: they too hold books in their hands. One of them looks respectfully at Gulbadan, while the other pores over her book. Marcus Fraser, honorary keeper of Islamic Manuscripts and Miniatures at the Fitzwilliam Museum, Cambridge, U.K., first drew my attention to the Chester Beatty Library's single miniature on an album page. Datable to circa 1600 (accession number is 43.2), it shows a female seated holding a book, with other women and further books around her. Linda Leach suggests that it is likely a stylized portrait of Gulbadan Begum, by association with the books and the portrait of Humayun on the verso: Linda York Leach, *Mughal and Other Indian Miniatures in the Chester Beatty Library,* vol. 2 (Dublin: Scorpion Cavendish: 1995), 610.

NOTE ON SOURCES

1. I engage with these questions in the following books: Ruby Lal, *Domesticity and Power in the Early Mughal World* (Cambridge: Cambridge University Press, 2005), chapters 1–3; Ruby Lal, *Coming of Age in Nineteenth-Century India: The Girl-Child and the Art of Playfulness* (Cambridge: Cambridge University Press, 2013), prelude and chapter 1.

2. Adrienne Rich, *On Lies, Secrets, and Silence: Selected Prose, 1966–1978* (New York: Norton, 1979), 13–14.

3. Over the centuries, people would spend long periods in Mecca, either studying or teaching, and so a mujawir was a student of the religious sciences. It was applied, for example, to students at al-Azhar in Egypt, who were said to be "staying in the neighborhood" of al-Azhar mosque. I am grateful to my colleagues Devin Stewart and Hossein Samei for an extended conversation on the word. Various meanings can be seen in William Lane, *Arabic Lexicon* (London: Williams and Norgate, 1867), https://archive.org/details/in.ernet .dli.2015.76952.

Acknowledgments

In the fall of 2020, the pandemic at its peak, I was at the Swedish Collegium for Advanced Studies in Uppsala on an in-person fellowship. I was to immerse myself in writing this book. It was an erratic time the world over; I didn't know what to expect of life in a locked-down universe. Within a month of my arrival in Uppsala, my father passed away in India. International borders were shut there, and I couldn't be with my mother as she bade goodbye to her companion of fifty-seven years. In the midst of the raging pandemic, my partner boarded a flight from Atlanta and headed to Sweden to be able to grieve with me.

A few months later, herself isolated, my sister insisted over the phone that I get outside, see the gorgeous snow draping the trees. A Scandinavian winter was a once-in-a-lifetime experience, she gently reminded me. I put on my long coat, wrapped myself head to toe, and went out to the city forest. Layers of grief, coming and going: that's how I remember those walks amid sea buckthorn, field maple, bird cherry, and so many trees that I didn't recognize, but was captivated by. In that tree-filled solitude, I began to mull over words in their richness and beauty. And thus I commenced writing this book. Physically locked in Uppsala, I was in my mind's eye on all the journeys of Princess Gulbadan. From the hills of Kabul to the rivers of northern India, across the seas to the Arabian lands, I was mesmerized. My grief began to take shape.

I have lived with the spectacular work of Mughal princess Gulbadan Begum for over twenty years, and the dynamic history that soaks it, the beauty of its content and language—and the magic of its disappearance. But writing about it in historic times—as the times *became* historic—I learned a great deal more about the spirit of history, the force of adventure, and above all the power of friendship. For reading many drafts of this book, my immense gratitude to Gyan Pandey, Bridget Matzie, Jaya Aninda Chatterjee, Anjali Puri, and Michael Fisher. For comments and conversations on early drafts, thanks to Leslie Harris, Lynne Huffer, Stephen Dale, Francis Robinson, Richard Eaton, Alexis Wick, Mary Odem, Ralph Gilbert, Michael Calabria, and Parth Mehrotra. Much gratitude to Bridget Matzie, Chiki Sarkar, Rudrangshu Mukherjee, Sonya Mace, Marcus Fraser, Nadia Cheikh, Allan Sealy, Daniel Weiss, Michael Elliott, Salman Rushdie, Irina Dumitrescu, David Page, Bruce Cleghorn, William Dalrymple, Steven Hochman, Walter Melion, V. Naryana Rao, Lois Reitzes, Khushru Irani, Gail O'Neill, Manasi Subrahmanyam, Daren Wang, Allison Warren, and Nimitt Mankad for years of intellectual care. Thanks to my 2020–21 co-fellows at the Swedish Collegium for Advanced Studies, and especially to Christina Garsten for her warm support, and to Inan Ozdemir and Outi Paloposki for our friendship. A special note of appreciation to Alison Keith, director of the Jackman Humanities Institute at the University of Toronto for inviting me to be the public humanities fellow for 2022–23, which gave me the much-needed time to complete and polish this work. I appreciate this memorable Toronto fellowship under the directorship of Alison and her associates, especially Kim Yates, and the solidarity of my

Acknowledgments

cohort of fabulous multi-generational fellows. Special thanks to Randy Boyagoda and Molly Crabapple for the exquisite conversation on art and history at the Jackman Humanities public event.

Only an utterly visual language can capture Gulbadan's itinerant world. For a number of years, I have leaned on the expertise of my brilliant art history colleagues and friends. I am grateful to Sonya Mace, Molly Aitken, Marcus Fraser, Cathy Benkaim, Monica Juneja, and Navina Haidar for suggestions, leads, readings—and camaraderie. For complex Persian passages, I have leaned on Hossein Samei. I continue to think of Homa Bazyar, my Persian tutor in Oxford, and our weekly afternoon readings of Gulbadan's book. Warm thanks to Alexis Wick for getting the orders of Sultan Murad and for several years of conversations on translation from Ottoman Turkish to English. And to Lubaba Al-Azami for her curiousity about sadaqat. I am grateful to Suraiya Faroqhi for her body of work on the Ottoman Hijaz and for a helpful afternoon conversation on na-meshru. Thanks to my Mughal cohort in India: Rana Safvi, Shadab Bano, Ira Mukhoty, and Avik Chanda.

People speak of dream agents. I have Bridget Matzie, a superb representative, guide, and friend. Huge thanks, Bridget, to you and to Aevitas Creative Management. Warm thanks to Jaya Aninda Chatterjee, my editor at Yale University Press, for her poised reflections, diligent edits, and solid support. Thanks to Amanda Gerstenfeld for helping with the production process and for her work on my manuscript to match up with the Yale guidelines. Cheers to Elizabeth Pelton and to the Yale production and publicity team for their excellent work. In India, thanks to Chiki Sarkar for her long engagement with my Mughal interests, and to Anjali Puri for reading the drafts of this work. Special thanks to Susan Laity for shepherding my book through editing and production, and to Robin DuBlanc for expert copyediting. Thanks also to the Juggernaut Books production and publicity teams. A special thanks to Suzanne Williams and Lauren Hodapp of Shreve Williams Public Relations.

Much appreciation to Emory librarian Gautham Reddy and Uppsala University librarian Christina Swedberg for chasing obscure references. Thanks also to Nur-Sobers Khan, director of the Aga Khan Documentation Center at MIT; Ursula Sims-Williams at the British Library, London; and Matt Saba, Rami Alafandi, and Lobna Montasser of the Aga Khan Foundation for their exceptional help with art permissions. Special thanks to Marcus Fraser and Richard Fattorini for permission to reproduce the Sotheby images. The following museums, libraries, and institutions were outstanding in their support and services: the Agha Khan Foundation (Boston and Zurich), the Cleveland Museum of Art, Harvard Art Museum (Boston), the British Library (London), Uppsala University Library, and the library of the University of Toronto. Thanks to Bill Nelson for the beautiful map, and to Barbara J. Anello and Rana Safvi for their evocative photographs.

For marvelous prose that keeps me alive, gratitude to Ocean Vuong, Patti Smith, and Olga Tokarczuk; to Krista Tippett for helping us think deeper; to Joni Mitchell for musical politics; to Andy Blackman for fostering ecumenical life force at the petroglyph-littered land of the Ring Lake Ranch, Wyoming. Molly Crabapple, thank you for our letters in Sweden and beyond—and for our collaboration on a remix of *Empress*. To my friends: Irina Dumitrescu, Linda Feng, Shyam Selvadurai, Molly Aitken, Susan Hunter, Lynda Hill, Lois and Don Reitzes, Mary Odem, Chet Van Duzer, Nada Moumtaz, Betsy Gorman, Laurie Patton,

Acknowledgments

Maggie Kulyk, Meenakshi Alimchandani, Wendy Farley, Leslie Harris, Lynne Huffer, Tara Doyle, Devyani Saltzman, Max Mandelis, Alison Cross, Sayali Bapat, Khushru Irani, Malaika Guntekunst, Smita Murthy, Navyug Gill, and James Fotheringham—I am lucky to have you in my life. Thanks to Karen Schwartz, Sally West, and Kimberly Saul for bringing light on clouded days; and to Jill Martin and Tamara Bradshaw for nourishing massages.

I am in awe of Prabba, my mother, and her exemplary resilience. To my sisters, Reena and Gudden, and to Prabhakar, I am forever grateful. To my nieces, Fanny, Aashna, and Ananya: you are just marvelous. To Gyan, so much love for our home, world travels, and friendship.

Illustration Credits

Illustration Credits

Nineteenth-century miniature painting of the Prophet's Mosque in Medina. Hijaz or India. (Hajj and the Arts of Pilgrimage, Khalili Collections, MSS 1176.2. © The Khalili Family Trust.)

Single-volume Qur'an, Egypt. (The Nasser D. Khalili Collection of Islamic Art, AH 844/1440 CE, Qur 241 [fols. 1b–2a]. © The Khalili Family Trust.)

Celebrations in the women's quarters at the time of Akbar's circumcision. The British Library blog notes, "One of the ladies is almost certainly Gulbadan." (Akbarnama, BL Or.12988, fol. 114r, British Library. With permission from the British Library/Granger.)

Index

Index

Index

Index

Index

Index

Index

Index